D1558671

INTIMATE STRANGERS

INTIMATE STRANGERS

Arendt, Marcuse, Solzhenitsyn, and Said in
American Political Discourse

ANDREEA DECIU RITIVOI

Columbia University Press
New York

Columbia University Press
Publishers Since 1893
New York   Chichester, West Sussex
cup.columbia.edu
Copyright © 2014 Columbia University Press
All rights reserved

Library of Congress Cataloging-in-Publication Data

Ritivoi, Andreea Deciu, 1970–
    Intimate strangers : foreign intellectuals and American political discourse /
Andreea Deciu Ritivoi.
        pages. cm
    Includes bibliographical references and index.
    ISBN 978-0-231-16868-7 (cloth : alk. paper) — ISBN 978-0-231-53791-9
(e-book)
    1. Politics and culture—United States—History—20th century.
2. Intellectuals—United States—History—20th century.   3. Rhetoric—
Political aspects—United States—History—20th century.   4. United
States—Intellectual life—20th century.   5. Arendt, Hannah, 1906–1975—
Influence.   6. Marcuse, Herbert, 1898–1979—Influence.   7. Solzhenitsyn,
Aleksandr Isaevich, 1918–2008—Influence.   8. Said, Edward W.—
Influence.   I. Title.

    E169.12.R538 2014
    320.97309'049—dc23

                                                    2014003432

Columbia University Press books are printed on permanent
 and durable acid-free paper.

This book is printed on paper with recycled content.
Printed in the United States of America

c 10 9 8 7 6 5 4 3 2 1

Jacket design by Julia Kushnirsky
Jacket illustration by R. Kikuo Johnson

It is a mistake to think of the expatriate as someone who abdicates, who withdraws and humbles himself, resigned to his miseries, his outcast state. On a closer look, he turns out to be ambitious, aggressive in his disappointments, his very acrimony qualified by his belligerence. The more we are dispossessed, the more intense our appetites and our illusions become.

—E. M. CIORAN, *THE TEMPTATION TO EXIST*

CONTENTS

ACKNOWLEDGMENTS

A FTER MAJOR flooding in the region where I live, my husband and I went to a food bank in a nearby church to donate food for the victims. We brought a large box of canned goods and left it in the car as we went scouting for the entry. We asked a member of the church staff where the food bank was, and she pointed to the back of the building, adding that we would have to return the next morning to *receive* food. I was initially confused by her answer, but then I realized she had assumed we were there to ask for food, not to donate it. My husband and I both look like white middle-class Americans. We are also immigrants. Her "clue" was our accent, which trumped race and class and, in her eyes, made us into indigent foreigners at the mercy of their hosts.

While this is a book about the negative representations of foreigners in American public and political discourse, I could have written a much different one about the welcoming reception of foreigners in American academic institutions based on my own experience. I have benefited not only from many suggestions offered by my colleagues and students at Carnegie Mellon University but also, and perhaps most important, from their openness and generosity. Unlike the protagonists of my book, who were often dismissed as unreliable and uninformed even though they were illustrious scholars and artists, I have been fortunate to have not only the intellectual trust of my colleagues but also their support and encouragement. My special thanks go to David Kaufer, former head of the English department at Carnegie Mellon University, who has a unique talent for helping me to understand my own thoughts better so I can write them down and whose faith in me has been one of the strongest motivations in my entire academic career; also to Roger Rouse, who taught me the most important lesson in collegiality and intellectual generosity by not only reading my manuscript with utmost care but also discussing it with me as the book I wanted to write and not the book someone else could have written; to Jon Klancher, who showed me, with pointed but ever so elegant comments, how to look at my work with the eyes of a cultural historian (which does not necessarily mean that I managed to do it successfully here); to Kathy Newman, for reading a draft of my manuscript in a very early stage and still seeing a book in it and for making me think about how to write in a way that puts individuals in the center, rather than their ideas; to Fred Evans, for the many stimulating exchanges we have had about political philosophy during our fruitful collaborations and for being such a model of erudition, passion, and kindness; to Peggy Knapp, with whom I share a secret love for the history of ideas, especially the ideas discussed in this book; to Jeffrey Williams, for asking me tough questions and suggesting some possible answers; to David Shumway, who suggested I look more deeply into Camus's *Stranger* (I did and it influenced my thinking even though I make no specific references to that novel here). My students at Carnegie Mellon are the most valuable resource I have had access to at this university. They have read drafts of my chapters and provided tremendous insight as well as motivated me with their excitement about the topic. My graduate research assistants have offered invaluable help, especially David Tucker at the beginning of the project and Emily Lane Ferris in the final stage. I am also grateful to Joe Monte who made useful editorial suggestions and inspired me, with his polite yet probing questions, to see more connections between the four exceptional immigrants that are the subject of this book, and immigrants in general.

This project has received summer support from the National Endowment for the Humanities, for which I am grateful. I thank my department head, Christine Neuwirth, and the dean of the Dietrich College of Humanities and Social Sciences, John Lehoczky, who supported my application for the NEH grant and my research over the years. I presented parts of this book to the research group on migrants and recognition at Carnegie Mellon University in 2010, with its members, Paul Eiss, Roger Rouse, Jennifer Gully, David Shumway, Lara Putnam, Richard Maddox, and Fred Evans, and received important and useful suggestions, and at the Center for Interpretive and Qualitative Research at Duquesne University in 2011, where I was pleased to discover a much more thoughtful response to Solzhenitsyn's Harvard address and my analysis of it than Solzhenitsyn received himself in the 1970s. Khalil Barhoum from Stanford University read my chapter on Edward Said, who was a close friend of his, and provided much encouragement for my analysis of Said's political agenda (although I am solely responsible for the claims I make in this book). And thank you to Alan Gross, for believing in me and inspiring me, no matter how far I strayed from the doctoral work I pursued under his mentorship at the University of Minnesota. Two old and very close friends deserve my deepest gratitude, not just for this project but for all of my scholarly pursuits: Michael Krausz, who has been a role model for me, albeit one impossible to emulate entirely, and Cǎlin-Andrei Mihailescu, whose vivaciousness and brilliance are matched by an incredible generosity and kindness. At Columbia University Press, I was fortunate to work with a patient and experienced editor, Wendy Lochner, and with her dedicated assistant, Christine Dunbar. I deeply appreciate their support and help. Michael Haskell and Margaret Puskar-Pasewicz offered invaluable technological and editorial assistance in the final stage of the process.

Finally, my gratitude to my family is hard to express in a few sentences. If it had not been for my mother, I would probably have been completely overwhelmed with the challenges of being a new mother myself when I started this book and required many more years to finish it. My father was patient and supportive while my mother spent months staying with us and helping in so many ways. My husband, Milu, is my lucky star. He was the first one to hear me talk about this project, on our first night out after the birth of our daughter, and he continued to support me in endless ways, hearing me read paragraphs out loud, listening and responding to my ideas, and helping me with his technological wizardry. I truly am most grateful of all to my daughter, Anouk, for offering to do illustrations for my book (even though I did not take her up on it) and to my son, Luca, for telling me to go work after I tucked him in every night. My children were born in America, and I am grateful to both of them for speaking English with me every day yet never hearing my accent.

This book is dedicated to Milu, Anouk, and Luca—you are my world.

INTIMATE STRANGERS

INTRODUCTION

I N 2010, the Arizona Department of Education decided to require schools not to employ anyone with a heavy foreign accent to teach students just learning to speak English. Officials argued that students who do not know the language—children of immigrants—should have teachers who can best model how to speak English. My fellow Romanian-born writer and university professor Andrei Codrescu commented sarcastically: "Come to think of it, the Arizona law doesn't go far enough. People with accents should be banned from any profession that involves communication. Politics, for instance. Henry Kissinger's accent would surely qualify for the ban."[1] Kissinger's successful career was the exception rather than the norm among immigrants. The intimidating barrier posed by a new language keeps them not only away from employment opportunities but also out of the public sphere. Politics often seems reserved for the native, those born and raised in the homeland.[2]

Yet despite such challenges and restrictions, accented voices (Codrescu's included) are heard in American public discourse. Whether or not they are models for correct grammar or proper pronunciation, some of them have made deep changes in American culture and society. It is, however, not just how their voices sound in English but, more importantly, what they say, their observations and their visions. Four foreigners in particular, Hannah

Arendt, Herbert Marcuse, Alexander Solzhenitsyn, and Edward Said, took American politics in new directions. Their ways of thinking stood both inside and outside America. All four were outspoken critics of and dissenters from what was considered at the time mainstream thinking and official political discourse in the United States. Their opinions were often dismissed in America with the argument that, as foreigners, they could not have an accurate understanding of an exceptional political system like American democracy.

Arendt, Marcuse, Solzhenitsyn, and Said relied on their cultural strangeness to formulate bold visions and introduce American audiences to radically different political perspectives. This book examines their contribution to American political discourse through what I term the "stranger persona," a strategic blend of detachment and involvement, of familiarity and strangeness projected by an author in discourse. I develop the concept of stranger persona to analyze the ways in which foreignness can constitute a strategy of rhetorical invention in response to a political and historical tradition that represents foreigners as dangerous and inferior. I examine these four intellectuals' criticisms of American society and politics around highly sensitive and controversial issues that affected the way in which Americans defined themselves as a nation in times of crisis: the emergence of totalitarian regimes; the desegregation of schools in the South; the counterculture movements and the New Left; the détente policy of relaxation in the Cold War against the Soviet Union; and America's relation with the Arab world and Israel.

As scholars and cultural critics, Arendt, Marcuse, Solzhenitsyn, and Said have an indisputable fame in American intellectual life. My selection of these four particular intellectuals is based on the prominence they achieved in the United States but also on the fact that all four became involved in *American*, rather than exilic politics.[3] They were not the only prominent intellectuals of foreign origin who took an interest in American politics. Leo Strauss, for instance, is broadly considered to have played a key influence on conservative politics in post–World War II America.[4] His books, it is rumored, lay on the night table of many congressmen and White House officials. The Russian-born Ayn Rand was a personal friend of Alan Greenspan, former chairman of the Federal Reserve.[5] The Republican senator Paul Ryan credits Rand with a formative role in shaping his political views.[6] At the other end of the political spectrum, Albert Einstein was a pacifist and passionate critic of big corporations' destruction of the environment. More recently, the British-born Tony Judt and Christopher Hitchens were distinguished scholars as well as vocal commentators in American politics.

None of these intellectuals, however, embodies the combination of scholarly or artistic capital with active participation in American political discourse in quite the same way as the four I discuss. Strauss, to my knowledge, never wrote political commentary and did not take a specific stance on a contemporary political matter. Einstein was a scientist rather than a philosopher. Rand left an intellectually mediocre body of work that cannot sustain a serious scholarly investigation.[7] Judt and Hitchens, impressive as they both were, did not achieve quite the same reputation as Said, for instance, nor were they as "foreign" as Marcuse, if only because they did not have to learn a new language or flee political persecution in their own country. Arendt's *Origins of Totalitarianism* was highly influential in the Cold War ideological battles, but her political involvement on the American scene went far beyond this one book as she commented on events and situations that were specific to American politics and history, from the desegregation of schools in the South to the Vietnam War. Marcuse's critiques of capitalism are thought to have influenced the New Left movement, with which he was closely connected. Solzhenitsyn's accounts of political prisoners in the Soviet gulag and his denunciation of communism as a totalitarian ideology and a crushing regime played an important role in America's Cold War politics. Finally, Said lambasted the United States for its support of Israel but also tried to mediate between the United States and the Arab world, both through his interventions in public debates and by participating in secret negotiations.

Arendt, Marcuse, Solzhenitsyn, and Said are not usually studied *as immigrants*, although much has been said about them as philosophers and writers with strong political views and commitments. Yet they were not spared the difficulties that immigrants arriving in America experience: culture shock, adjustment to new customs, (re-)building a career, making new friends—in other words, having to create new habits and new routines in order to make their existence in the United States meaningful and fulfilling. Examining their philosophical-political work as the expression of an immigrant consciousness affects how I read their texts. I examine the contrast, even conflict, between their political ideas and style and what most American readers believed. Lack of familiarity with a political culture became a source of insight, no matter how paradoxical this might seem.

The practices of statecraft rely on strict differentiations between citizens and aliens.[8] This book argues that the distinction is also salient for understanding the dynamic of political discourse when it involves disagreements between the foreign born and the native born on matters that directly concern the nature of a polity—such as the type of organization it prefers, its values, or its attitude toward other nations. In the exchanges I analyze, these foreigners argued *as citizens*, regardless of the identity that was stamped on their passports. Even Solzhenitsyn, who is the only one in the group not to have acquired American citizenship, addressed his American audience using the rhetoric of citizenry (in a commencement address). Arguably, Arendt, Marcuse, and Said were more involved civically in America than Solzhenitsyn; his Harvard address might seem an isolated case in his political activity, which was focused on his native country (though I argue that it was not). Yet all four shared, in degree and scope, their rejection *as foreigners*, and all four made similar use of a stylistic of foreignness as a source of insight. Often the response to their criticism addressed them as *noncitizens*, again regardless of their actual status. They belong together not because they were similar in views or immigration status but because they were treated so.

Of the numerous definitions of the nation, Jürgen Habermas's puts in perspective how *strange*, not just foreign, those who come from another country appear to us: "a nation of citizens (as) composed of persons who, as a result of socialization processes, also embody the forms of life in which they formed their identities."[9] Different national communities have different forms of life, even when they might seem universal. The solidity of Arendt's marriage to Heinrich Blücher, who was involved for several years with a friend of the couple, was a constant source of surprise (and probably gossip) among American friends who saw it as the product of the interwar

Berlin culture, with its relaxed sexual mores and tolerance for extramarital affairs. Margarette von Trotha's film vividly captures the difference between forms of life for Arendt's German circle in New York and her American acquaintances: at a gathering in Arendt's elegant apartment, Mary McCarthy and an American professor of German studies from the New School watch from a distance the excited conversation in German of the hostess and her German guests. Neither can follow the discussion, and the movie makes it clear that this is not a matter of linguistic difference.[10] We presume the foreigner's way to be *different* even before we know it for what it is or even though we might be familiar with it. Said recounted frequent inquiries from colleagues and students who wanted to know what he eats for breakfast and how his residence looks, as though his political views and Palestinian identity made it seem implausible that he could live like so many other Americans who drink coffee in the morning and rent an apartment.

How these intellectuals were perceived in the United States affected the reception of their ideas. Classical theories of rhetoric would explain this phenomenon as a problem of ethos. Rhetoric handbooks recommend that attempts at persuasion strive not just to present a logical sequence of arguments (*logos*) but also to project credibility (*ethos*).[11] The presence of the latter is all the more important because, as Eugene Garver explains, "we infer from ethos to logos."[12] If we trust the speaker, we are more likely to attend carefully to and even be convinced by his or her arguments, irrespective of their inherent merit or logic. Communication relies on a "labor of codification and normalization" of linguistic strategies, patterns of argumentation, stylistic choices, dramatic personae, and emotional display (or its avoidance).[13] This labor emerges as a generalization of existing usages that belong to a dominant group. The official language—in the United States, American English, through status and use if not law—functions as the most palpable proof of what is ultimately a projection, the idea of a unified, coherent community of individuals willing to trust members of their national community more than they are willing to trust outsiders. Those who are already inside the national polity are loosely subjected through habit to the norms and codes of the standard language rather than explicitly coerced to follow certain rules that bestow on them their status as natives. They have a citizen's ethos, unavailable to newcomers or outsiders who are introduced to these linguistic codes and norms by those not only authorized to impose them but also deemed the ideal representatives—such as a teacher who can model good English by not having an accent.

Rather than stay away from the public sphere because they lacked a citizen ethos, the four intellectuals I discuss in this book turned this lack into a rhetorical strategy, taking it on as a part they would play in the theater of American politics, a *persona*. Their stranger persona had both a cognitive and a stylistic component: it was a way of generating original ideas—as in the rhetorical canon of *inventio*—and of arranging them in patterns of argumentation—*dispositio*. As such, their political discourse is significant beyond these intellectuals' own ascent to or fall from political authority. Across the period spanned by their writings—close to half of a century— the backlash against foreigners raises questions about the inclusiveness of the American polis and the strength, or rather rigidity, of its national bond. The American response to the stranger persona persisted despite changes in the political climate and variations in the national origin of the foreign critic in question. The Russian anticommunist Solzhenitsyn was dismissed in equal measure as the German socialist Marcuse, the German liberal Arendt, or the Palestinian anti-Zionist Said. All four shared the same fate, no matter how different their political views or cultural background. They got caught in a clash of vision and style, a clash between "us" and "them" that resonates all too powerfully with the so-called clash of civilizations, no matter how much the participants in this political discourse were all intellectuals in the Western mold.

I am aware that putting too fine of a point on the *foreignness* of these intellectuals is risky. It ignores differences among them, ignores the extent to which some changed over the years spent in America, reifies the category of *American* intellectuals, and creates a dichotomy between the native and the foreigner that is far too simplistic given the overall cosmopolitanism of both American and European intellectuals after World War II. American-born intellectuals not only differed greatly by ideological beliefs, styles of thought, taste, and values but also conceived of their own Americanness differently depending on their social background. Some were children of immigrants and still felt like new arrivals. Some struggled financially more than the immigrant intellectuals. Some had lived abroad, and others had never left their country. No doubt, intellectuals have complex ties to a national polity and challenge the simple dichotomy of belonging versus not belonging. As a sociological category, intellectuals have always been part of a transnational rather than national order, even before terms like transnationalism and cosmopolitanism became fashionable. According to Jacques Le Goff, in the Middle Ages the category of intellectuals consisted of scholars, mainly humanists affiliated with a European university, committed to abstract ideals rather than particular institutions.[14] Medieval intellectuals were heavily involved in translation projects, actively pursuing knowledge assumed to transcend cultural and national borders—just as they themselves did. Richard Pells views modern intellectuals as, by the very nature of their mission, outsiders or marginal in relation to any form of power—whether represented by the state, the market, or the university—so as to be able to reflect critically on it.[15] Yet at the same time, no matter how unencumbered by national or political interests, intellectuals have historically been central to the formation of national consciousness. Paradoxically, they are both involved in and detached from the national order.

Yet it would be impossible to deny that uprooted intellectuals face a different predicament than their native-born colleagues. The four I study here wrote and thought differently, even when agreeing with American intellectuals or communicating with American friends and even though they saw America as their own country. They frequently engaged in philosophical, cultural, and political debates with American-born intellectuals. Sometimes, their intellectual training, artistic taste, and social status formed a strong shared foundation for agreement. But their national origin never went unnoticed or was completely forgotten, and this is not a trivial point. Arendt was a German Jew who had come to America as an experienced political activist and thinker. The German cultural and political tradition that had shaped her intellectual and personal identity, as well as Marcuse's, was markedly different from that of her American friends. Solzhenitsyn's anticommunism was the stance of a political dissident from the Soviet Union. While his enemy was the Communist Party in power in the Soviet Union, for American anticommunists the enemy was often more broadly defined, and it extended to the people of the Soviet Union, and specifically to Russians. Said, although he had spent his entire adult life in the United States, had a different perspective on Israel as a Palestinian whose family were victims of Israeli policies than American critics like Noam Chomsky. In the United States, these intellectuals shared a stranger's ethos not because they were immigrants (not all were) or because they opposed government policies but because they faced the common predicament of being on the fringes, marginalized and disenfranchised when their criticism of America offended patriotic sensibilities. Although they differed widely in political agenda, intellectual vision, and style, they were also similar insofar as they shared the rejection of the foreigner. Their foreignness was projected on them, no matter how different their political views and status.

All four were foreigners also because, while they lived in America, they did not identify the United States as their sole or main national affiliation. Their interest and involvement in American politics did not preclude Arendt and Marcuse from maintaining an interest in postwar Germany, manifested in frequent trips, writing, and public lecturing. Said traveled extensively to the Middle East and increasingly assumed a Palestinian identity. Solzhenitsyn never became a naturalized American citizen and indeed returned to Russia after the collapse of the Soviet Union. His stay in the United States, however, was almost two decades long. He became a fixture in American political discourse, appearing often in public at lectures and meetings, publishing in highly visible American media outlets, and, most important, being frequently invoked by American commentators. All four used their familiarity with other cultures and traditions as a strategy for questioning the American way though their American critics dismissed this as mere lack of familiarity with America. They charged that without an intimate knowledge of American practices and traditions, the foreigner had no solid foundation upon which to formulate a valid opinion and thus no right to pass judgment. A respectable American scholar once argued that since Arendt never had a driver's license, she could not have been able to travel much in America and therefore could not be familiar enough with American society.[16]

Arendt admitted that she had never traveled to the South, but she still expressed her views on the desegregation of schools in Arkansas, arguing against the use of federal troops. Many American intellectuals disagreed with her perspective, but some dismissed her *right* to weigh in and question the government's decision (especially since it received wide support from American liberals). When Solzhenitsyn criticized the role played by the media in manipulating public opinion in the United States, American critics on the left and the right dismissed his position as that of a Russian who had no experience with democratic institutions. Marcuse's criticism of American capitalism was often met with complaints that he was merely a hostile and ungrateful foreigner. Said's attacks of American Zionism brought him the charge of being not just anti-Semitic but also anti-American. Such charges denied them a fundamental right, "the recognition of the individual as a being who is entitled to moral respect, a being whose communicative freedom we must recognize."[17] Being dismissed or shut down *as a foreigner* constitutes the mark of a xenophobic politics that deems the foreigner's position wrong by default.

To accept that a foreigner's political views might be right is not a sign of tolerance but of recognition, in the sense proposed by Paul Ricoeur, which I discuss in the conclusion. Such a shift requires a reframing of our understanding of the relation between foreigners and the nation-state beyond the perspective inherited from the political philosophy of the Enlightenment. For Kant, foreigners had the right to hospitality, not to be "treated as an enemy when he arrives in the land of another."[18] Dismissing the foreigner's views and arguments as wrong because they are a foreigner's is a way of treating him as an implicit enemy. The Kantian conception of a foreigner's rights assumes the foreigner as visitor. The hospitality was temporary as foreigners may have been welcomed in the land but were also expected to leave. But in a country like the United States, whose national identity is founded on the myth of an immigrant past, foreigners have historically also enjoyed the right to stay and acquire full political membership in the nation. Such membership requires the right to be not only physically present on American land but also present in American public discourse by being granted freedom of speech and also political recognition.

To unsettle the habit of mind that deems the foreigner wrong by default requires more than mere shedding of prejudice, if this is even possible. It demands a rethinking of the traditional narrative that records and interprets encounters between Americans and foreigners coming to this country, the tropes on which this narrative relies, and the symbolic constructions it makes available. In the remaining part of this introduction, I outline briefly the contours of this narrative, focusing on the ambiguous figure of the foreigner who ventures to criticize America.

THE FOREIGNER AS ENLIGHTENED TRAVELER

From the early days of the republic, a steady stream of Europeans traveled to the United States and produced a literary tradition of American travelogues. The key representative of this tradition inaugurated a discourse of praise that was hard to rival. Alexis de Tocqueville traveled to America in 1831, accompanied by Gustave de Beaumont, to study the penal system of the country. Both voyagers were public prosecutors, and the purpose of their trip required them to spend most of their time and attention on American jails. The result, however, is much different from the somber account one might have expected. As we know, the book turned out to be more than a presentation of American legislation. *Democracy in America* has been repeatedly hailed, in the words of the editor of the Perennial edition, J. P. Mayer, as "the most comprehensive, penetrating, and astute picture of American life, politics, and morals ever written—whether by an American or, as in this case, a foreign visitor."[19] Thirteen editions were published during Tocqueville's life alone, followed by dozens more after his death. *Democracy in America* is a canonical text for political theory, still recognized today as a key contribution to the study of democracy. It is also a canonical text for American history insofar as it is read as an accurate depiction of American life. These two levels of significance can be easily conflated. *Democracy in America* has been depicted as making the case that American politics is synonymous with democracy, in other words, that democratic governance originates in distinctly American practices and institutions. Sheldon Wolin has argued that Tocqueville's ability to understand and theorize democracy at a time when it was still a new form of politics was directly determined by his firsthand experience of American life.[20] Tocqueville's account, then, represents not just the recognition of America's greatness but also the highest compliment ever paid to it.

But was this really a foreigner's compliment, or rather self-flattery? Ali Behdad has drawn attention to the American secondary sources of Tocqueville's account, suggesting that their effect on *Democracy in America* was far greater than that of the author's direct experience. Following William E. Connolly, Behdad claims that Tocqueville's travelogue was "constructed from the dominant archive of the nation—works such as Cotton Mather's *Magnalia Christi Americana, or the Ecclesiastical History of the New England, 1620–1698* and Nathaniel Morton's *New England Memorial*." Rather than documenting the workings of American democracy, Tocqueville was a symbolic witness to its existence as it had already been established by American commentators through whom he had discovered it. Tocqueville also relied on non-American sources, such as travelogues by eighteenth-century European travelers, adopting their Enlightenment ontology along with its racial overtones. This European influence comes through in his depiction of Native Americans, which focuses on their inability to assimilate into "the political economy of white civilization." Such a perspective was not only convincing for an American audience but also convenient. "Above all, what made Tocqueville a 'friend' to Americans," Behdad suggests, "is not the political theory of democracy he gave them but a canonized history of how their nation-state was imagined in an 'exceptional' way by pilgrims."[21]

Tocqueville's account was flattering to Americans because it praised their country and also implicitly criticized Europe, specifically France, his own country, the bastion of European civilization. In the preface, the author insists that the American context is unique and that he did not wish to present it as a model for political life in Europe. At the same time, he writes, "American institutions, which for France under the monarchy were simply a subject of curiosity, ought now to be studied by republican France."[22] This was a weighted statement when it appeared in the preface to the edition published in 1848, the year of European revolutions that brought national emancipation in several European countries.

Since the book was intended for a French audience, its author makes it clear in the introduction that his interest in the subject—and theirs, he implies—was not just "to satisfy curiosity, however legitimate; I sought there lessons from which we might profit."[23] In the particular context of the book's production—postrevolutionary France with its emergent political landscape defined by republicanism—such lessons were directly connected to the "shape of democracy itself . . . its inclinations, character, prejudices, and passions. I wanted to understand it so as at least to know what we have to fear or hope there from."[24] The most important lesson America offered to Tocqueville and his French readers was one in equality, from "political mores and laws" to "opinions, . . . feelings, . . . customs." While describing equality as "the creative element from which each particular fact (in America) derived," Tocqueville took great care to present equality as a political condition not dependent on American life and thus exportable and importable:

> When I came to consider our own side of the Atlantic, I thought I could detect something analogous to what I had noticed in the New World. I saw an equality of conditions which, though it had not reached the extreme limits found in the United States, was daily drawing closer thereto; and that same democracy which prevailed over the societies of America seemed to me to be advancing rapidly toward power in Europe.[25]

The America seen by Tocqueville was a source of political inspiration for Europe. Such a model had to be presented carefully to audiences reluctant to admit that they needed one. "Anyone who supposes that I intend to write a panegyric is strangely mistaken," warns Tocqueville, a classic instance of someone who protests too much, indirectly admitting his anxiety over appearing so admiring of a country other than his own.[26] Yet in his effort to avoid being seen as a proselytizer, he ended up not only presenting America as a paragon of democracy but also promoting American democracy as a natural political order toward which all civilized nations would ultimately gravitate.[27] Tocqueville's legacy was a narrative of enchanted self-discovery in the eyes of the foreigner, a satisfied confirmation that to be American is to be superior, an important reassurance for a nation remembering its birth as emancipation from a European power.

This discourse of praise sits in tense relation with a discourse of harsh criticism, associated mainly with British accounts. To the nineteenth-century British traveler, Simon Schama writes, "the hallmark of Jacksonian America seemed to be a beastly indifference to manners, the symptom of a society where considerateness to others was a poor second to the immediate satisfaction of personal wants."[28] Schama reminds us of Frances Trollope, wife to the novelist, who made her own literary reputation on the basis of a single book, *Domestic Manners of the Americans*, a highly critical portrait presenting to European audiences a boorish materialist people.[29] Her account was popular with the British because, as Schama points out, the American Revolution was still relatively fresh in the minds of readers pleased to receive confirmation of their own stereotypes of Americans. However, the book was also noted in France and seemed to have informed the views of influential authors such as Stendhal and, later, Charles Baudelaire. In 1842, Charles Dickens published his *American Notes*, a travelogue documenting his voyage through New York, Boston, Philadelphia, and Cincinnati and into Illinois. Dickens's dark vision, centered on disrepair, immorality, and insanity, emerges partly from the sites he visited—prisons and asylums—and partly from his own novelistic aesthetic. He was hardly a chronicler of idyllic, happy settings. Schama notes the climax of Dickens's dark representations in his rendition of a key cultural trope in American self-representation, the Mississippi River. Observing it from Cairo, Illinois, Dickens offers a dystopian vision of the American rundown town: "The hateful Mississippi circling and eddying before it, and turning off upon its southern course a slimy monster hideous to behold; a hotbed of disease, an ugly sepulchre, a grave uncheered by any gleam of promise: a place without one single quality, in earth or air or water, to commend it."[30]

Matthew Arnold did not think there was anything worth seeing in America, and his decision to avoid it reveals a common stereotype about the U.S. as an intellectually and culturally barren country.[31] Schama credits

Rudyard Kipling with introducing the idea of an America moving away from this position of inferiority to Europe and being on the verge of an "imperialist awakening"—a view that would lead to twentieth-century anti-Americanism that saw America as a superpower trying to take over other national cultures through pernicious influences such as Coca-Cola-ization if not direct military means. Finally, for Schama, the most important recurrent complaint in European intellectuals' representation of Americans is their arrogant sense of national pride. America's "national egocentricity" contributes, according to the European writers Schama reviews (and with whom he agrees), to its cultivated isolation and emphasis on its exceptionalism. These are attitudes that lead to defensiveness rather than openness to the criticism of outsiders.

In the aftermath of World War II, as the United States strengthened its economic and political presence in Europe, anti-Americanism intensified. European resentment imagined a greedy imperialist America, as I show in chapter 4. At the center of this anti-Americanism was the perception of difference—America as unlike the rest of the Western world yet also determined to attempt a cultural and economic invasion of Europe. Some European intellectuals traveling to America after 1945 conveyed this general resentment toward America, only to admit to their change of heart upon discovering a fascinating and complex nation. Albert Camus, who came in 1946 at an invitation from the exiled École Libre, found himself waxing poetic, in the diary entries recorded in his notebooks, about American restaurants, women, and architecture. For the most part, however, Camus was not very interested in the United States, and his trip to New York was only the first leg of a longer voyage to Mexico and South America. He liked the rain in New York more than the city itself. Upon entering the New York Harbor on arrival, he observed "in the distance, the skyscrapers of Manhattan against a backdrop of mist." This vista prompted the following comment: "Deep down I feel calm and indifferent, as I generally do in front of spectacles that don't move me."[32]

A year later, in January 1947, Simone de Beauvoir arrived in New York with a letter of introduction from her partner, Jean-Paul Sartre. After spending two months in New York, where she met with the most prominent American intellectuals of the time, she traveled from coast to coast by train, bus, and automobile. Many French intellectuals rallied behind Sartre and de Beauvoir in their infatuation with the Soviet Union, but in America the ideological climate was much more muddled by the split between anti-Stalinists, anticommunists, and anticapitalists. In *America Day by Day*, de Beauvoir declares herself in love with America, especially New York, a city whose contradictions and complexities seduced her to the point that she claimed in her journal to love it as much as she loved Paris. Her reflections on American life and society are not only insightful, as many American critics have hailed them, but also infused with affection and admiration. Even when arguing intensely with American intellectuals over politics, or when she disagreed vehemently with their position, de Beauvoir found Americans welcoming and open, concerned with making a foreign guest feel at home and at ease. From taxi drivers (a category she grew especially fond of) to the fiercely political editors of the *Partisan Review*—whose politics differed from hers—Americans struck the French guest as committed to surrounding themselves "with a climate of trust, cheer, and friendship." The American "benevolence," as she called it, was not only rare or inexistent in France as a social feeling toward others, but also extended toward anyone, including foreigners. "I am a foreigner: this seems to be neither a defect nor an eccentricity here," noted a surprised de Beauvoir. Although grateful each time a newly made acquaintance organized a party for her, which opened new doors and made new contacts, de Beauvoir's overall characterizations of American (especially intellectuals) are critical. Her criticism is not harsh but is firmly delivered, which makes the praise seem condescending. The reproaches she levels at Americans differ from the old epithets, and it was not Americans' superficiality, boorishness, or obsession with material values that disappointed de Beauvoir, but their lack of wisdom:

If Americans have so little sense of nuances, it isn't that they are incapable of grasping them . . . but that they would be troubled by them. To accept nuances is to accept ambiguity of judgment, argument, and hesitation; such complex situations force you to think. They want to lead their lives by geometry, not by wisdom. Geometry is taught, whereas wisdom is discovered, and only the first offers the refreshing certainties that a conscientious person needs. So they choose to believe in a geometrical world where every right angle is set against another, like their buildings and their streets.[33]

Presenting the American intellectual as unable to cope with uncertainty, the foreign visitor is simultaneously asserting her own superiority. *She* is wise. The implicit contrast serves as a way of elevating the foreigner. This trick may have been all too obvious to the American intellectuals who interacted with de Beauvoir during her visit, and it certainly irritated them once her book was published. "Indeed, 'authoritative' was the word for her on most subjects," wrote William Barrett in his reflections on her trip; he had read de Beauvoir's travel memoir and did not agree with most of her characterizations of America. His response to her representation of America, however, is more than disagreement. Barrett dismisses de Beauvoir as a foreigner prone to misunderstanding because of a basic lack of linguistic proficiency. While de Beauvoir admits she had difficulty understanding English at times, Barrett portrays her as barely knowing any English at all. Her linguistic incomprehension becomes pure arrogance, as Barrett sneers: "I wondered at times why she had come here at all, since she already had her case complete on us and our country. Perhaps it was only to add some confirming details to the picture she already had. She seemed to me like a traveler carrying an invisible visa form in which all the main items had already been entered and she had only to fill in a few blanks."[34]

In September 1947, the journal *Commentary* published an article by Mary McCarthy, titled "America the Beautiful," which offers a portrait of American culture using the pretext of a foreign visitor, a female "Existentialist" who had asked about the uniquely American characteristics. The rather transparent reference to de Beauvoir, who had met McCarthy in New York, is part of a broader rhetorical strategy in McCarthy's piece, which uses the motif of the foreigner as an inquisitive mind to contest for anyone except the native the ability to form accurate impressions of a culture or a nation. Reporting that the visitor had asked to be shown a distinctly American thing—whether a food, a sight, or an institution—McCarthy derides the very attempt at distinguishing America in a way that might impress favorably a European visitor. "For the visiting European," she quips, "a trip through the United States has, almost inevitably, the character of an expose, and the American on his side is tempted by love of his country to lock the inquiring tourist in his hotel room and throw away the key." By contrast, McCarthy feels no compulsion at acknowledging the inferiority of America by European standards, manifested in the less impressive architecture, food, even women's fashion. Yet she also argues that such inferiority is precisely the result of America's immigrant heritage. If Europe appears more cultured and civilized than America, McCarthy argues, it is because of the "thousands and thousands of European peasants and poor townspeople who came here bringing their humanity and their suffering with them." Europe's shortages have become American's abundance. The chiasmic relation posited by McCarthy between Europe and America —"the concavity of hunger" in one converted in the "convex of abundance" in the other, as she memorably put it—establishes an antagonism that makes criticism of America ring hostile, always reproach rather than mere observation.[35] "America the Beautiful" bespeaks a hurt national pride, yet McCarthy spent many years living in France and her closest friend in America was not a fellow American but a German Jew, Hannah Arendt. The America McCarthy defended from a European's scorn was a culture she criticized more harshly than most foreigners. Why, then, would the foreigner seem so especially cold, detached, and unsympathetic?

USURPERS AND ENEMIES

In the late 1930s and early 1940s, war-torn Europe began to send to America not curious visitors who could make insightful (or even condescending) observations about a complex country from the blurred landscapes captured from a train window, a few handshakes with the locals during an overnight stop, or distant vistas seen from the balcony of a Manhattan apartment. Those arriving now knew their stay would be longer and that they would need to make an effort to function in American society, if only to survive. Walter Lacquer speaks of an entire elite generation of scholars who were immigrant children, arriving in America with their families escaping Nazi Germany.[36] For them, returning to Germany after the war was not an option. The fact that the majority of these intellectuals came from Germany or from regions once in the Habsburg Austrian Empire deeply marked the position of the foreigner as intellectual in America. The wartime German intellectual became the paradigmatic representation of an alien and evil influence infiltrating American minds, its marked difference from the Puritan and Anglo-Saxon mold of America a threat greater than if it had been any other sending nation.

The wartime mass migration of intellectuals marked an important shift, yet one insufficiently noticed in a political culture built on the self-image as a nation of immigrants. Whether contested or accepted, the iconology of immigrant America has always implied an ethos of hard work, but most often physical work; determination, but often conceived as physical endurance; intrepidness, but mostly as practical spirit rather than reflection; and, finally, optimism and hopefulness, not the pessimism or skepticism of those who had seen their ideals betrayed or destroyed—this was what Americans expected in their immigrants. A case in point is the account of the rescue mission that brought Walter Benjamin from France into Spain as recounted years later by an assimilated immigrant, Lisa Fittko. A German Jew and guide to hundreds of political refugees who crossed the mountains from Nazi-occupied France into Spain, Fittko recounts Benjamin's rescue with disdain rather than admiration, focusing on a symbolic element that identifies him as an intellectual: a heavy briefcase, carried along with much effort by an ailing Benjamin, which slowed him and the rest of the group. This lost burden, presumed to have been Benjamin's last manuscript, is a vestige of the European world of ideas, but for Fittko it was merely a nuisance:

> I had my hands full guiding our little group upward. Philosophy had to wait until we were over the mountain. I was busy rescuing some human beings from the Nazis, and here I was with this odd character, Old Benjamin, who under no circumstances would let himself be parted from his ballast, the black leather briefcase. And so, for better or worse, we had to drag that monstrosity over the mountains.[37]

Dark irony has it that the thinker of the messianic internationalist order arrived at the Spanish border on the only day that passage was closed. Benjamin committed suicide. Fittko and the others crossed into Spain the next day. In a narrative of survival that represents the foreigner as a hero facing extreme danger and overcoming it, the death of the intellectual is not only anticlimactic but also a symbolic dramatization echoing the frontier myth: to succeed takes physical endurance in a hostile environment, courage, and determination, not intellectual sophistication. Fittko's depiction of the briefcase suggests an anti-intellectualist bent that was shared by many Americans and used especially aggressively against foreign intellectuals.

In turn, the European intellectuals who came to America had their own reservations about this country. This was not where most of them would have preferred to be, if they had had an option. Many of those who had to flee Germany (or, shortly afterward, Austria and France) had already been exiles in other European countries and only embarked on a transatlantic voyage when nothing else seemed to work. It was not easy for them to travel to the United States. Immigration policies passed in the 1930s and 1940s imposed strict visa quotas and made entry to the United States difficult by increasing the number of requirements imposed on those who applied for visas.[38] Against the general reluctance of American society to allow more foreigners—even enlightened ones—into the country, a few foundations, organizations, and academic institutions (notably Rockefeller, the Emergency Rescue Organization, and Columbia University), aided by key public and political figures (notably Eleanor Roosevelt) helped large numbers of European intellectuals arrive safely in the United States.

Once here, these formed the classical "receiving networks" that facilitate the entry of fellow nationals.[39] The European intellectuals already in America often filled out affidavits of support for visas that would get others out of countries newly fallen under German control. Such documents confronted the immigrants with the American bureaucracy and killed any illusion they might have had that prestige and talent were welcome in the New World. For some, entering the country posed such difficulty that it left them with a strong feeling of being undesirables in America. In some cases, this feeling even led to suicides, as Stefan Zweig's example shows. For others, like

Thomas Mann, immigrating to America was the final recourse they had postponed as long as they could, rather than a choice embraced happily. All struggled with the bureaucratic hurdles of immigration. A few who were already internationally renowned came as part of a contingent that benefited from the financial support and moral lobbying of the Emergency Rescue Committee. Formed in June 1940 at the initiative of prominent immigrants already in the United States, the Emergency Rescue Committee was trying to compensate for a highly restrictionist immigration policy. Through its appointed representative, the journalist Varian Fry, the committee identified exceptional European intellectuals whose lives were in danger and arranged for their visa formalities and trip to New York. While awaiting departure, the fortunate chosen stayed at Fry's luxury villa, Bel Air, a name that came to symbolize the paradox of the intellectual refugee, both deprived (awaiting an entry visa) and privileged (guaranteed a safe haven in the midst of a world in political turmoil).

It is hard not to have mixed feelings—like Fry himself—about this rescue mission and not to question its elitist bent and emphasis on intellectual value over political involvement. Among those he helped to bring into the United States were more avant-garde painters and poets than anti-Nazi dissidents because he was "employed by a committee that depended for its financial support on an American public that was largely indifferent to the fate of the masses of unknown refugees."[40] And while Fry managed to extend his list beyond his assigned roster of "celebrity refugees" by applying criteria other than intellectual merit, the contingent he brought into the United States came under the joint premise of political innocuousness and a peculiar kind of racial neutrality. Arendt, for instance, was included in this rescue effort not because she was Jewish or a political dissident in Hitler's Germany but because she was regarded as an outstanding philosopher. But in the political turmoil of the war years, intellectual merit was hard to separate from a political agenda. Some of Germany's luminaries held socialist views at a time when American officials and segments of the public dreaded socialism and readily equated it with Stalinism. The relation between political activists and intellectuals *engagés* was already fraught in Europe; in America, it would become explosively dangerous as being involved in politics could be equated with being a radical and potential anarchist.[41] In a period of five years, between 1953 and 1958, the Immigration and Naturalization Service completed 60,371 investigations of foreign-born residents deemed "subversives."[42]

Yet the European intellectuals arriving in America had the appeal that the continent that had sent them had exerted on Americans for centuries: sophistication and erudition. But this fascination was paralleled by a similarly long-standing distaste for the Old World and another set of features associated with it: old-fashioned ideas, rigidity, and lack of progress. European intellectuals had to carve out a difficult niche in response to the admiration lavished upon them simultaneously with contempt. These opposing responses were strangely synergistic in their outcome, which was to peg onto real people generic descriptions designed to stress difference and incompatibility. What resulted was a frequently invoked clash between mindsets and worldviews, in Francis Goffing's rendition, a clash between the European mind, "hierarchical, systematic, and abstractly conceptual in its analysis of the world," and the American mind, "lateral, free-wheeling, and concretely empirical."[43]

Perhaps even better representatives of this European mindset than their German colleagues, French intellectual war refugees were an ephemeral presence on the American scene. In the early 1940s, several prestigious French intellectuals escaping the Vichy government found refuge in the United States. The Catholic and socialist thinker Simone Weil, the anthropologist Claude Lévi-Strauss, the novelist Antoine de Saint-Exupéry, the Nobel laureate poet Saint-John Perse, and many others lived and worked in New York without being perceived by most Americans as a cultural or political threat. In turn, they did not show much interest in participating in American politics as their focus remained on France and its own political situation. In a letter to Lévi-Strauss, Archibald MacLeish encouraged all French exiles to keep their eyes on France, and so they did. All of them returned promptly after the war and France's liberation. Their decision can be explained partly on the strength of their ties to France, but they also experienced a different clash with the American public. From 1942 to 1944, Mount Holyoke College hosted several encounters between American intellectuals and French exiles. Modeled after the Pontigny *entretiens*—a series of lively dialogues in a picturesque setting in southern France sponsored by the philanthropist and intellectual M. Paul Desjardins—these encounters produced some interesting exchanges but were short-lived. Rather than establish a deep French-American connection, they proved its impossibility. As Laurent Jeanpierre points out, "Pontigny-en-Amerique acknowledged—and, to a degree, mourned—the passing of the old-style French intellectual . . . his notion of 'good will' had failed . . . and that failure had called into question the European—and above all, French—model of the 'universal intellectual.'"[44]

Unlike the short-lived Pontigny-en-Amerique or the New York–based École Libre, the academic institutions formed around the German scholars were more prominent, and some became landmarks in American higher education. The New School, along with the Graduate Faculty, and the Institute for Social Research—all based in New York—were not only havens for displaced scholars but also highly productive intellectual centers that formed a strong reputation and launched their own intellectual traditions, sometimes against a rather cold, if not downright hostile reception. Despite the significant impact in America of the work done under the auspices of the Institute for Social Research, its leaders, Theodor W. Adorno and Max Horkheimer, experienced major difficulty in their early years at Columbia University, their host in New York. In addition to having to face the anti-Semitism of those years in forms that were unfamiliar to them, they got caught in scholarly disputes concerning the legitimacy of their methodological approach, which was deemed by the Americans too abstract, insufficiently empirical, and devoid of practical applications. Recalling his experience with the Princeton Radio Research Project and the difficulties he encountered in modifying his usual frame of work, Adorno confessed that he felt "a strong inner resistance to meeting this demand by turning [himself] inside out" and insists that he "probably couldn't have done it even if [he] had wanted to more than [his] intellectual orientation made possible." Aside from his own professed unwillingness to change in order to be accepted into his new scientific circle, Adorno was disturbed to discover "a certain resentment" toward himself in American colleagues. "The type of culture that I brought with me," he reflected, "appeared (to Americans) to be unjustifiable arrogance. (They) cherished a mistrust of Europeans such as the bourgeoisie of the eighteenth century must have entertained toward the émigré French aristocrats. However little desire I, destitute of all influence, had to do with social privilege, I appeared . . . to be a kind of usurper."[45]

The reference to class as a metaphor of political rivalry is not incidental in Adorno's reminiscences. European intellectuals like him clashed with their American counterparts in part because they represented different class mentalities. Regardless of their socialist agenda, Germans like Adorno had a solid bourgeois background. In America, their intellectual partners were more often first-generation college graduates. Yet the particular metaphor of political rivalry chosen by Adorno also reveals the fear that Americans had no real sympathy for the European intellectual refugees. Americans tolerated but did not approve of them. Accurate or not, such belief could explain the unwillingness of many European intellectuals to become involved in American politics, even though so many were highly politically aware and had been politically involved in their own countries.

The European intellectual refugees were frequently accused of not really understanding America. Some readily admitted to being rather perplexed by this country, and many writers whose outlet for creative expression was entirely dependent on language were discouraged by their struggles with English (the American exile put a tragic end to several promising literary careers). In 1941, the New York–based German Jewish newspaper *Aufbau* published an almanac for recently Americanized immigrants to familiarize them with American institutions and life. One section was devoted to American English, and it introduced the immigrants to bizarre (to them) and colorful colloquial terms that captured their sense "that American culture is like these idioms—glib, sensual, mercenary."[46]

Even when Adorno and other foreign intellectuals had become household names in the mainstream American academic and intellectual milieu, their style, if not the content of their work or their method, continued to be attacked. Regardless of how well some actually did speak and write in English, all of them faced the assumption that their discourse must be *deficient*. And the assumption moved surreptitiously from the level of pronunciation and vocabulary to logic and content. Adorno is a case in point. As he re-counts, when his book *Der Philosophie der neuen Musik* (*The Philosophy of New Music*) was being translated for publication in the United States, the American editor requested a rough draft of the translation. "Upon read-ing it, he discovered that the book (the original book) with which he was already familiar was 'badly organized' [*schlecht organiziert*]. In Germany, I said to myself, despite everything that had happened there, at least I would be spared this."[47]

The comparison between the harassment received from a publisher and anti-Semitic Nazi Germany is doubtless over the top. Indeed, in the next sentence Adorno himself retracted the analogy: "Compared to the horrors of National Socialism my literary experiences were insignificant trifles."[48] Yet such "trifles" played a key role, by his own admission, in his decision to return to Germany after the war. Adorno did not simply object to being corrected by native speakers. He resented the implication that his approach needed correction because it was that of a foreigner. The implication may have existed. As I have already mentioned, Simone de Beauvoir's English fueled not just criticism but the rejection of her views of America as inac-curate and misconstrued.

Many German intellectuals were, like Adorno, Jews. In the United States they came up against the stereotype of the "smart Jew," which functioned as a strategy for "articulating Jewish difference" in post-Holocaust America. While seemingly a positive one, the image of the "smart Jew" was more ambiguous than it appears not only because it served as a strategy for imag-ining a unitary category of the Jew primarily in order to differentiate it from Americans but also because it hides a negative stereotype underneath a seemingly positive representation. In his analysis of popular representations of the "smart Jew" in American film, novels, and popular culture, Sander Gilman has found that the Jew's intelligence is always pinned against a flaw, be it moral or physical. The "smart Jew" is especially depicted as lacking virtue, which renders intelligence useless. The fact that in many representa-tions of the "smart Jew," he or she is also either a victim or needs to be res-cued from a dangerous situation suggests that "intelligence, especially when connected with the supposed superiority of the intellectual, is clearly an in-sufficient quality in this world."[49]

For the newly arrived European Jew, being Jewish posed additional chal-lenges because their particular kind of Jewish identity was disconnected from the emancipatory discourses on Jewish American identity emerging in the aftermath of the war. The postwar conception of Jewishness in America, coming out of "university campuses, rabbis' studies and the pages of Jew-ish and non-Jewish periodicals, grounded Jews in American patterns—and thus, American success."[50] But where would the non-American Jew, who had no recourse yet to "American patterns," fit? The foreign origin of Eu-ropean Jews coming to America was not easily compensated by a shared religion, especially when the newcomers did not go to live in a New York settlement. However lucky they were in this regard, they also missed out on a sense of shared identity and stood out as different.

When not perceived merely in broad terms as European or Jewish, the foreign intellectuals' reception was heavily dependent on representations about their national origin. For most German intellectuals, such percep-tions posed significant problems around the war years. During the war, elite journals like *Commentary* and *The New Republic* published mostly negative articles of "works by German exiles . . . (which) would routinely fault their 'Germanness' and their Teutonic clumsiness."[51] The Federal Bureau of In-vestigation had an even more severe and more consequential indictment of German authors on account of their national origin. Several exiled German writers, most famously among them Bertolt Brecht and Thomas Mann, were suspected of communist activity and placed under surveillance.[52]

In April 1949, *Life* magazine launched a series of attacks against Thomas Mann based on the accusation that he was a "communist dupe," along with Albert Einstein and several American intellectuals. In April 1951, the *Los Angeles Times* published on its front page the news that Mann had been put on a list of forty people considered by the House Committee on Un-American Activities as affiliated with communist organizations. Mann had never become involved in American politics proper, and the focus of his po-litical activity in exile remained Germany. His views of America were a mix of high praise and rather condescending generalizations. His correspondence with German friends is peppered with phrases such as "the good-natured barbarians" (the Americans) and "curiously emptied and amiably stereotyped" (about American faces).[53] Already in 1946, Mann started to worry about the political situation in the United States, which he deemed dangerously similar to the one in Germany right before the ascent of fascism to power. By the early 1950s, Mann was making dark predictions about the fate of democracy in America and was afraid that his American passport would be revoked and that he would be forbidden to ever enter the country again (he had returned to Switzerland). While the 1950s were a politically difficult time for many intellectuals and artists who lived in America, including those born here, the danger was markedly increased for a foreigner. This was a time of deportations increasingly decided on ideological grounds.[54] Foreignness made immigrant intellectuals politically suspect. As targets of the state that had taken them in, they were reminded of their difference. Mann left America disappointed and humiliated. The man who had once seen in President Theodore Roosevelt a political god (and had immortalized him in *Joseph and His Brothers*) also saw in President Dwight Eisenhower the reincarnation of Field Marshal Hindenburg.[55] Some Americans accused him of being a communist. Mann, in turn, was convinced that many Americans were rising fascists.

Such cross-firing gives a measure of the clash between American intellectual and media circles and European intellectual refugees. Brecht, who also eventually left the United States, was placed under even more intense political scrutiny than Mann. Unlike many of his fellow Germans in exile, Brecht had come to America excited to join a culture embodying everything he could no longer find in Germany: vitality, imagination, and nonconformism. In 1920 he had written in his diary: "How this Germany bores me! . . . What's left? America."[56] But once he decided to emigrate, encounters with American immigration officials radically modified this idyllic image of America. After obtaining the necessary visas with difficulty, Brecht arrived in a country that was not eager to share his artistic or political vision. His publicly declared communist beliefs were enough to make him a suspect. The FBI surveillance file reveals a strong emphasis on his national status and not just ideology. Subtle shifts in word choice in the section that identifies Brecht's immigration status illustrate how suspicious his foreignness appeared:

> The records of the Immigration and Naturalization Service, Los Angeles, disclosed that EUGEN BERTOLT FRIEDRICH BRECHT was born at Augsburg, Germany on February 10, 1898, and that he arrived in the United States at the port of San Pedro on July 21, 1941 on the S.S. Annie Jackson from Helsingfors, Finland. Accompanying BRECHT were his wife, HELEN WEIGET BRECHT and two children STEFAN and (illegible), then eighteen and twelve years of age respectively. The above records also revealed that BRECHT married in Berlin in 1928. BRECHT declared his intention to become a citizen of the United States on December 8, 1941, at Los Angeles.[57]

Standard, routine information—date of birth, nationality, marital status—suddenly suggests a clandestine status, prompting the use of verbs like "disclose" and "reveal" instead of neutral ones like "show" or "state." The suspiciousness is later reinforced through the inclusion of an excerpt from Brecht's literary work, titled "On the Designation 'Emigrant,'" in which the author takes poetic license with the status of the German refugees, lamenting that "we didn't emigrate, we, of our own free will, choosing another country. . . . The country that accepted us is no home, but a place of exile. We sit restlessly as near the Border as possible, waiting for the day of our return, observing every little change beyond the Border, questioning every newcomer eagerly, forgetting nothing and giving up nothing."[58]

The poem included in the file is meant as evidence that Brecht could not have been genuinely interested in American citizenship. The FBI file presses the non-assimilability of the foreigner on moral, not merely legal, grounds: Brecht appears cunning and untrustworthy and his petition for American citizenship a devious ploy rather than the expression of a genuine commitment to the new country. The capitalization of a common noun into

"Border" sanctifies the limit that sets apart citizens from noncitizens. This restless being who hovers around the "Border" is the ultimate embodiment of nonbelonging: the foreigner lurking on the margins of to the nation.

In a country that was highly suspicious of the newcomers, citizenship and visa requirements became moral tests rather than mere bureaucratic procedures. One of the key concerns American officials had vis-à-vis foreign intellectuals was their political activity in the homeland and the risk that it might be resumed in the United States. But political missions have different meanings in different contexts. Being socialist in Weimar Germany was not the same as being socialist in America. Caught between different cultural and ideological worlds, anxious to be allowed to stay in America and evade a tragic fate in Europe, some foreign intellectuals hid their political beliefs. As Heilbut comments, "many people felt insecure even in their citizenship, and regarded the course of their emigration as a transit from affidavit to subpoena.[59]

Over time, such anxiety, along other disappointments the émigrés experienced in America, became grave enough to convince them to leave. Whether they died, like Zweig, returned to their homeland, like Brecht, Adorno, and Horkheimer, or chose another European destination, like Mann (who left the United States for Switzerland), European-born intellectuals were a diminished presence in Cold War America. As the Soviet Union tightened its grip on Eastern and Central Europe, a new category of intellectual refugees started trickling into the United States. Yet those fleeing Stalin were neither as numerous nor as famous as those escaping Hitler had been. Later, political dissidents, such as the Czech Václav Havel and the Polish Adam Michnik, remained in their homelands and suffered imprisonment and other kinds of persecution. Eastern European dissidents could and did emigrate to France, Germany, or Britain rather than the United States as Western European states were closer and now also secure (unlike during World War II). The intellectual refugees who came after 1956 (the year of the Hungarian Revolution) or after 1968 (the Soviet invasion of Czechoslovakia) were less politically minded, even if they were escaping political persecution. The Polish poet and philosopher Czeslaw Milosz, who immigrated to America in 1960, became known mainly as a poet and literature professor at Berkeley rather than as the author of *The Captive Mind*, his critical account of communism as a totalitarian ideology. The Eastern and Central European intellectuals fleeing communist dictatorships found a sympathetic reception, at least among anticommunists.[60] Since Cold War America fashioned itself as the political and cultural opposite to the world these refugees left behind, they were all the more welcomed because they reinforced the American "narrative of choiceworthiness," to use Bonnie Honig's term.[61] The very presence of a Solzhenitsyn, Milosz, or Nabokov confirmed America's ascendancy over the Soviet Union and its satellite states. At the same time, they were still foreigners, inheriting the profile of the World War II intellectual refugee: admired, envied, feared, and resented. Even a fierce anticommunist like Solzhenitsyn had an uneasy reception in American intellectual circles, including the most conservative anticommunist ones because he was so strikingly Russian, as I discuss in more detail in chapter 4. Like shared religion or, in time, even a shared language (with many foreign intellectuals publishing and lecturing in English), shared ideological beliefs did not eliminate the gulf between the foreigner and the native.

The history of foreigners' discourse about America is a mix of praise and criticism as America itself changed in their perception from an exotic sojourn and locus of wonder to a more accessible and familiar destination, albeit also a final one. The reception of this discourse in the United States reflects a pattern of rejection that is more than just xenophobic. Foreigners represent "agents of legitimation," expected to confirm and renew a nation's positive self-image.[62] Whether they extolled the virtues of American society as a model for the rest of the world or provoked Americans to assert the exemplarity of their nation, the foreigners' discourse activated a narcissistic impulse that makes one impervious, if not allergic, to criticism. At the same time, the foreigner's linguistic difference, as nonnative speaker of English (when not completely unacquainted with the language) became an iconic representation of inferiority.

"I still speak (English) with a foreign accent and I often don't speak idiomatically," admitted Hannah Arendt in an interview given when she had already lived for several decades in the United States.[63] Her admission sounded both confessional and apologetic, as though she had failed some important test, no matter how much she had published in English or how important her works had been, along with her lectures at the New School and the University of Chicago. It was the test of linguistic membership in the nation. The mark of the stranger persona is deviation from the "universe of sedimented discourse" that persuasion draws upon, not just a national language but also a stock of familiar arguments and common stylistic patterns.[64] Native speakers also deviate from conventions and norms, whether they make grammatical mistakes, have a regional accent, or issue unorthodox claims, but their departures can pass for provisional and perfectible or merely original. The stranger persona, on the other hand, is not just eccentric but also heretic. It reinforces exteriority to the imagined community of the nation and renders it dangerous. As Pierre Bourdieu put it, authority comes to language from the outside—the nation-state.[65] What identifies speakers as citizens or noncitizens, more than documents, is the way they speak. It is no coincidence that, at the same time the Arizona Department of State prohibited the hiring of teachers who spoke English with an accent, the state introduced new deportation procedures that allowed law enforcement to demand identification documents from people suspected of being illegal aliens. What made them look foreign was sometimes how they sounded.

In chapter 1, I examine the political tradition of foreignness in theories of democracy and its effect on creating a discursive polis in which the available means of persuasion, as Aristotle defined rhetoric, are restricted to citizens. Reading theories of the nation-state alongside the sociology of the stranger and the development of a political style centered on citizen-orators, I argue that foreignness affords insights otherwise unavailable but that it is also highly constrained historically and conceptually, and thus rhetorically unstable. In the case studies that follow, I offer four instances of the stranger persona, each shaped by the historical and political context in which these foreign intellectuals built their American political career. I focus on their most controversial writings, in which they made claims either directly about or highly consequential for U.S. politics. In chapter 2, I examine Arendt's criticism of the use of federal troops in Little Rock, Arkansas, and the scandal surrounding her "banality of evil" thesis as it emerged from the *New*

Yorker reports on the trial of Adolph Eichmann. Both these works led to a vilification of Arendt in American intellectual circles and continue to provoke interest decades after their initial publication. Arendt was in many ways the most important protagonist in my cast of characters. Her ideas resurface in the work of the other three, whether the influence is acknowledged or not. She is the first, chronologically, to have launched a career of political commentary in and on America (even though Marcuse arrived in New York two years before her, he remained initially within the bounds of his circle of German associates). Arendt also offers the most comprehensive discussion of estrangement, rather than merely using it as a technique. Even though she put it under the rubric of the pariah, Arendt envisioned a stranger persona that inspired much of my own thinking in this book. Finally, the Arendtian works I study in this chapter contain a critique of American society (explicit and implicit) that captures the political agendas of the other three, no matter how different they were.

In chapter 3, I analyze the critique of capitalism presented by Marcuse in *One-Dimensional Man* and *Essays on Liberation* but also in lesser known public speeches. I argue that Marcuse saw American capitalism as the most dangerous embodiment of a political and economic system present in other Western societies as well. In America, this fervent critic of the bourgeoisie and former revolutionary during the Berlin 1919 uprising found himself in the belly of the beast. I analyze Marcuse's relationship with the American student radicals and the making of his reputation as their alleged guru. In chapter 4, I examine Solzhenitsyn's 1976 commencement speech at Harvard University, in which the Soviet dissident appears as a fierce critic of the United States, and the paradoxical response it received in America, both a dismissal of his arguments and a reaffirmation of his understanding of the role America should play as an imperialist power. Solzhenitsyn's political views differed substantially from those of Arendt, Marcuse, and Said, and this contrast is, in part, what justified my selection. The rejection of completely different, indeed, opposed political agendas reveals the magnitude of the reluctance to accept a foreigner's perspective, no matter what this perspective was. In chapter 5, I investigate Said's political activism on behalf of Palestine and his criticism of Zionism as the founding ideology behind

Israeli policies in the Middle East, compatible, in his view, with the key tenets of Orientalism and American imperialism. I analyze Said's political rhetoric not only in his political journalism but also in his scholarly and literary work, especially *Orientalism* and his memoir *Out of Place*. I make the case that Said strategically used a stranger persona based on his origin as a Palestinian despite the fact that he had inherited American citizenship from his father and had lived most of his adult life in the United States.

My analysis of these intellectuals' political texts places them in the "spaces within which *the dialectic of political rights and cultural identities* unfolds,"[66] identifying the traditions of thought and social practice that may have shaped some of their views and considering the ways some of these views could also have been relevant to the American polity. To study their stranger personas, I analyze these intellectuals' stylistic devices as techniques of estrangement, in the sense originally proposed by the Russian formalist Viktor Shklovsky, but I adapt this to the specific task of rhetorical invention in political discourse and trace their use of specific rhetorical tropes, from analogy, metonymy, and synecdoche to narrative techniques and irony or despair. Yet it is not a particular trope that uniquely defined the styles of these four intellectuals as much as the very tropological nature of their political discourse, which constituted a way of departing from shared understandings and casting into question common assumptions.

Foreigners being introduced to new customs and practices, in some cases vastly unfamiliar to them, can have some problematic cultural blind spots. I do not deny or overlook this. Yet lack of familiarity with their new culture not only does not justify dismissal but can also lead to missed opportunities. What the reception of these four intellectuals illustrates is the rhetorical dynamic of a political culture that retains a habit of exclusion even as it purports to be committed to pluralism. In the conclusion of this book, I consider the implications of the stranger persona for a polity, beyond the particular reception of these four intellectuals, for eliminating this habit of exclusion. The political membership for foreigners I argue for in this book requires a modification in the very positioning of these intellectuals in the foreign/native binary. The distinction was affirmed by those who responded, especially those who responded critically, to the political ideas of Arendt,

Marcuse, Solzhenitsyn, and Said. Yet the stranger persona used by these four intellectuals constitutes a discursive avenue into a polis that does not operate along this distinction anymore. By that, I do not mean that I advocate a political world without nation-states but that I see major political risks in promoting an oppositional rhetoric that takes the distinction among nations at face value and essentializes it to represent a distinction among individuals and among ideas. A language habit even more deeply entrenched in political discourse since the Cold War, the argumentation framework built around the insider-outsider distinction is what a stranger persona can throw into question. The rhetorical merit of these four intellectuals is that they created an argumentation stance that undermines the assumption that the commitment to a polis cannot be shared beyond national origin, cultural background, or common life experiences. Thus, the main contribution of this book regards the political implications of the stranger persona as a discursive phenomenon, which need not be restricted in use to individuals who were born in another country. We can all do with an increased dose of estrangement in political discourse. We should look at our civic world with the eyes of a stranger, but not any stranger: one who is involved and committed to the society in which he or she lives. An intimate stranger, just like an intimate friend, can be not only a trusted aid but also a source of enlightenment.

This is all the more the case for these four intellectuals, who were exceptional individuals. The story of their involvement in American political discourse is not simply one of triumph or rejection.[67] Perhaps their most impressive achievement is that they got to the forefront of public discourse and captured the attention of American audiences against a long tradition of American discourse sneering at criticism from foreigners or treating it with condescension. None of them faced the obstacles of a political refugee from Kosovo or Somalia. They were not illiterate, destitute, or racially different from many Americans. They came well equipped with the rhetorical ability required for political participation. The controversies that ensued as they tried to make their voices heard in American discourse represent a litmus test for the negotiation of discursive and political rights that could be afforded to all foreigners, regardless of their profession, prestige, or rhetorical prowess.

1

THE STRANGER PERSONA

I N THE days after Hurricane Katrina, the uproar over the lack of disaster preparation and mismanagement of emergency funds dominated political discourse while a less noticed controversy was unfolding over the use of the term "refugee" for the hurricane victims. The *Washington Post* interviewed some of the victims seeking shelter at the New Orleans convention center and reported that they all felt insulted by the term. Elijah Cummings, democratic representative from Maryland and member of the Congressional Black Caucus, echoed the response: "They are not refugees. I hate that word." The term even prompted a presidential intervention. Upon visiting the destroyed region and meeting the survivors, President George W. Bush urged the use of alternative phrases to describe the status of those recently made homeless. He even offered a few suggestions: "evacuees," "victims," or simply, "displaced citizens." This last phrase seemed ready-made to address the frustration of Annette Ellis, one of the displaced Baton Rouge residents interviewed by the *Washington Post*, who insisted in simple and clear words: "We ain't refugees. I'm a citizen."[1]

"Why is the term such a dirty word to some?"—asked the *Washington Post*.[2] After all, it was only a metaphor. However much the victims had lost in the hurricane, they still had their citizenship. To call them "refugees" was to throw into question some of their most important rights. The disaster left its victims homeless, unemployed, and in precarious health. They were dependent on state and federal assistance and the rest of the American citizenry now saw the displaced as a political problem and an economic burden. Their status was not radically different from that of a refugee arriving from Somalia or Rwanda.

More than terms like immigrant or exile, "refugee" emphatically references the foreigner as a noncitizen and an overall rather sorry figure. Public imagination captures this representation well through (often racialized) images of extreme poverty, illiteracy, and disease—features of a diminished subjectivity. The objections of Katrina victims at being identified as refugees show the anxiety created by the subjectivity assigned to them, the subjectivity of the noncitizen deprived of rights, at the mercy of others. The figure of the refugee emerges from historical, political, and policy documents as a "pure victim *in general*: universal man, universal woman, universal child, and taken together [all refugees] universal family." "This universalism," Liisa Malkki claims, "can strip from them (the victims) the authority to give credible narrative evidence or testimony about their own condition in politically and institutionally consequential forums."[3] Even more so it strips from them the authority to draw on their own experiences to offer insight into the politics of their adoptive nation.

Readers looking at Arendt's picture on the covers of her books did not see a poor refugee in the woman seated comfortably in an armchair and smoking a cigarette. Nor did they see one in television interviews with Herbert Marcuse, a white-haired man in black suits and bow ties. Said's physical appearance, that of a scholar with a pensive look, hardly inspired Palestinian refugees. Even Solzhenitsyn, a hirsute in Russian peasant garb, looked defiant and self-assured, not destitute and needy. Such intellectuals cannot be refugees, it would seem. If they were poor, their poverty was bohemian; if they were ill, their disease was romantic. They were certainly not illiterate; if anything, it was American students who must have fidgeted under the professorial gaze of these foreigners . Yet all four of them were, or self-identified at some point, as refugees: Arendt and Marcuse in the most straightforward sense of the term, as political refugees from Nazi Germany; Solzhenitsyn as a member of a larger category of refugees from the Soviet

Union and Eastern European countries (even though he, in particular, was expelled); and Said as a spokesperson for Palestinian refugees forced to live outside their homeland.

We find it difficult to think of them alongside refugees from the Third World and "the babies in Africa that have all the flies and are starving to death"—to use an image that was especially disturbing to one of Katrina's victims.[4] Intellectuals who have fled their countries, or were forced to leave, are more commonly called exiles rather than refugees or émigrés rather than immigrants. Word choice matters. It could be that the term "refugee" is deemed too unsavory to be assigned to an elite group but even more likely that it is *made* unavailable. In 1940, as the first waves of middle-class, intellectual Europeans fled to America, *Life* magazine scorned them as "refugees de luxe," depicting them as well-to-do foreigners in fur coats at upscale restaurants, living in luxury hotels or vacationing at expensive resorts, while presenting themselves as refugees.[5] *Fortune* magazine was equally dismissive of these refugees' plight: "The pilgrims of the seventeenth century came here to make their fortune; the *émigrés* of 1940 have come here to protect theirs."[6] To not identify these intellectuals as refugees is to keep them symbolically at a distance from their new political environment, as their commitment is expected to be to the homeland, and their sojourn, temporary. Intellectual refugees (writers, artists, and academics) once seen as uprooted from their homeland can be in an even more precarious situation than other refugees.

Underlying all other representations of the foreigner in a nation-state—exile, immigrant, refugee, and asylum seeker—is a subjectivity defined by inferiority to the citizen as native born. The litmus test of this inferiority is that foreigners must face racially and morally inflected residence and naturalization requirements (such as passing IQ tests or the expectation to not have been involved in prostitution), which decide if they deserve to be allowed into the national community. At the other end of these requirements for admission is a deportation system designed to eliminate those deemed undesirable to the nation-state. The modern deportation regime emerged from a conception of citizenship as full membership in the constitutional community of the nation, which assumes that the citizens are "the people," "whereas noncitizens are something less."[7] Deportation decisions can resort to denaturalization if someone who is legally a U.S. citizen is deemed undesirable. The foreign origin, then, makes one vulnerable in a way that can never go fully away. Even when legally drawn into the nation, the foreigner inhabits a precarious position, not just politically, but also ontologically, because citizenship is not simply a political category but also commonly imagined as a natural condition and articulated in a series of metaphorical representations of place and nationhood as roots that ground the citizen. The uprooted, by such logic, falls outside not just a national but also a natural order. "The powerful metaphoric practices that so commonly link people to place," Malkki argues, "are also deployed to understand and act upon the categorically aberrant condition of people whose claims on, and ties to, national soils are regarded as tenuous, spurious, or non-existent."[8]

While they can fulfill some residence and naturalization requirements more easily than others, intellectuals are potentially the most threatening instance of foreignness from the perspective of the nation-state. In 1919, Emma Goldman, a Russian national who had lived in New York since 1885 where she was an active writer and public speaker on women's rights, social issues, and anarchist politics, was denaturalized without notice and deported to Russia as an "alien radical." Goldman is not the only case of a foreign intellectual deported on the basis of dangerous political ideas. In 1955, Jamaican writer C. L. R. James was deported after fifteen years of living in New York and being involved in socialist politics. At the height of the Eichmann controversy, Arendt said to friends, more or less jokingly, that she hoped she would not be deported. Marcuse and Said received hate mail that demanded they leave the country. Solzhenitsyn was invited to go back to communist Russia if he did not like American democracy. These intellectuals, like Goldman and James before them, were highly critical of the U.S. government, yet hardly alone in their opposition. They had American-born allies and partners who did not suffer a similar fate because the state could not force them to leave. One can only wonder: "a citizen might be immune from deportation, but how was a refugee to be sure?"[9]

The noncitizen's inferiority cuts across other categories, such as race, class, or national origin, even though each of these has been at times deemed inferior for separate reasons.[10] What all noncitizens share is their uprooted-ness perceived as a fall from the national order, which renders them fundamentally deficient and suspect. Being white, Western European, and highly educated has only been a partial remedy to such deficiency. Granted, American immigration law has consistently privileged white European immigrants, especially if they had a Christian, preferably Protestant, religious orientation. These were often seen as the stock America was originally made of, and hence more likely to fit in the fabric of the nation.[11] Yet the push and pull of immigration also meant that these white European Christian immigrants belonged to a particular class: they were usually farmers or unskilled laborers who arrived empty-handed and achieved socioeconomic success. Ironically, low class status could facilitate Americanization; as throughout much of the nineteenth century and the early part of the twentieth, the process of Americanizing immigrants was forged through education.[12] By contrast, intellectual migrants came with a completed education and were unlikely enrollers in Sunday school or after work language and cultural programs. Indeed, some encountered other Americans by acting as their teachers rather than students. Challenging Hannah Arendt's negative remarks on American foreign policy, Nathan Glazer once referred to her sarcastically as "our teacher."[13] While seemingly acknowledging her intellectual authority, Glazer questioned her political wisdom by emphatically putting her on a different level from "regular" Americans and rendering her inassimilable to the community that she was addressing. How could a perspective like hers be other than irrelevant, theoretically sophisticated perhaps, but surely impractical?

Laura Fermi estimates the financial contribution wartime European intellectuals made to American society by being ready to contribute immediately to the workforce at $32 million, without any investment from the U.S. government required for their training.[14] Yet, as the label "refugees de luxe" suggests, their reception was far from enthusiastic. As I show in the introduction, American officials suspected many of them of subversive political activity, even as the State Department employed several intellectual refugees in the war intelligence effort.[15] Surveys published in popular magazines and newspapers of the time along with articles and letters to the editors indicated a general anti-immigration sentiment in America. Almost 80 percent of the population expressed negative feelings about intellectual refugees from Europe.[16] As the *Life* magazine article shows, intellectual refugees got caught in a double-bind of rejection, on the one hand simply as foreigners, and on the other hand, as impostors. Ironically, then, they were doubly inferior.

Yet no matter how critically they were received at times, Hannah Arendt, Herbert Marcuse, Alexander Solzhenitsyn, and Edward Said succeeded in becoming political commentators in the United States and frequently voicing their opinions, even the most critical ones. How did they formulate their ideas and position given the constraints exerted by a political discourse structurally and historically set up to keep foreigners at bay? To begin my investigation, in this chapter I look more closely at the politics of foreignness and its rhetorical valence in postwar America to articulate the general framework in which I examine the particularities of the stranger persona in each of my four case studies. My goal is to conceptualize foreignness at the intersection of political practices of stratecraft and rhetorical practices of de-familiarization (or estrangement), drawing on Victor Shklovsky's work. These practices converge in the figure of the *stranger*, which I take from, but also expand upon, the sociology of Georg Simmel and Alfred Schutz.

This chapter, then, lays the foundation for the overall argument of the book: the four foreign intellectuals I study here developed a stranger persona that was not the mere consequence of maladjustment, or a rejection of American mores, but rather a strategy of invention and delivery created in response to the political subjectivity of the foreigner. In their criticism, these intellectuals offered a portrait of the American nation. In their audiences' responses, we discern a different image of America. Looking at these images side by side, I am less concerned with whose depiction was more accurate and more interested in the tension between the underlying representations. It is this tension that gives us a unique measure of civic engagement in America, of its ambivalence toward plurality and its cautiousness toward ideas that could inspire political renewal.

THE CITIZEN'S ETHOS

Political life relies on rhetorical acts: decisions that are made and enforced by the members of the community based on the arguments they find most compelling. Aristotle saw such political-cum-rhetorical activity as the rational byproduct of the natural inclination of human beings to live together and achieve certain goals that are valid and desirable for all, rather than only particular individuals. Politics—and political discourse—brings individuals together in a "sort of partnership."[17] But did foreigners also belong in this partnership? A foreigner himself, Aristotle did not participate in Athenian politics, but he was a key player as advisor to Alexander the Great, whose thinking and policy he influenced directly. What kept foreigners out of political deliberation was not only their inferior social status, but also, and connectedly, their lack of a citizen's ethos.

In the classical rhetorical tradition, the genre of political deliberation required that in order to convince an audience the speaker display ethos, or moral character, usually associated with a well-defined set of characteristics: practical wisdom, virtue, and goodwill. The complete list of virtues included courage, temperance, magnanimity, liberality, gentleness, prudence, and justice. Greek culture did not define these virtues in the abstract terms of a moral theory but as ethical conventions shared by a community. Practical wisdom, for instance, referred to the capacity to identify what is beneficial for the community in certain circumstances, which, in turn, depended on what the members already took for granted as being "beneficial."[18] Virtues were context- and culture-specific, set up by "an ethics of citizenship to parcel up humanity into different natural types."[19]

The classical conception of ethos carries an unacknowledged legacy of ethnocentrism, not only because ancient rhetoric saw the circumstances of a person's birth as an "intrinsic and essential part of an individual's identity," but also by disadvantaging rhetorically those whose status was deemed socially and politically inferior. Moreover, in the *Nichomachean Ethics* Aristotle implicitly linked ethos to the self-image of a community by claiming that ethos develops through custom and education, in other words through familiarity and adherence to the values and beliefs of a particular community that can consistently recognize and reward behaviors assumed to be praise-worthy.[20] Ethos, then, presumes membership in the rhetorical community formed by the speaker and audience and is "virtually co-extensive with the activity of judgment that partly defines citizenship."[21] This judgment almost inevitably left out the foreigner as the ancient Greeks inhabited a moral and political universe that often asserted its identity in contrast to outsiders, the "barbarians." Roman rhetoric was no different in this regard, as the art of oratory was taught "in the context of a telos—the development in students of the capacity to see themselves primarily as citizen-patriots, dedicated to working on behalf of republican ideals."[22] Romans tended to dismiss non-citizens from the field of rhetorical transactions, and the focus on citizenry comes through in Cicero's *De Oratore* in Crassus's insistence that the ora-tor be familiar with Roman citizenship laws. The very idea that an orator would be 'ignorant of these . . . laws of his own community" strikes him as "supremely scandalous." While Cicero considered various qualities that the ideal orator would need, its public significance for the state goes unques-tioned. The republic saw itself reflected in the character of the noble orator. In the words of Crassus: "the wise control of the complete orator is that which chiefly upholds not only his own dignity, but the safety of countless individuals and of the entire State."[23]

The Romans reluctantly admired some contributions made by foreign-ers, starting with the rhetorical treatises of the Greeks. Cicero preferred a speaker who would "show, first, as little trace as possible of any artifice, and secondly none whatever of things Greek."[24] Yet he was willing to bow to the Greek's accomplishments and believed "it would be brutish and inhu-man not to lend an ear, and . . . to pick up their sayings by eavesdropping and keep a look-out from afar for their talk."[25] Even at the risk of receiving condemnation from their fellow citizens, the Roman rhetoricians remained receptive to foreign influence, especially when it was Aristotle's. Cicero was hardly the only one to carry on the Aristotelian legacy over the centuries. It was not only Greek precepts that traveled across time and space in the rhetorical cultures of Europe but also one of their key philosophical dilem-mas regarding the moral neutrality of a rhetorical education. Was the ideal orator morally virtuous or only verbally skilled to the point of being able to feign virtue? The answer depended both on the audience's familiarity with the orator in question and on the particular epistemic climate whether it was committed to the ideals of truthfulness and authenticity or more cynically inclined and constantly alert to the risk of deception and manipulation. Either way, foreigners were at the short end of the stick, whether because they were the ones audiences did not know and therefore did not readily trust or because they were deemed a priori untrustworthy. The regulation of trust within the confines of a political community depends on how that community is structured around individuals, relations among individuals, institutionalized ties, or an abstract system of rules.[26] The ancient rhetorical culture was centered on an ideal of civic republicanism that influenced the Anglo-American tradition of civil society.[27] In this tradition, civic virtue— or the citizen's ethos—is predicated on the assumption that the community sees its public values reflected in the private ones of its members so that individuals readily and easily agree with a "General Will," as Jean-Jacques Rousseau would put it, that reflects their collective consciousness.

In the "transformation from a rhetorical, oratorical style to a modern, bourgeois one," oratory not only converted ancient civic republicanism to the value of politeness in a Christian aristocracy but also sought to serve an emerging culture of sentiment in which foreignness becomes the measuring rod for impartiality, the principal civic virtue.[28] The impartial spectator envisioned by Adam Smith was "characterized by the absence of already existing commitments," which allowed him to be detached and objective.[29] Yet this spectator was still a member of the community whose impartiality represented a cultivated epistemic stance rather than mere consequence of an outsider status. Indeed, the spectator was attached to his fellow citizens not only through shared membership in their nation but also through a faculty of imagination that allowed him to understand and empathize with other members of the community. This imagination, in turn, was activated by the sentiment of sympathy towards one's fellow citizens. The emphasis placed by Enlightenment political theorists on sympathy as the foundation of the faculty of imagination that allows one citizen to relate to another and

Bernard Anderson's definition of the nation as an "imagined community" are not by accident the same. Sympathy was the byproduct of familiarity, and thus focused on one's fellow citizens rather than strangers. As Jürgen Habermas puts it, the nation "is Janus-faced. Whereas the voluntary nation of citizens is the source of democratic legitimation, it is the inherited or ascribed nation founded on ethnic membership (*die geborene Nation der Volkgenossen*) that secures social integration."[30] Whereas ethnic membership, which sustains the everyday life of the nation, leaves foreigners out, the rule of law, which cements the nation around a presumed consensus, is predicated on foreignness or on the figure of an impartial and detached evaluator. Rousseau mentioned approvingly "the custom of most Greek cities to entrust the establishment of their laws to foreigners," a custom later adopted by the modern republics of Italy.[31] When Rome did not follow this practice, it frequently ended up with tyranny, and according to Rousseau, a political framework limiting access to citizens only leads to corruption and destruction.

In Rousseau's view, the legislator is "in every respect an extraordinary man in the state. If he ought to be so by his genius, he is no less so by his office, which is neither magistracy nor sovereignty. This office, which constitutes the republic, does not enter into its constitution."[32] In this tradition, the foreigner is the figure of a" godlike man . . . able to discover the best rules for a society, see all of men's passions yet experience none of them; have no relationship at all to our nature yet know it thoroughly." Cast in positive terms, the foreigner is the ultimate impartial observer with objectivity the very consequence of disinterestedness. From westerns to religious narratives like the Book of Ruth, there are abundant representations of a wise and virtuous outsider who can help the community when its own members fail to do so. Yet at the end of the story, the foreigner either goes native or departs "in a timely fashion."[33] The figure of the foreigner is absorbed into the group or eliminated if it becomes resistant. Thus, the ethos of the foreigner is based on exceptionality, and its tenuous nature comes from the very fact that it lacks the virtues associated with citizenship: disinterested rather courageous, detached rather than magnanimous, and objective rather than gentle. There is no absolute opposition between these virtues but a marked contrast: while one set of values signals connection and inclusion, the other one emphasizes dissociation and distance.

With distance comes danger, as the American deportation system again illustrates. Daniel Kanstroom has shown that the roots of the American deportation law lie in the laws designed to justify the removal of Native Americans from their land and those overseeing the treatment of fugitive slaves from the late eighteenth century to the middle of the nineteenth century. "They all involved the application of majoritarian power," Kanstroon claims, "against a particular group of people, largely identifiable by race or nationality, to compel their removal from one place to another."[34] Deportation law depicts the foreigner proposed to be deported as a criminal but not just any criminal—no matter how petty the crime, the foreign convict is regarded as more dangerous than the native one. What the legal system deems "criminal," however, can vary from shoplifting to anti-U.S. government activity, the spectrum wide enough to produce a regime of political rejection designed to detect danger in foreignness.

Historically, foreigners became suspect political subjects in the political landscape created by World War I with the emergence of the modern European nation-state marking the conjunction of sovereignty and territorial control through border-enforcement. As Saskia Sassen explains, "the coupling of state sovereignty and nationalism with border control made the 'foreigner' an outsider."[35] The first decades of the twentieth century saw increased movements of foreigners with large refugee flows reaching European borders at the same time as the United States, previously the major in-taker of immigrants, was introducing immigration restriction policies.

America, of course, has historically defined its national identity in relation to foreigners. In the Declaration of Independence, one of the grievances listed against the British sovereign concerns the restrictions imposed on the naturalization of foreigners who came to the American colonies. Thomas Jefferson, however, was making a political rather than moral complaint as he was not concerned with the welfare of foreigners as much as interested in their strategic value as agents of nation-building. As Aristide Zolberg explains, in the United States naturalization procedures "achieved unprecedented practical and theoretical prominence because foreign immigration—as against mere transfers within the empire—made a much greater contribution to its population than had ever occurred in any European nation."[36]

In American political and legal discourse, the foreigner is an alien, caught "at the nexus of two legal worlds": the world of government restrictions, national communities, and border control as well as the world of social relationships among the people present in a territory. In the United States, these relationships define a polis formally committed to norms of equal treatment.[37] In the name of such commitments, Michael Walzer has argued that foreigners make important contributions to the community of citizens and therefore must be allowed to have political membership. To deny such membership would amount to relegating foreigners, in Walzer's view, to a "metic status" that makes foreign residents into the "subjects of a band of citizen tyrants, governed without consent."[38] The very fact that Walzer emphasizes the lack of consent and the tyranny of a citizenry turned against foreigners reveals his commitment to allowing foreigners political membership, effectively making them eligible for participation in the consent of the nation. But Walzer has also argued that nation-states are justified in restricting access to foreigners as a way of preserving their way of life. In his view, the members of a national community express their beliefs and values in the political decisions they make regarding which and when to accept foreigners and when to keep them out. Linda Bosniak explains Walzer's seemingly conflicted views toward foreigners by pointing out that he endorses both the right of states to restrict admission to foreigners and their obligation to grant them political membership because he subscribes to a conception of justice grounded in the principle of separation. Once *inside* the political community of a nation-state, foreigners are subject to the principle of equality governing that sphere. The contradiction is further explained by the fact that the American "moral tradition simultaneously embraces external boundedness and internal inclusive equality." Foreigners heighten this ambivalence by activating the pressures of treating them in accordance with the principle of inclusive equality as well as reminding a community of its own cultural imperatives. But the tension is absorbed in a "nationalist narrative of choiceworthiness" that asks, and indeed assumes foreigners are willing, to assimilate in the land of their dreams to become citizens and adopt the lifestyle of the native.[39] American national sentiment is based on immigration as a trope that is "not simply an expression of . . . openness," but also "operates as continuing reference point for making decisions about membership in the nation and the terms of that membership and ultimately serves to renew American nationhood."[40] Does this symbolic value of immigration also mean that the citizenry is open to assimilating a newcomer's opinion, no matter how critical it might be? Not necessarily. The American "rhetoric of consensus," as Sacvan Bercovitch articulates it, is a "strategy for absorption," for subsuming diversity under a set of ideals.[41] Chief among these ideals is that of a chosen nation, a "community of grace" in which the strongest bond consists in the very fact of belonging.[42]

Already in 1820, John Quincy Adams, while only Secretary of State, urged new Americans—significantly, those of German origin—to

> cast off their European skin, never to resume it . . . [to] look forward to their posterity, rather than backward to their ancestors; . . . (to) be sure that whatever their feelings may be, those of their children will cling to the prejudices of this country, and will partake of that proud spirit, . . . that feeling of superiority over other nations . . . (which) arises from the consciousness of every individual that . . . no man in the country is above him.[43]

Becoming an authentic American was more than a matter of acculturation. It implied acquiring a citizen's ethos centered on authenticity as a prerequisite for honesty and reliability. Questions of authenticity have been central to American political discourse from the birth of the nation to contemporary media depictions of the character of key political leaders. As Shawn Parry-Giles defines it, political authenticity is a "symbolic, mediated, interactional, and highly contested process" by which the veracity of a political leader's public character is assessed.[44] While the politics of authenticity relies on a complex ideological repertoire of assumptions about race, gender, sexuality, and class, it is first and foremost rooted in an ideology of nationalism. To be authentic becomes entangled with being an authentic American or authentically committed to America. This concern with political authenticity creates a culture defined not only by suspiciousness but also by defensiveness. Tocqueville had noticed that the American citizen "feels a duty to defend anything criticized there, for it is not only his country that is being attacked, but himself."[45] The citizen's ethos is one with the nation's ethos. As such, criticism cannot come from outside.

A STRANGER'S EMBRACE

The assimilation of immigrants is not only a benign way of eliminating foreignness; it is also a strategy of re-invigorating national self-enchantment. In Honig's terms, "the myth of an immigrant America depicts the foreigner as a supplement to the nation, and agent of national re-enchantment that might rescue the regime from corruption and return it to its first principles."[46] The intellectuals I examine in this book were hardly assimilated immigrants, but they believed in America's founding principles. They were seduced by the *idea* of America, even though they disliked some of its concrete manifestations. Arendt extolled the wisdom of the Founding Fathers in the making of a nation committed to plurality and held together by civic pride rather than ethnic bonds. Although he spent most of his career criticizing American society, Marcuse maintained a vision of the land of freedom that had greeted him upon arrival from Nazi Germany. Solzhenitsyn saw in the United States a potential rescuer of nations. Even Said hoped that the absence of a history of European colonialism might redeem Americans and inspire them to act differently in the Middle East.

Despite the fact that they nurtured visions of America as an enchanted land—each having his or her own enchanted vision—the intensity of and arguments used in rejecting their criticism suggest that in their audiences' eyes, they were guilty of anti-Americanism. The accusation is not merely xenophobic or unfair but also an illustration of the paradoxical position of the foreigner: both inside and outside a national community, drawn to and by it, as well as repelled. Their criticism seemed at times detached and uncaring as if it was simply the dismissive reaction of a temporary visitor who was about to return, rather disappointed, to his or her own country. Each of them was not only a foreigner by virtue of having come from another country but also a stranger in the sense defined by Georg Simmel as a "*potential* wanderer . . . his position in this group . . . determined, essentially, by the fact that he has not belonged to it from the beginning, that he imports qualities into it, which do not and cannot stem from the group itself."[47]

The stranger, according to Simmel, embodies a "synthesis of 'nearness and distance,' physically present and thus close, but also a vestige of a world that is remote and unfamiliar." When Montesquieu's hero Rica arrives in Paris, he is surprised to see the excited reaction of the French to his appearance: "Oh! Oh! Is he a Persian? What a most extraordinary thing! How can one be a Persian?"[48] But the interest of the French is only aroused if alerted to the fact that Rica is a Persian. When he starts dressing in European clothes, nobody in Paris notices him anymore. He is a foreigner, whether noticed or not, but he becomes a *stranger* when the natives interact with him and (re)mark his difference. Simmel explains this phenomenon by stressing that to be a stranger "is a form of interaction. The inhabitants of Sirius are not really strangers to us, at least not in any sociologically relevant sense: they do not exist for us at all; they are beyond far and near. The stranger . . . is an element of the group itself." The stranger does not share the "peculiar tendencies of the group." The stranger can observe and assess the society around him because he has no stakes in it, which makes him into an "objective individual . . . bound by no commitments which could prejudice his perception, understanding, and evaluation of the given." The boldness of a stranger's reflection is the result of "not (being) tied down in his action by habit, piety, and precedent." Simmel believed that the "unity of nearness and remoteness" characteristic of strangers makes them attractive to the members of the group who come to value their knowledge, seek their advice, or entrust them with secrets. The stranger "often receives the most surprising openness—confidences which sometimes have the character of a confessional and which would be carefully withheld from a more closely related person."[49]

Simmel's optimistic and indeed cosmopolitan view did not withstand the test of real life. His concept was based largely on an abstraction and inspired by his longstanding interest in the philosophy of economics, which drew his attention to the trader who travels back and forth, never staying long enough to assimilate or to be perceived as a threat. Ironically, though, the ultimate source of inspiration was Simmel himself as an assimilated Berliner Jew. As Pierre Birnbaum has remarked, Simmel "historicize(d) the quality that affected him throughout his own life.[50] But he also gave it a positive valence and glossed over the rejection of the stranger before he would have the misfortune of experiencing it directly in his later struggles with the anti-Semitic academic establishment of 1900s Berlin.[51]

In a 1963 Lecture at Leo Baeck Institute in New York, Albert Salomon, a former student of Simmel's, questioned the idea that the stranger can receive a legitimate place among those who seem to accept him.[52] A Jewish refugee from a Germany even more violently anti-Semitic than Simmel had experienced it, Salomon criticized his former teacher for having offered a politically utopian, if not complacent, conception of the stranger. Simmel had also ignored, in Salomon's view, that "the world of everyday life, the social world, is as strange to the stranger as it is to the people who live by their social roles for the fulfillment of social goals."[53] Making the stranger into the main figure of modernity, Salomon also brought it into the post-Holocaust conversation about the role of Jews in the international political order. The concept of the stranger became laden with the assumptions of nationalist ideology that maintained a clear separation between the native and foreigner, whether to avoid conflict or to preserve national distinctiveness.

The American sociology of marginality and alienation influenced by Simmel's concept of the "stranger" shifted in instructive ways from the original sense of the term.[54] Robert Park, who uses the concept in his own work to describe immigrants, focuses on their assimilation more than Simmel himself ever did.[55] Moreover, Simmel stressed that the stranger is "by nature no 'owner of soil'—soil not only in the physical, but also in the figurative sense of a life-substance which is fixed."[56] The stranger is a category that includes several characters—the poor, the anarchist, or just the anonymous person in an urban crowd—as all can exist inside a group without being fully recognized by the other members. Simmel's strangers shared more than a condition of marginality: he called them "sundry 'inner enemies,'" thus emphasizing their opposition to the group, whether an actualized or a potential one, real or only imagined by the members of the group.[57] The stranger would not only be a noncitizen in many countries that restrict property to citizens but also a non-national insofar as the nation is the main provider of a stable "life-substance," in Simmel's terms. This makes the stranger bound to suffer restrictions in his or her activity. For Simmel, such a restriction is illustrated by taxation laws imposed on Jews. Arendt, Marcuse, Solzhenitsyn, and Said were "taxed" differently, in their right to criticize America. They were allowed the freedom of speech afforded to any American, but the systematic and intense rejection of their views invoking their foreign origins suggests that this freedom was, for them, limited. Moreover, those who contested their right, or prerequisite knowledge, to criticize saw them as having no stake in the welfare of American society. They were not, after all, "owners of soil," even in the most literal of senses. Both Arendt and Said rented a small apartment their whole life, Marcuse moved across the country, and Solzhenitsyn built a Russian estate in the heart of Vermont.

It is hardly a coincidence that Simmel's understanding of the stranger reemerged in the work of an exiled intellectual from Austria, Alfred Schutz, in the very article that debuted his entry to American sociology in a 1944 issue of *The American Journal of Sociology*. While still dealing with abstractions and using Simmel's terminology, Schutz narrowed the sphere of application for "the stranger" to a permanent immigrant rather than a traveler. The shift from the sojourner to the permanent immigrant led Schutz to a recasting of the concept of the stranger in less optimistic terms than Simmel. The change is captured by the different take on the synthesis of distance and closeness that fascinated Simmel. For Schutz, this is not even a synthesis anymore but "hesitation" leading inevitably to "uncertainty, and . . . distrust."[58] Foreign intellectuals like Schutz felt caught in the gap between their cultural universe and that of America. The figure of the refugee intellectual lurking in the backdrop of Schutz's model is important because it explains the double bind of the foreigner in the new world, one who is not a "sundry inner enemy" by choice but by political necessity. This makes Schutz's stranger, like so many of the immigrants in his cohort and like himself, into someone pining for "an 'ex-world'" while facing the daunting task of a "breach of cultural and psychological difference" in order to make a new home.[59]

In a letter that echoes Salomon's critique of Simmel, philosopher Aron Gurwitch critiqued Schutz's concept of the stranger in part because it had over-stressed, in his view, the inadaptability of the newcomer.[60] One can read between the lines Gurwitch's irritation that Schutz did not seem to acknowledge the successful assimilation of prestigious immigrants (which both men were). The emphasis on the inadaptability of the stranger, however, had little to do with the question of assimilation as mere ability to function in a new society. It was more a way of stipulating a cognitive imperative. The stranger can understand the new world upon studying its "cultural pattern of group life" that hold together "all the peculiar valuations, institutions, and systems of orientation and guidance (such as the folkways, mores, laws, habits, customs, etiquette, fashions) which . . . characterize—if not constitute—any social group at a given moment in its history."[61]

Those inside the group know and follow these values tacitly. Theirs is a "knowledge of acquaintance"—a term borrowed by Schutz from William James—and thus merely "a halo knowledge *about* what seems to be sufficient." The members of a group navigate social life based on familiar procedures that they take for granted, forming what Schutz calls "thinking as usual." Strangers, by contrast, have a fresh perspective on the group in which they seek membership precisely because they have no access to its "thinking as usual." What the members of the group take for granted, strangers need to ponder and decipher before they can understand. What insiders know tacitly, strangers have to learn, and to learn, they must also analyze and interpret. The group members have "trustworthy *recipes* for interpreting the social world and for handling things and men in order to obtain the best results in every situation with a minimum of effort by avoiding undesirable consequences." Lacking such recipes, the stranger "becomes essentially the man who has to place in question nearly everything that seems to be unquestionable to the members of the approached group."[62]

By positing such a sharp contrast between the stranger and the group, Schutz reified the cohesion of a group around insiders' cultural knowledge. It is a strategic reification meant to suggest that the insiders recognize their

own insider status by interacting with outsiders. Thus, what makes the beliefs, behaviors, and values of a group familiar to its members is defined by
their very lack of familiarity to nonmembers. Put differently: "a stranger, in
fact, serves to demarcate, by his or her very strangeness, the boundaries of
the familiar and (in that sense) of the real."[63] From the boundaries of the
real, "the stranger discerns, frequently with a grievous clear-sightedness, the
rising of a crisis which may menace the whole foundation of the 'relatively
natural conception of the world,' while all those symptoms pass unnoticed
by the members of the in-group, who rely on the continuance of their cus-
tomary way of life."[64]

By depicting the stranger as an oracle, Schutz stressed the intellectual
superiority of the stranger as one who overcomes the initial ignorance or
inexperience of the newcomer and ends with a wisdom that can foresee the
future. It seems an apt depiction if we consider that Arendt correctly saw
that the desegregation of schools would not be a quick remedy for racist
discrimination. Marcuse anticipated not only the collapse of the American Left but also the perpetuation of politically and economically disastrous
wars involving the United States in faraway regions. Solzhenitsyn insisted
that the post–Cold War political world would remain "split." Finally, Said
thought that the Palestinian-Israeli conflict would continue indefinitely, a
verdict that still stands a decade after his death. The clarity of their vision is
the result of their ability to de-familiarize, to scrutinize "with care and precision" where the native merely pursues "thinking as usual."

Russian Formalist Viktor Shklovsky, the famous theorist of estrangement (*ostrenenie*), reflected on the effects of what Schutz called decades
later "thinking as usual": taking things for granted, assuming that the way
things are is the way they should be, in other words, living life on automatic
pilot. "Automatization eats away at things, at clothes, at furniture, at our
wives, and at our fear of war," complained Shklovsky from his German exile, writing to another exiled friend, Roman Jakobson, in America.[65] Habits
dull our impressions and make "life fade into nothingness."[66] To revive our
perceptions, we have to escape routine and habit by creating images that
"do not draw our understanding closer to that which (the image stands for),
but rather . . . allow us to perceive the object in a special way, in short, . . .

lead us to a 'vision' of this object rather than mere recognition."[67] Estrangement offers renewal by allowing us to "question how mythical narratives are made, to lay bare the devices and to offer a new architecture and geometry of understanding."[68]

For Shklovsky, estrangement was primarily an aesthetic technique associated with formalism, but it also had strong political implications. It was not just art he wanted to renew but also society. One of Shklovsky's famous examples of estrangement comes from a story by Tolstoy in which the narrator is a horse who can understand human language. The horse observes the institution of property by puzzling over the use of expressions like "my house" or "my wife." Stripped of their habitual meaning, these phrases reveal the arbitrariness of social life with its practices and institutions. Like Tolstoy's horse, the stranger persona begins the reflection with a puzzlement caused by not knowing or understanding certain practices and conventions. Unencumbered by "thinking as usual," the stranger sees that they are not only arbitrary but also noxious. Estrangement becomes a way of revealing a hidden layer of the world, which we no longer notice. By exposing the contrast between alternative meanings of the same act or event—what those caught in routine assume it means and what those unfamiliar with the habituated meaning interpret—estrangement acts as a delegitimizing device, operating at epistemic and political levels.

In Shklovsky's conception of estrangement, foreignness meets strangeness, as the writer himself reached this understanding while living in exile in Berlin. Banished from Moscow for his involvement with the Socialist Revolutionaries, Shklovsky spent his Berlin years in the company of other prominent Russian artists and writers. From Russian Berlin, he pined for Moscow and observed German life with melancholy, when not with contempt. It is hard to pin down where his criticism of Germany stops being the result of careful reflection and becomes merely an expression of homesickness for Russia. Indeed, the two might be connected, as revealed in Shklovsky's discovery that the pronoun "we" functions differently in German and, respectively, in Russian: in one, it refers to the speaker and other people while in the other to the speaker and the hearer. This is not a matter of translation but of pragmatic meaning. The German "we" strikes

Shklovsky as detached from the interlocutor and thus deceptive by contrast to the Russian "we" signifying solidarity.[69] At the same time, such linguistic speculation comes with an air of irony that defines most of Shklovsky's exile writing. Estrangement is a pose designed to exhibit, as much as to hide, nostalgia for the homeland.

The technique of estrangement was connected, from its initial design by Shklovsky, to striking a pose in the context of a theatrical performance (later developed by Bertolt Brecht as *Verfremdung* specifically for the performing arts). Taking on a persona defined by cultivated eccentricity becomes "an exercise of thinking the world as a question." The boldness of this persona has some natural affinity with the American sensibility, especially with the oratorical ideal of a New World Adam, a "self-reliant, unconditionally free and innocent individual."[70] But the American ideal orator has always also been "a sort of representative figure—representative in the sense of being one *with, one of* the democratic audience."[71] Such a persona requires a citizen's ethos and demands that it be an authentic one. Through their stranger persona, Arendt, Marcuse, Solzhenitsyn, and Said challenged this assumption of citizenship in the sense of belonging to the nation as to a natural order from the beginning (of one's life). Their rhetorical (not just political) achievement was to create a vantage point that forced a leveling of the ground for reevaluating arguments and premises that were framed *within* an ethics of citizenship. American audiences were offered a critique of the U.S. détente policy toward the Soviet Union from the perspective of a Gulag survivor and arguments for a binational Israeli-Palestinian state from the vantage point of a Palestinian-born scholar of the Western tradition. Arendt presented a view of segregation and racism from the perspective of a Jewish pariah refusing to be a parvenue; Marcuse called for a revolution in America's political and economic system, targeting capitalism as a former German socialist and as a citizen of the world. These personae were not only associated with a different nationality but also with different discursive norms.

The stranger persona of Arendt, Marcuse, Solzhenitsyn, and Said has its origin in estrangement conceived as "*depaysement*" in a broad sense, not merely being uprooted from one's homeland, but also not sharing the same discursive resources available to one's new community.[72] In this sense, estrangement creates new perspectives by virtue of employing a different language. This language is poetic not in the aesthetic sense, but in its opposition to the everyday linguistic habits of a community. This language was, as Shklovsky's friend, Jakobson, would have put it, "not a supplementation of discourse with rhetorical adornment but a total reevaluation of the discourse and of its components whatsoever."[73]

In a 1967 interview, at the height of his literary fame in America, Vladimir Nabokov confessed that he considered "the absence of a *natural* vocabulary" in English to be his greatest stylistic flaw. "My English," he reflected, "is . . . a stiffish, artificial thing, which may be all right for describing a sunset or an insect, but which cannot conceal poverty of syntax and paucity of domestic diction when I need the shortest road between warehouse and shop. An old Rolls-Royce is not always preferable to a plain jeep."[74] It is hard to imagine a better metaphor for the stranger persona than this image of a foreign luxury car. While ironically performing the very inability he admitted having—efficiency and simplicity—Nabokov pinned down the chief characteristic of the style associated with the stranger persona: it is artful and especially apt for nonmundane matters. His choice of metaphor field is significant: the Rolls-Royce suggests futile luxury against the practicality of a domestic vehicle. This was sagely put for the political visions of the four intellectuals I study in this book were also frequently dismissed as impractical and their vision of American politics utopian.

The stranger persona is indeed utopian for it requires a redefinition of the terms foreign and native as forming a *positive* relation, as Simmel envisioned it, rather than a dichotomy. It is a difficult task, and one that brought Simmel charges of political utopianism, if not defeatism.[75] Nevertheless, his notion of the stranger bespeaks a commitment to a social and political order in which the foreigner gains acceptance, not through assimilation but in a kind of embrace though which the stranger takes hold of, while also trying to adopt, the world of the natives. This is the fundamental stance that I trace in the next four chapters.

2

HANNAH ARENDT: THE THINKER AND THE AMERICAN REPUBLIC

O
N JANUARY 29, 1946, Hannah Arendt wrote from New York to her friend and mentor, Karl Jaspers:

> There is much I could say about America. There really is such a thing as freedom here and a strong feeling among many people that one cannot live without freedom. The republic is not a vapid illusion, and the fact that there is no national state and no truly national tradition creates an atmosphere of freedom or at least one not pervaded by fanaticism.[1]

Arendt had arrived in the United States in 1941, as a stateless person. The connection she saw between freedom and the absence of a national state bespeaks the relief of a victim of nation-states.[2] The freedom she discovered in America was also a freedom of speech and that must have been its most important aspect to the vocal social and political critic Arendt already was. What she took for lack of a national tradition was reassuring to a cosmopolitan and a nontraditionalist like her. America was Arendt's new Rome.

Intellectuals like Arendt were allowed entry into the United States not as Jews and also not as Germans, French, Spaniards, or any other nationality represented in the pool rescued by the American Emergency Committee but as individuals of exceptional talent. The designation was apt: the career she made in the United States is impressive even for someone in this elite category she occupied along Franz Werfel, Victor Serge, Siegfried Kracauer, Heinrich Mann, and others. She held academic positions at the New School, University of Chicago, and Princeton University while publishing regularly in *Partisan Review*, *The New Yorker*, *Commentary*, *Nation*, *Dissent*, and *Encounter*. Her writing approached philosophical questions that were not only politically significant but also controversial in a way that fostered new ideas, clarified assumptions, and sharpened positions. Responses to her works, even when critical, brought to the fore complex and significant questions about the nature of totalitarian regimes, the mechanisms of evil as a political phenomenon, the social dimensions of racial discrimination, the purpose of civil disobedience, and the relationship between imperialism and postwar American foreign policy. The texts I examine in this chapter, "Reflections on Little Rock, Arkansas" and *Eichmann in Jerusalem: Report on the Banality of Evil* (originally a series of articles published in *The New Yorker*), were Arendt's most controversial writings.[3] These essays surprised, excited, outraged, and disappointed many American readers as much because of their content as because of their style. It was the style of an impartial observer who readily admitted to be presenting her views *as an outsider*.

But just how was she an outsider? Compared to other German intellectuals who had fled to America during the war, she not only stayed afterwards but also became one of the most assimilated into local circles and came to be referred to as a member of the New York Intellectuals group.[4] As a Jew, she worked alongside American Jews on matters pertaining to the creation of Israel and the new status of Jews in postwar America. As a European, she was difficult to pin down, inasmuch as she was as much at home in France as she was in Germany and often just as critical of Europe as she was impressed with America.[5]

Since she was already a respected scholar when she left Europe, Arendt's challenge for gaining acceptance among American public intellectuals was not merely one of matching her own rhetorical self-image against their expectations but also one of developing a style in a language other than her native German. This was the language in which she had read the Western philosophical canon and had written her study of Saint Augustine as well as numerous articles on Jewish politics. "I write in English," she said when she was already widely published in America, "but I have never lost a feeling of distance from it."[6] The stylistic particularities of her American writings have been noticed more than in the case of the other protagonists of this book. However, commentators have remarked mainly the uncommon turns of phrases, idiomatic idiosyncrasies, and grammatical mistakes, all marks of a foreigner, a nonnative speaker.[7] Her style was also strange, not just foreign: she employed irony when reflecting on matters that others insisted on treating with the utmost seriousness, such as the Holocaust, or tried to convey compassion that struck readers as mere condescension. Her style reflects a perspective on American society mainly at odds with other views, and this unfamiliar thinking and expression made her ideas seem insightful and compelling at times and outrageous at others. Her stranger persona was the rhetorical expression of a political consciousness inextricably connected to being Jewish. Trained as a philosopher by mentors who became icons of German thought, Arendt turned to politics as a Jew. As she put it: "if one is attacked as a Jew, one must defend oneself as a Jew. Not as a German, not as a world-citizen, not as an upholder of the Rights of Man."[8] She was also a German, a European, and an upholder of the Rights of Man. These affiliations functioned as "terministic screens," funneling assumptions and expectations about who she was and what she should say.[9] Her stranger persona emerged at the nexus of these terministic screens but was also consciously crafted by Arendt after her conception of the Jew as *pariah*. In this chapter, I analyze some of her most strikingly original conceptions, that discrimination need not be the product of racism and that victims—especially Jewish victims of the holocaust—can contribute to their own destruction. I do not defend her views as much as trace their connection to the stranger persona, but I do argue that these views have important positive implications for how we envision the American polis.

BECOMING A JEW

Like many other German Jewish intellectuals before World War II, Arendt came from an assimilated, well-respected family living in the town of

Königsberg, where Jews occupied prominent places in the social hierarchy. She was, however, exposed to Jewish religious and cultural life as a child. Both sets of her grandparents were reform Jews who were well acquainted with Rabbi Herman Vogelstein, one of the most influential leaders of liberal German Jews in Königsberg and a convinced Zionist. She was raised by a progressive mother who had many social democrat friends and who believed that daughters should be educated for careers that were once reserved only for sons. Martha Arendt supported the Spartacist movement and was not intimidated by the growing atmosphere of anti-Semitism in Germany during the 1920s and early 1930s.[10] Königsberg was not as anti-Semitic as other German cities during Hannah's childhood yet it did provide the "opportunity" to discover that being Jewish amounted to being different:

> The word "Jew" was never mentioned at home. I first encountered it—though really it is hardly worth recounting it—in the anti-Semitic remarks of children as we played in the streets—then I became, so to speak, enlightened. . . . As a child—now somewhat an older child—I knew, for example, that I looked Jewish. . . . That is, that I looked a bit different from the rest. But not in a way that made me feel inferior—I was simply aware of it, that is all.[11]

Arendt's awareness of being Jewish was influenced by the circles her family frequented, which placed her "at the center of attraction for a group of talented sons and daughters—mostly sons—of Jewish professional families."[12] Her older friends had studied at prestigious German universities, and they were familiar with and talked to her about the intellectual idols of the time, including Martin Heidegger. Arendt was a precocious child and excelled in school; her intellectual abilities so powerful that even the intolerant atmosphere of Prussian schools—from one of them the fiercely independent Arendt was expelled for insubordination—could not prevent her from reaching the university level. She studied at the University of Marburg with Heidegger, who also became her lover. The (well-guarded) secrecy of this relationship is known now to have been a burden for Arendt, especially as it exposed her to the anti-Semitic remarks circulating in Heidegger's entourage, including those of his wife, Elfriede.[13] Through Heidegger, Arendt also met Hans Jonas and Karl Löwith, future important thinkers whose ideas were beginning to take shape, like hers, in a tense relation with their mentor's philosophy.[14] Arendt left Marburg for a semester of study with Edmund Husserl in Freiburg and never returned. She finished her academic studies with Jaspers, who became her doctoral dissertation advisor at the University of Heidelberg.

Although surrounded by increasing anti-Semitism and although she counted among her friends Jewish students who took an active interest in Zionism, Arendt herself spent her university years focusing mostly on her studies. But in 1926, she met Kurt Blumenfeld, the most influential proponent of Zionism in Germany, at a meeting organized by Jonas. As Elizabeth Young-Bruehl explains, "the lecture did not convert Hannah Arendt to Zionism, but it did convert her to Kurt Blumenfeld."[15] He became her "political mentor" and through him she became more and more involved with Zionism, especially after the Reichstag was set on fire on February 27, 1933, as pretext for a series of arrests of Communist political figures. In the spring of that year, Blumenfeld asked her to help the German Zionist Organization by distributing leaflets (which was illegal). She was arrested by the Gestapo but released after only eight days. Soon afterwards she fled Germany, first to Prague and then to Paris.

In her later reflections, Arendt took great care to present her decision to leave Germany as motivated not by a Jew's fear of Nazi repression but by her disappointment in German intellectuals. Her "personal problem," as she put it, was not one of fearing persecution but of discovering the political apathy or even cowardice of German intellectuals and tracing these attitudes to their philosophical interests:

> The problem, the personal problem, was not what our enemies might be doing, but what our friends were doing. This wave of cooperation—which was quite voluntary, or at least not compelled in the way it was during a reign of terror, made you feel surrounded by an empty space, isolated. I lived in an intellectual milieu, but I also knew many people who did not, and I came to the conclusion that cooperation was, so to speak, the rule among intellectuals, but not among others. And I have never forgotten that. I left

Germany guided by the resolution—a very exaggerated one—that "Never again!" I will never have anything to do with the "history of ideas" again. I didn't, indeed, want to have anything to do with this sort of society again.[16]

The German intellectuals she believed had let her down included her future colleague at the University of Chicago, Leo Strauss, another Jew, whom she considered in Germany as much as later in America politically naïve and philosophically as conservative as the ideologues of fascism.[17] Arendt left Germany with a firm commitment to politics, which was grounded in her experience as a Jew more than in a particular ideology but did not extend to an automatic solidarity with all Jews. In this regard, a comparison between her and Heinrich Blücher, her lifetime partner, is instructive. The two met in France in 1936, where both were involved in antifascist political activities. Blücher came from a non-Jewish family, had joined at age nineteen the Soldiers' Council, and had participated in the left-wing movement led by Karl Liebknecht and Rosa Luxemburg before becoming a member in the German Communist party.[18] While Arendt would always remain an idealist in politics, Blücher was a man of action.[19] Yet they came together in their interest in politics as emancipation and social justice.

In France, Arendt did practical work for organizations that helped Jewish refugees to emigrate to Palestine but without emigrating there herself (as Martin Buber and Gershom Scholem would). Commitment to the Jewish cause did not spare her some disappointing discoveries, for example, that some Jews, especially affluent ones, were convinced that assimilation would protect them from the Nazis. In her view, these Jews—"parvenus" as she would later call them—were unable to understand the real political problem posed by anti-Semitism because they concentrated on their personal welfare instead of on the Jewish situation in general. Her political experience was doubly estranged—not just from anti-Semites but also from Jews seeking assimilation.

In the French internment camp of Gurs where she was sent as an enemy alien in 1940, Arendt discovered how adversity creates its own logic that conflates and confuses levels of identification. She must have felt the same way as Lisa Fittko, the Jewish communist who was also interned at Gurs:

To the French we émigrés were simply Germans. We came from there, we spoke with the despised *accent boche*. Even during the years of emigration we always remained, in the eyes of many Frenchmen, the "*sales Boches.*" And now—we were prisoners, so we must be spies. Probably Nazi parachutists, the ones the newspapers and radio had warned them about.[20]

In the chaos of the early days of the Vichy government, when Germany was no longer officially an enemy, Gurs opened its gates. Unlike many prisoners who stayed at Gurs hoping that it would be easier to be found by their families, Arendt left. She met Blücher at Montauban, and they crossed the border into Spain. Soon afterward, Arendt crossed the ocean to America.

BECOMING A STRANGER

As early as 1925, Arendt reflected on estrangement as the mark of an enlightened, albeit isolating, life of the mind. In one of the early letters addressed to Heidegger in the course of their affair, she offers a self-portrait entitled "The Shadows," which describes her in the third-person as a young woman who is keenly aware of the discrepancy between the everyday circumstances of life in a "Here-and-Now" and the "Then-and-There" of another time and place. This awareness leads to

> independence and idiosyncrasy [which] were actually based in a true passion she had conceived for anything odd. Thus, she was used to seeing something noteworthy even in what was apparently most natural and banal; indeed, when the simplicity and ordinariness of life struck her to the core, it did not occur to her, upon reflection, or even emotionally that anything she experienced could be banal, a worthless thing that the rest of the world took for granted and that was no longer worthy of comment.[21]

Later in life, Arendt's experiences would be anything but banal, but this early reflection on estrangement depicts her ability to defamiliarize as spontaneous rather than deliberate, a way of being rather than a conscious act.

The state of which Arendt spoke in this letter is not merely the poetic expression of a young woman's crush on a famous philosopher. Using Heidegger's vocabulary, the text describes the ontological estrangement that defined more generally the Weimar Republic sensibility.[22] Like other German intellectuals who shared this sensibility, Arendt became aware early on of the great fracture in German *Kultur* and of the disappearance of the tradition of tolerance she had studied in the works of Jaspers, her other mentor. No matter how much she was intellectually a German, this awareness made her stop identifying as one, as she relayed to the incredulous Jaspers.

To say that she began to identify, instead, as Jewish, would be an oversimplification. She explored her options in the biography titled *Rahel Varnhagen: The Life of a Jewess*, which she wrote in Germany in 1933, finishing the last two chapters during her stay in France in 1938.[23] Yet the book was published for the first time only in 1957 in English translation in London under the auspices of the Leo Baeck Institute. Shortly afterwards it also appeared in America and in 1959 in Germany. This was one of the first books Arendt worked on after crossing the ocean.

Rahel Varnhagen is the story of a German-Jewish writer who hosted one of the most prominent salons in Europe during the late eighteenth and early nineteenth centuries. Articulating a historically situated view of Jewish identity, *Rahel Varnhagen* introduces the idea of estrangement as the result of a confrontation between the two irreconcilable alternatives open to European Jews: to become accepted by the majority of the society through complete assimilation or to maintain their distinct Jewish identity at the price of remaining on the margins of that society. Arendt's interest in revisiting this early work suggests that the ideas discussed in it still mattered to her twenty years later and perhaps that it was especially important to her in America. A rich, complex, and occasionally abstract text, *Rahel Varnhagen* can be read for different purposes. Arendt took great pains to explain the purpose *she* intended for the book:

> It was never my intention to write a book *about* Rahel; her personality, which might lend itself to various interpretations according to the psychological standards and categories that the author introduces from outside;

nor about her position in Romanticism and the effect of the Goethe cult in Berlin, of which she was actually the originator; nor about the significance of her salon for the social history of the period; nor about her ideas and her "Weltanschauung," insofar as these can be reconstructed from her letters. What interested me solely was to narrate the story of Rahel's life as she herself might have told it. My portrait therefore follows as closely as possible Rahel's own reflections upon herself, although it is naturally couched in different language and does not consist solely of variations upon quotations.[24]

Seyla Benhabib finds it, quite rightly, "astonishing" that someone could presume to know another person's story and thus, be able to narrate it just as that person experienced it. "What hermeneutical mysteries," Benhabib wonders, "does this little subjunctive phrase, 'might have told it,' contain?"[25] For Richard Wolin, however, the mystery is easy to decipher: in recounting the story of a Jewish woman who went from desperately seeking assimilation to one who embraced firmly her Jewishness, Arendt was telling her own narrative. "In all . . . respects," says Wolin, "Varnhagen must have appeared to Arendt as an eerily perfect *doppelgänger*."[26]

The similarities between author and character are indeed remarkable: both Jewish, both highly educated, neither particularly attractive as a woman yet profoundly influenced by the non-Jewish men who were attracted to them. Varnhagen sought to become assimilated through several love affairs and relationships to men who were inferior to her, spiritually and morally, but who were Gentiles and as such could have provided a respectable social status. All these relationships failed—a failure that in the end forced her to understand and then take ownership of her Jewishness.

Wolin believes that Arendt's painful and humiliating love affair with Heidegger played a similar role, pushing her to face and accept her difference and to renounce her youthful naivety and hope in the intellectually egalitarian German culture.[27] Yet it could not have been only the therapeutic effect of her work on *Rahel Varnhagen* that enabled Arendt to take charge of her Jewishness but also the broader political awakening she was experiencing at the time. Benhabib argues:

In the early 1930s Arendt's own understanding of Judaism in general and her relationship to her own Jewish identity were undergoing profound transformations. These transformations were taking her increasingly away from the egalitarian, humanistic Enlightenment ideals of Kant, Lessing, and Goethe toward a recognition of the ineliminable and unassimilable fact of Jewish difference within German culture. In telling Rahel Varnhagen's story Arendt was engaging in a process of collective self-understanding and redefinition as a German Jew.[28]

Estrangement is the key aspect of this process of self-understanding. Arendt viewed the German Jew as defined by a relationship of exteriority to the dominant group, as conveyed by "a widely accepted Enlightenment precept [which] held that the Jews, a backward and uncultured people, could only gain acceptance once they shed their Jewishness, an ungainly medieval atavism."[29] The exteriority of the Jew qua *Jew* is what leads to discrimination, oppression, and finally extermination. As an outsider, the Jew can be relegated to the role of an undesirable, unacceptable Other and subjected to political mechanisms of exclusion that claim to be legitimate because the cultural exclusion already exists and society takes it for granted. Arendt had emphasized this point in *The Origins of Totalitarianism*: "social discrimination, and not political anti-Semitism, discovered the phantom of '*the*' Jew."[30]

To explain the distinction further, Arendt associates assimilation and conscious marginalization with the symbolic figures of the parvenu and the pariah. Through intermarriage, for example, the parvenue may hope to be accepted by society at the price of disguising or even abandoning her Jewish identity, as Rahel Levin Varnhagen hoped to become Countess von Fincklelstein. That relationship ended, and with it, Rahel's chances for assimilation. However, even when assimilation is complete, the Jew remains in the eyes of the dominant society still a Jew, only an exemplary, "ideal" Jew whose Jewishness is deemed innocuous, reduced to an exotic feature. Thus, the parvenu is faced with a paradox, well captured by Lisa Jane Disch: "The parvenu views membership as a problem to be solved by performing the inherently contradictory role of the individual 'exception Jew'—one who is both Jew in the sense of having exotic appeal and non-Jew in the sense of honoring no cultural traditions and displaying none of the 'undesirable traits,' stereotypically associated with Jewishness."[31]

The Germany of Arendt's youth had many parvenus among its Jewish intellectuals. Arendt herself was accused of being a parvenue when she criticized certain aspects of Jewish life or Jewish history—as in her report on the Eichmann trial. Her critics charged that she was acting as an assimilated German Jew "superior to Eastern Jewish ghetto-dwellers."[32] Yet Arendt herself fashioned her Jewishness as that of a pariah—and in that regard criticisms and accusations reinforced her status through the very act of marginalization and even exclusion they constituted. Benhabib explains that while the parvenue tries to hide her difference, "the pariah is the outsider and the outcast who either cannot or chooses not to erase the fate of difference." Moreover, the pariah realizes both the risks and the opportunities difference affords. The pariah, then, "transforms difference from being a source of weakness and marginality into one of strength and defiance."[33] Arendt's break with the German intelligentsia bespeaks such defiance and reflects a firm rejection of the position of a parvenue. She made a similar choice in America.

Here, the figure of the pariah could have significant appeal, especially in the years after World War II and to a readership increasingly appreciative of nonconformism and drawn to rebellion.[34] Arendt rejected the notion of a pariah that would simply amount to "an empty sense of difference . . . in all its possible psychological aspects and variations from innate strangeness to social alienation."[35] The figure of the pariah continued to interest Arendt throughout her philosophical career. In *Men in Dark Times*, published in 1968, she argued that

[a pariah] is often accompanied by so radical a loss of the world, so fearful an atrophy of all the organs with which we respond to it—starting with the common sense with which we orient ourselves in a world common to ourselves and others and going to a sense of beauty or taste with which we love the world—that in extreme cases, in which pariahdom has persisted for centuries, we can speak of real worldlessness.[36]

"Worldlessness" was a derogatory term in Arendt's political vocabulary.[37] It connoted apathy, escapism, and political anomie. Taken to the extreme, pariahdom could amount to merely being an outsider and "altogether incapable of public judgment."[38] How, then, to change a polity in order to be recognized as a legitimate member of it while at the same time not adjusting to it? This was the question Arendt faced squarely, not only as a Jew in Europe, but also as a political refugee in America. In was a question she implicitly posed in her reflections on racism in American politics or on the legacy of the Holocaust.

In seeking an answer to guide her own political conduct, Arendt reviewed four models of pariahdom inspired by fictional characters and also by a historical figure: the pariah as "*schlemihl*," as featured in Heinrich Heine's poetry, who treats the world with indifference and withdraws from it; Charlie Chaplin's "little man," who plays the fool to reveal the absurdity of the world around him; Franz Kafka's character K. in *The Castle*, who is the victim of an absurd and inhumane system to which he does not acquiesce; and the radical French Zionist, Bernard Lazare. Significantly, Arendt identified most closely with Lazare not so much because she shared for a while his Zionist beliefs but because she admired his courage to confront the world. Lazare—who supported Captain Alfred Dreyfuss when he was wrongly convicted of treason in France in 1894—had asked that

> the pariah relinquish once and for all the prerogative of the *schlemihl*, cut loose from the world of fancy and illusion, renounce the comfortable protection of nature, and come to grips with the world of men and women. In other words, he wanted him to feel that he was himself responsible for what society had done to him. Politically speaking every pariah who refused to be a rebel was partly responsible for his own position and therewith for the blot on mankind which it represented.[39]

Arendt admired Lazare for a quality aptly described by Disch as "situated impartiality," which defines a stance informed by concrete experience and historical events rather than by abstract ideas or a political ideology.[40]

Lessing, as author of *Nathan the Wise*, was, for this reason, another one of Arendt's heroes. She admired his "forever vigilant partiality . . . always framed not in terms of the self but in terms of the relationship of men to their world, in terms of their positions and opinions."[41] At the same time, the pariah does not just refuse to conform to existing conventions but more importantly has the ability to critique these conventions by de-scrutinizing them with the "care and precision," to use Schutz's terms, of someone who does not take them for granted. By being on the margins, the pariah is well positioned to engage in techniques of estrangement.

Arendt was a pariah not only as a Jew but also as a political refugee. World War II political refugees constituted a political subject fallen outside the legal domain defined by nation-states. They lacked civil as well as *human* rights because, as Arendt explained, the very notion of the Rights of Man was the conceptual product of a political order based on nation-states.[42] While refugees nominally represented the group most in need of human rights intervention, the very reinforcement of human rights depended on political institutions that could only operate within the boundaries of a nation-state. These institutions could no longer function in the era of massive displacement, and "those who were refugees or stateless thus became rightless, 'foreigners' beyond their borders and in strange lands where they were outside the law and denied full legal recognition."[43]

"We, Refugees," published in New York in the journal *Aufbau* in 1943, is one of the few writings in which Arendt expressed compassion for the refugees who had lost their home—a personal as well as political loss because political participation, in her view, is possible only when one feels "at home" in the world.[44] At the same time, she mocked the refugees who make desperate, parvenu-like efforts to become assimilated in the countries that had taken them in. She sketched a sarcastic portrait of a Mr. Cohn, an assimilated Jew who is "150 percent German, 150 percent Viennese, and 150 percent French." Mr. Cohn is a sorry figure because as a World War II refugee he is even more disadvantaged than a Jew dealing with anti-Semitism in wartime Europe. Refugees like him faced the threat of "discrimination as the great social weapon by which one may kill men without bloodshed; since passports or birth certificates, and sometimes even income tax receipts, are no longer formal papers but matters of social distinction."[45]

Refugees, as Arendt herself was, represent a modern type of pariah, for whom "there is no autonomous space within the political order of the nation-state."[46] This pariah inhabits a state of liminality, and is constantly pushed to another place.[47] For Arendt's stranger persona, liminality was an ideal stance for engaging in the exercise of defamiliarization insofar as it allowed her to position herself in one social framework in order to reflect on events occurring in another. Yet liminality also put her between the Scylla and Charibdys of conflicting images and values associated in America: being German and being Jewish, being a philosopher and being a political activist.

A REDOUBTABLE WOMAN

In the United States, Arendt kept her distance from other German intellectual émigrés, especially those who claimed to represent "the good Germany" that could be actively reinstated once the Nazis were defeated.[48] Rather, she contacted and worked for American Jewish organizations representing the Jewish cause. In November 1941, she became a writer for the New York–based German-language newspaper *Aufbau*. In the pages of *Aufbau*, she argued as a Jew who did not ask or expect Americans qua Americans to make sacrifices for the European Jews, targeting instead American Jews qua *Jews*. In her biweekly columns, she advocated the need for Jews to defend themselves and fight the war that had been waged against them by Hitler.[49] Arendt was briefly a Zionist and supported the formation of Israel, but she later insisted, against the general opinion of Jewish American circles, that it be from the onset a bi-national state. She abandoned Jewish politics after the Biltmore conference held in New York in 1942, which called for a Jewish state in Palestina.[50]

Despite her disappointment with American Zionism and the complicated nature of Jewish American politics after the war, as a Jew who had experienced discrimination and had opposed and escaped the Nazi regime, Arendt carried a special authority and legitimacy with her American colleagues. This legitimacy was especially useful to her arguments about totalitarian regimes and ideological terror, which formed the basis of her most important work, *The Origins of Totalitarianism*, written on the heels of the war in 1945–1946. Despite some negative reviews, the book became a major success in the 1950s in no small part because it put Stalinism on par with Nazism at a time when anti-Soviet sentiment and anticommunism in America were on the rise.[51] Arendt's goal in this book was to offer, as she explained,

> an insight into the nature of totalitarian rule, directed by our fear of the concentration camp, (which) might serve to devaluate all outmoded political shadings from left to right and, beside and above them, to introduce the most essential political criterion for judging the events of our time: will it lead to totalitarian rule or will it not?[52]

In this book, Arendt emerged clearly as a critic of bourgeois society and of liberalism, which she deemed responsible, among other things, for creating conformism and thus a mob mentality that would result both in willing submissiveness and the total domination associated with totalitarianism.[53] One of the skeptical readers of the book was American sociologist David Riesman, who challenged Arendt using arguments that would later be often charged against her: that she was making hasty generalizations, that she had exaggerated the power of totalitarianism to take over individual minds and inhibit any kind of resistance, and that she did not have a rigorous methodology of study.[54] These were criticisms frequently made against German scholars in America, and the Frankfurt Institute members also did not escape them, as I showed in chapter one. Most importantly, the scholarly objections raised by Riesman were entangled in a complicated web of political attitudes toward communism and the Soviet Union, which I discuss more in chapter 4. *The Origins of Totalitarianism* made Arendt into a potential ally to the anticommunists and thus an enemy of those who remained on the left even during the Stalin era, especially after she participated in the 1951 meeting of the American Congress for Cultural Freedom and became associated with the Harvard Center for Russian Studies, which was financed by the CIA.[55] Arendt herself, however, never identified her political stance as either liberal or conservative and declared herself uninterested in such distinctions.[56] Her closest friends, however, were liberals and leftists. It is not always clear whether they accepted her for being a sophisticated intellectual or because they shared similar political views.

Yet it is clear that Arendt felt most at home in America among her friends. She met most of them while working as an editor at Schocken Books in New York in the mid-1940s: Riesman, Robert Lowell, Randall Jarrell, Alfred Kazin, and later Mary McCarthy. As this was a close-knit network, one acquaintance or friendship led to several others. Her philosophical training with Jaspers and Heidegger gave her political ideas a philosophical depth that impressed many of her new friends and colleagues, especially at a time when their own professed cosmopolitanism favored cultivation of European ideas. But it also turned others off, especially as she never escaped being linked back to Heidegger's influence and never offered a public condemnation of her former teacher (quite the contrary, she resumed her correspondence with him after the war).

Whether they contested or approved of her views, and even when they were her friends and close allies, prominent liberal intellectuals in America revolved around her and were proud to be in her entourage. They also related to her as to someone who did not quite comprehend their way of life, even though she could offer interesting insights. Hyperbole is the trope that informs their depiction of Arendt. Here is William Barrett remembering his first meeting with Arendt, occasioned by a request for an article on existentialism:

> She was a redoubtable woman, and that first meeting still lingers in my mind. She knew Rahv [Philip Rahv, the editor of *Partisan Review*] only slightly, and she was thus cast into the situation of confronting four strangers—and possibly four antagonistic males—but she never faltered. She was very hardly shy (it would be hard to imagine her ever shy), and in very short order had locked horns with Rahv. His usual authoritative manner could

not pass muster with her, and he was thrown off stride by encountering an aggressively intellectual woman who talked back to him. It was a novelty for me to hear him becoming somewhat faltering and tentative in tone. He, who usually laid down the law to other people, now rather put himself in the role of the inquiring learner. . . . What impressed me was her great gusto and the vibrancy of her character. She came at things with energy and eagerness.[57]

This overly flattering portrait is presented in a narrative of confrontation. Arendt, emphatically gendered, confronts four prominent American men and manages to dominate them. Interestingly, Barrett refers to the Americans as the "strangers," because his recounting places Arendt at the center. The narrative authority Barrett assigns to Arendt as a character enhances the overall impression of the hold she had over her American colleagues. In this story of power and competition, Barrett's language is replete with terms of conflict ("locked horns," "laid down the law," "authoritative," "aggressive," "faltering," "thrown off stride"), and Arendt emerges as the victor in a battle. Regardless that there was no actual confrontation, Barrett hyperbolizes the antagonism to emphasize Arendt's power. The result is that Arendt is not depicted simply as an outsider to the group but as the omnipotent, dominating stranger, more powerful than even the leaders among the insiders, and thus both more threatening and impressive. This status is further emphasized by Barrett's re-gendering of Arendt:

She was dressed rather informally that afternoon, with her hair set back loosely. And finding herself at ease with me, she was much more womanly than I had expected. She was also much younger then and more attractive than her later photographs, when she became a more public person, could show. I couldn't help thinking throughout that she was a very handsome woman indeed. Later I reported this judgment to William Phillips, who pondered it judiciously for a moment and then declared, "I think of Hannah rather as a very handsome man." He could only think of her in intellectual argument.[58]

Juxtaposed against Phillips's evaluation of Arendt, which de-genders her completely, the emphasis on her femininity in Barrett's depiction reads almost as implausible, as if Barrett himself is surprised to remember Arendt as a desirable woman. Through these conflicting representations of Arendt as both unfeminine and as an attractive woman, she becomes de-gendered and symbolically disembodied. Barrett sanctions his own lingering on physical detail—her clothes and her hair—by invoking Phillips's remark, which is hard to interpret as a compliment or not. The portrait, although focused on images of Arendt's body, has precisely the opposite effect: not to bring to life the image of a physical person but to suggest that it is inappropriate to think of Arendt in such terms.

This description of Arendt, especially set against Phillips's characterization, functions as a hyperbolic representation of her intellectual ability, but it also dehumanizes her. Arendt has a powerful mind but hardly a body. Such constructions of Arendt feed into other representations of her as omnipotent ruler of the New York intellectual scene. Nowhere is this depiction more evident than in Martin Jay's recounting of his experience upon submitting in 1975 to *Partisan Review* an article that was very critical of Arendt's work. *Partisan Review* had published harsh reviews of *Eichmann in Jerusalem*, which led to a brief break-up between Arendt and the journals' editors. By 1975, Arendt and the editors had reconciled. Jay's article traced Arendt's politics to her philosophy of existentialism and German formation, insisting on connections between her thought and Heidegger's.[59] Williams was reluctant to publish the piece because he worried that it might upset Arendt and that a new reconciliation would never be possible. When Arendt died unexpectedly of a heart attack, Phillips deemed it all the more inappropriate to publish a piece that took a negative stance toward her work. In the end, Jay's article did get published, albeit with a modified, less acerbic, title, and adjoined by another paper that reviewed all the strengths of her political work. The incident inspired Jay to reflect on intellectual fields and power:

> Although all intellectual fields are inevitably pre-structured, that of the New York Intellectuals was especially replete with the residues of previous conflicts, personal as well as intellectual, which made it impossible to enter without setting off hidden landmines. . . . Writing for a journal like *Partisan Review* entailed assuming the baggage of its previous history, which meant that contributions represented not merely the opinion of the writer

but also to a greater or lesser degree the general line of the journal. Rather than having sovereign control over his words, the contributor was in danger of becoming a bit like a script writer in the Hollywood cinema production process.[60]

Even though this passage does not even mention Arendt, it relies on the same language of conflict used by Barrett, now intensified through more aggressive war metaphors. If the New York intellectuals occupy, in Jay's view, a war zone, and the conflict is between combatants who fight for "prestige and power," it is clear that Arendt was the ultimate authority behind the lines, a veritable general who issues orders from a distance.

In many stories about her, Arendt emerges as a rather exotic figure towering over the American-born intellectual. Yet the American criticism of her most controversial works did the opposite, dwarfing her not only through quantity, but also intensity.

THE AMERICAN DILEMMA

When her "Reflections on Little Rock, Arkansas" were published in 1957, *The Origins of Totalitarianism* had brought Arendt recognition as an important thinker, but she had never spoken on a matter so specific to American politics. In 1954, the United States Supreme Court held in *Brown v. Board of Education* that segregated schools violated the Fourteenth Amendment of the Constitution. This decision paved the way for the Court's 1955 ruling that schools must integrate "with all deliberate speed."[61] This phrase, notoriously ambiguous, gave enough latitude to school officials trying to find ways to satisfy the Court ruling but with the minimum of compliance possible to postpone integration indefinitely, reasoning that, done too "hastily," it might lead to social unrest, violence, and increased racism. In the fall of 1958, with the support of the local National Association for the Advancement of Colored People (NAACP) branch, nine black students decided to attend Central High School in Little Rock, Arkansas. They were met by an angry mob that was backed by members of the Arkansas National Guard, who had been ordered by the Arkansas governor to prevent the black students from entering the school. In response, the NAACP and Martin Luther King Jr. asked Dwight Eisenhower to enforce the Supreme Court's decision, and the president decided to deploy federal troops to protect the black students for the rest of the year.

Arendt compared the problem of schools segregation to other domestic problems characteristic of the Cold War—such as the "security hysteria" and a "runaway prosperity" leading to "sheer superfluity and nonsense" that inevitably "wash out the essential and the productive"—to argue that unlike those, it had deeper roots in American history.[62] The comparison was instructive and reveals the connection between her work on totalitarianism, with its twin focus on the rise of a mass society and total domination, and racism. As she had done in *The Origins of Totalitarianism*, her method was to employ a "political criterion for judging the events of our time: will it (desegregation of schools) lead to totalitarian rule or will it not." The peremptory intervention of the federal government and the elision of a democratic consent on the matter could only worry Arendt as both failed her test.

Arendt's position on the desegregation of schools was twofold. First, she argued against the deployment of federal troops in the South on the grounds that federal power should not trump local jurisdiction because this would violate the political principle that was at the core of the American Republic. Second, she argued that school integration represented an attempt at opposing a *social* practice and, as such, could not resolve the problem of *political* discrimination. It is hard to defend her arguments, especially against massive agreement that she was deeply mistaken, and that she had "severely misinterpreted what was at stake in some of the issues involved."[63] What was at stake in the desegregation of schools in the South? According to its backers—and critics of Arendt's position—it was the elimination of racial inequality that had plagued the nation from its inception and that contradicted so flagrantly the principle of equality on which the republic was based. According to Arendt, however, the stakes were different and concerned the preservation of diversity in a body politic founded on the "endless variety of a multitude whose majesty resided in its very plurality," as Arendt put it, with undisguised admiration, in *On Revolution*. The federally mandated desegregation of schools trumped diversity by ignoring those voices in the South who disagreed and forcing them to obey. From the beginning, then, Arendt and most liberal American intellectuals were at odds.

Even before it was in print, Arendt's article had caused a stir. Originally commissioned by Norman Podhoretz for *Commentary*, the article eventually came out a year later in *Dissent*, after *Commentary*'s editorial board refused to issue it. *Dissent* published it with an emphatic disclaimer that informed readers that the editors did not share Arendt's position on the desegregation of schools. *Dissent* published the article along with two strongly worded rejoinders by David Spitz and Melvin Tumin, who both accused Arendt of failing to understand the political importance of school integration.[64] Tumin even suggested, in no ambiguous terms, that her lack of comprehension betrayed racism. In the subsequent issue of the journal, Arendt published a response to Spitz only, sticking to her original position, and offered a note explaining what compelled her to write the article.[65] In this note, she described the shock that she experienced upon seeing the photograph of Elizabeth Eckford, one of the nine African American students admitted to Little Rock Central High School in the fall of 1957, surrounded by an angry mob as she tried to enter the school building. Arendt claimed that, had she been a mother, she would never have wanted to see her child used in a political battle and would have expected the government to prevent, rather than precipitate, a situation that endangered a child's life.

"Reflections on Little Rock" was awarded the 1959 Longview Foundation Award for the year's outstanding magazine article. Fifty years later, on the anniversary of the desegregation of Little Rock Central High School, the essay was still considered significant enough to inspire at Princeton University a conference focused on it.[66] There is a certain fascination with this piece in America reflected in the ongoing discussions about Arendt's position and arguments.[67] "Reflections" is a difficult text because it cannot be summarily dismissed as racist since Arendt had expressed clearly, on other occasions, her support for the civil rights movement. Even in this piece, she did not claim that segregated schools should be allowed to exist but rather that racism had not started in segregated schools and would not end in integrated ones. Instead, she argued, to end racism requires political equality for African Americans, which, in her view, would have to start with new legislation that recognized African Americans' human rights and repealed anti-miscegenation laws.

Arendt defined discrimination radically differently from how her American readers might have expected, and she defamiliarized its common meaning by ignoring its usual connection to racism. Indeed, she used a conceptual dissociation to separate racism and discrimination.[68] Arendt viewed discrimination as the right to associate preferentially with some individuals rather than others. "If as a Jew I wish to spend my vacations only in the company of Jews, I cannot see how anyone can reasonably prevent my doing so," Arendt ventured. To present discrimination in terms synonymous with voluntary associations was no doubt risky because it resonated with a familiar perspective, the conservative southerners' slogan of "equal but different." She allowed, however, for situations in which discrimination would be "scandalously unjustified and positively harmful to the political realm," using the example of refusing the right to sit where one pleases in a bus—clearly endorsing Rosa Parks's protest and the acts of civil disobedience it had inspired.[69]

Arendt defended her controversial position by arguing, in turn, from the perspective of a European, a Jew, and an imagined parent (first African American, and then white). These self-identifications are strategies of rhetorical invention, as each shed light on a different aspect of the issue, and inspired Arendt the distinction she made among three realms: political, social, and private. From the perspective of a European, Arendt reasons as an outsider, a theorist focused on ideas and abstractions, in this case the *idea* of the American Republic. The perspective of a European is supposed to lend objectivity to her analysis while the second one, as a Jew, signals her sympathy—from one victim of discrimination to another—for the civil rights movement, which she had expressed on other occasions as well.[70] It might come as a surprise that she recognized from the outset that she was an outsider. "I have never lived in the South," Arendt admitted, "and have even avoided occasional trips to southern states because they would have brought me into a situation that I personally would find unbearable. Like most people of European origin, I have difficulty in understanding, let alone sharing, the common prejudices of Americans in this area."[71] Her confessed lack of understanding is rhetorical rather than a genuine ineptitude as it launches the defamiliarization mechanism while also trying to deflect suspicions against her as a white woman arguing against desegregation.

It is as an impartial observer that Arendt announced her worry that the scandal over school desegregation might damage America's international reputation. If this were to happen, she continued, it would be "unfortunate and even unjust," and would cost America "the advantages she otherwise would rightly enjoy as a world power." At stake, for Arendt, is the integrity of an idea, that of the American Republic, now threatening to become a "vapid illusion." Arendt distinguished racial discrimination in America from "the color problem in world politics [which] grew out of the colonialism and imperialism of European nations—that is, the one great crime in which America was never involved."[72] Arendt used the contrast to Europe to argue that the race problem existed within American society from its inception and is endemic to it, rather than in relation to another nation, and thus, if not impossible to eliminate then at least impossible to solve by feat. The Fourteenth Amendment, she argued in "On Civil Disobedience" in 1969, was long ignored by the southern states and only reformed American society when the Supreme Court enforced it, especially when the civil rights movement brought into the open Americans' responsibility from their forefathers for the country's greatest crime—slavery.[73] Yet, confusingly, Arendt also bracketed the violent face of this legacy of discrimination, racism, in order to focus on the violent nature of federal military intervention. She did so because she believed that the solution to the problem of racism that was specific to America could only be available "within the political and historical framework of the [American] Republic." The political framework of the republic, she reminded her readers, "rests on the principle of division of power and on the conviction that the body politic as a whole is strengthened by the division of power."[74] Federal intervention contradicted this principle.

Political power could not solve the problem of racial discrimination, Arendt believed, so long as it allowed the anti-miscegenation legislation in the South to infringe on African Americans' "elementary human rights," and thus assigned to them a second-class status. Yet Arendt's insistence that racist legislation be abrogated is not out of concern with the human rights of African Americans but with the principle of political equality upon which the republic was founded. In this regard, she saw herself thinking just like Thomas Jefferson, who, in pleading for the abolition of slavery, "trembled not for the Negroes, not even for the whites, but for the destiny of the [American] Republic because he knew that one of its vital principles had been violated right at the beginning. Not discrimination and social segregation, in whatever forms, but racial legislation constitutes the perpetuation of the original crime in this country's history."[75]

In her 1946 letter to Jaspers, Arendt had reported with distinct enthusiasm that freedom exists in America because it is not constrained by a national tradition. Now, her enthusiasm was starting to falter. Were Americans going to stay faithful to their own founding principles? By reminding her readers of the political tenets of their republic, Arendt was seeking a rhetorical communion with her audience. She identified as a European, but she was more faithful to the political framework of the republic than even an American. To some critics, arguing as a European was what had sent her arguments astray. George Kateb, for instance, warned American readers to be wary of Arendt because she thought too much like a European and because theoretical schemes devised by European thinkers in general should be approached with great skepticism when applied to American political and social matters.[76] Insofar as she sought confirmation from other Americans, especially those in the South, Arendt settled on an unfortunate choice, William Faulkner, who had also expressed reservations about the federally enforced desegregation. For such statements, Faulkner was facing his own media battles, especially since he had made them mostly while intoxicated.[77]

Most of Arendt's "liberal critics," as she identified them rather derisively, dismissed her arguments as philosophically invalid and politically misguided.[78] Sydney Hook, for instance, trivialized her position when he held that Arendt seemed to be arguing that "Negroes should give priority to agitation for equality in the bedroom rather than to equality in education."[79] In the rejoinder published by *Dissent*, Spitz praised her method of drawing distinctions (such as between the social and the political) but dismissed her "misguided courage" to be at odds with the liberal consensus and questioned the political wisdom of the concepts she proposed. Spitz was troubled by the dissociation of discrimination and racism because it seemed to apply only when one appealed to a "standard external to society itself" and suspected that Arendt saw herself as the one holding such standard. He concluded: "she is an aristocrat, not a democrat, at heart." The other author featured by *Dissent* was far more dismissive. Tumin, an African American Princeton sociologist, found it "appalling" that Arendt had "ignored the most courageous people in the nation . . . in the interest of showing up her decrepit metaphysics with even more decrepit non-facts."[80]

Such vehement contestation is in part the result of Arendt's confusing *political* position—was she in favor of segregation or just against federally enforced desegregation?—partly because it required more philosophical elaboration than she was able to offer in the article.[81] She explained the distinction between the political and the social sphere through the use of a chiasmus, a complex and easily confusing rhetorical figure that relies on an inverted parallelism: *"What equality is to the body politic—its innermost principle—discrimination is to society.* Society is that curious, somewhat hybrid realm between the political and the private. . . . For each time we leave the protective four walls of our private homes and cross over the threshold into the public world, we enter first, not the political realm of equality, but the social sphere.[82] Spitz challenged this definition with an intriguing example from Vladimir Nabokov's novel *Lolita*, which had been published in 1958 in the United States, after having been banned in Europe. According to Spitz, the affair between the middle-aged male character and his teenage stepdaughter is not a private matter but a case of incest and pedophilia that is relevant socially and politically, as it needs to be combated with legal action. The example of domestic violence would have been a better choice for pointing out the porous contours of the private, social, and political realms, but Spitz's selection of Nabokov's famous literary masterpiece reveals a social and moral conservatism that Arendt did not have. Her own tolerance made Arendt more optimistic about the possibility of a strictly benign discrimination than many Americans could have been at that time.

The America that interested Arendt was first of all a political concept, defined by both equality and pluralism. The latter, however, resides in the social realm and is maintained through what amounts to a positive discrimination, in the name of "differences by which people belong to certain groups whose very identifiability demands that they discriminate against other groups in the same domain." Using her own example, to associate with people who identify as Jews, by this logic, one needs to leave out non-Jews. Arendt was arguing as the former activist who had worked for Jewish organizations dealing exclusively with Jewish causes. "Discrimination is as indispensable a social right as equality is a political right," as she put it, because it allows such organizations to function.[83]

Read in this chiasmic logic, the conception of discrimination proposed by Arendt acquires an important nuance: discrimination remains positive only under conditions of political *equality*. At stake, then, is "not how to abolish discrimination, but how to keep it confined within the social sphere, where it is legitimate, and prevent its trespassing on the political and the personal sphere, where it is destructive."[84] Arendt had little to say on how discrimination might be safely contained beyond her plea for abolishing racist legislation. Granted, that was not her task in the article. The lack of a concrete solution made her seem less invested in thinking alongside Americans of a way to deal with the problems of racism and more in issuing warnings and pontificating from the sideline. Her emphasis on legal reform was not taken seriously by her contemporaries, even though half of a century later, debates about legislation regarding same-sex marriage prove that Arendt's focus on marriage laws as a way of influencing political equality was not only valid but prescient. In 1957, however, as Tumin complained, she seemed to privilege legal reform haphazardly or almost as a strategy for drawing attention away from school segregation.

The notion of the social realm distinct from the political and the private domains was a conceptual stopgap for many critics, and it has continued to prompt negative assessments even in response to a far more carefully elaborated version presented in *The Human Condition*.[85] Arendt's stranger persona not only made her conception of discrimination seem removed from the everyday experience of an average American but also made Arendt seem removed from the social realm, any social realm, and only concerned with conceptual problems. She admitted not to know the South, but it was also clear that her familiarity with African Americans was limited to newspaper photographs. But in the segregated South, white and black Americans faced one another every day. They were already neighbors and played together as children. Even in the North, many American intellectuals' perspective on racism was deeply informed by their experience of sharing the social sphere with African Americans (or parts of it), rather than inhabiting it in a segregated manner. Podhoretz's essay published in *Commentary*, "My Negro Problem—and Ours,"[86] provides a stark contrast to Arendt's "Reflections." Podhoretz recounts his childhood in Brooklyn, "beaten up, robbed, and in general hated, terrorized, and humiliated" by black children who were physically stronger and psychologically freer to do whatever they pleased," and describes his feelings about African Americans as "twisted" and in conflict with the moral convictions he had developed as an adult.[87] The article has a shocking bluntness about it as Podhoretz admits to having a deep-seated dislike of many African Americans. His reflections end with an unexpected confession: despite such dislike, he would not oppose his daughter's decision to marry a black man. Podhoretz comes off supporting interracial marriage—in his own family—just as much as Arendt, precisely as a political duty, and despite his personal feelings. Podhoretz, in other words, illustrates precisely the argument Arendt had made: he was committed to political equality even though he seemed to believe in discrimination in the social realm.

Yet the rhetorical difference between Arendt and Podhoretz is important: her detachment and impartiality contrast with his pathos and sincerity. His autobiographical style gives him an air of authenticity while she sounds aloof and arrogant even when referring to her experience as a Jew. Their arguments, while reaching the same conclusion also take a different conceptual route: the frame of the republic and the law, abstract and impersonal in Arendt's case, or in contemporary American society and family, concrete and deeply personal in Podhoretz's case. The result is that Arendt seems to be lecturing her readers while Podhoretz's voices many of their fears and experiences. She had constructed an elaborate and interesting argument as an impartial observer while interventions like Podhoretz's reminded American readers that they cannot be impartial in such matters.

By defamiliarizing discrimination, she removed the term from the reference shared by most Americans in their social experience of racism. This removal played a conceptual role but is also reflected in a language that troubled her readers because it had a rather awkward ring, such as when she referred to racism as "the country's attitude to its Negro population."[88] This is a strange construction not only as a euphemism but also because it breaks the link between the American nation and African Americans. Calling African Americans "population," awkward as it seems, emphasizes their position of exteriority to the nation. For Arendt, this is the position of the pariah. Rosa Parks had behaved more as an Arendtian pariah than the leaders of the NAACP did when supporting the Little Rock Nine because Parks had confronted a discriminatory practice in the political sphere and one manifested publicly. By refusing to give up her seat in the section of the bus that was for black people, Parks had acted as a pariah and had mobilized wide support. It was such support, from the ground up, Arendt wished to see in Little Rock, not federal intervention.

Arendt's defamiliarization of discrimination was connected to a metonymic representation of African Americans in the image of Elizabeth Eckford as the "unwanted child." By looking at the picture of Eckford metonymically, as that of the unwanted, Arendt seemed not to see real African Americans as much as her own political abstraction. Arendt believed that by forcing a child into a world that rejects it will lead to the child's internalizing of its own undesirability and create the instinct of a parvenu rather than a pariah.[89] Critics have charged that Arendt "failed to see that African-Americans seeking to integrate public schools were not parvenus, striving for acceptance where they were not wanted. Instead, they were escaping the master's house, struggling to get out from under their enforced servility and to emerge into the light of the public realm as equals."[90] Along these lines, the most devastating criticism came from Ralph Ellison, who accused Arendt of not understanding the historical specificity of the African American experience. In Ellison's view, this experience, a simultaneous confrontation of "social and political terrors" was a rite of passage for African American children. The parents who risked their lives facing angry mobs in front of Central High School were "aware of the overtones of a rite of initiation which such events actually constitute for the child, a confrontation of the terrors of social life with all the mysteries stripped away. And in the outlook of many of these parents (who wish that the problem didn't exist) the child is expected to face the terror and contain his fear and anger precisely because he is a Negro American."[91]

This was the only criticism to which Arendt conceded. In a personal (unpublished) letter sent to Ellison, she admitted: "it was precisely this attitude of sacrifice that I did not get."[92] But this was hardly a concession, and it did not cancel her arrogant dismissal of the NAACP's position in support of school desegregation over the abrogation of racist legislation. "Oppressed minorities have never been a good judge of their own situation," she proffered, clearly implying that *she* was a better judge.[93]

Elizabeth Eckford's photo played an evidentiary role in Arendt's arguments about the importance of maintaining the social realm separate, by introducing another distinction, from the private sphere. Arendt thought that the government had violated the privacy of family by making decisions she held that only parents are authorized to make, such as what school a child attends.[94] Her own mother had decided what schools the young Arendt should attend, even in difficult times when such a decision was drastically limited by anti-Semitic legislation. Arendt believed that Eckford and the other eight black students had been used as pawns in the political battle of adults. "The girl, obviously, was asked to be a hero," Arendt continues, "that is, something neither her absent father nor the equally absent representatives of the NAACP felt called upon to be." "Have we now come to the point," she asked rhetorically, "where it is the children who are being asked to change or improve the world?"[95] She did not comment on the fact that the students and their families had been advised by the NAACP *not* to go to school on that day. Tumin took this to be evidence of how unfounded her arguments were: "Ms. Arendt obviously knows little or nothing about what actually happened in Little Rock."[96]

Arendt's arguments on the desegregation of schools in the American South reflect her commitment to the American political tradition—as she understood it—rather than a concrete America—the society in which she herself lived. Her cultivated impartiality came across as uncaring detachment and undermined the solidarity she was trying to convey for the civil rights movement. The "Olympian authority"[97] of "Reflections on Little Rock" was especially troubling to an audience struggling with the realization of their most difficult "dilemma of difference."[98] To American readers who were incensed, worried, or scared by the events taking place in the South, the problem was not conceptual as much as practical, and their own attitude was not detached and analytical but intensely emotional.

Did Arendt think that her persona was responsible for creating confusion over some of her arguments and for alienating her American audience? Nothing she said in response to criticisms—not even in the concession she made to Ellison—suggests any interest in adjusting her style. Her main strategy of defamiliarization, to dissociate discrimination from racism, played a key role in the distinction she made between the social and the political sphere, which is one of the best known, if controversial, contributions of her political thought. At the time Arendt wrote this article, relationships between the African American and Jewish American communities were tense. Ernest Green, one of the nine black students admitted to Central High, recalls the exchange he had with a friend who was the son of a Jewish family who frequented the Jewish country club where Green worked as a towel boy: "He came up to me and said, 'How could you do it?' I said, 'what do you mean, how could I do it?' He said, 'you seem like such a nice fellow. Why is it you want to go to Central? Why do you want to destroy our relationship?'"[99]

This exchange would not have surprised Arendt. The relationship—no matter how awkward and inadequate the term seems here—that was being "destroyed" by giving a black student access to a white school is based on the right to difference. It is disturbing to think of it as a *right*, and not to be incensed in our moral instinct by the words of this white young man. But his response reveals how difficult the American dilemma can be: how to maintain plurality and equality at the same time, without allowing one to rule insidiously over the other, either compromising equality or eliminating plurality? As James Bohman has argued, the main point of "Reflections" is "a warning about the use of political power," which can maintain the balance between equality and plurality.[100] Whether Arendt was mistaken about the importance of desegregating schools, she was right about the dilemmas of difference in American politics. On this front, as one commentator acknowledges, "Arendt broke the ice."[101] Assessing her arguments decades later, Bohman claims that they were dismissed too easily by her contemporaries. Arendt was "urging us to accept clear-mindedly the real moral costs of holding both diversity and consent as necessary political values."[102] Nonetheless, she clearly failed to convince most readers, even the most well intended and sophisticated, that she was sufficiently in favor of civil rights for them to accept her morally neutral notion of discrimination. The one way in which she tried to establish communion with her readers not at the level of a political ideal defining the American Republic, but in the social sphere, was as a Jew. But this was far from a guaranteed successful strategy of identification. When she first submitted her article to *Commentary*—a journal with a predominantly Jewish readership—Arendt hoped that her credibility would be enhanced by the fact that she had experienced discrimination as a Jew. She asked her readers to accept that she would naturally have empathy for "oppressed minorities everywhere."[103] That most did not make this allowance is the result of more than the fact that these were different kinds of discrimination. There were also different kinds of Jewishness involved.

A GERMAN JEW IN NEW YORK

At the time of her arrival in America, mainstream political discourse frequently featured arguments that the Nazi problem only concerned Jews and Europeans and not average Americans. Public sentiment was reflected in official immigration policy, as until the end of World War II very few Jewish refugees fleeing the Nazi regime obtained entry.[104] Arendt was a European

Jewish immigrant at a time when most Americans opposed increases in immigration quotas to aid Jews from Austria and Germany. She, however, was not *any* Jew. Ezra Pound would not have seen her, to use his disturbingly anti-Semitic language, as a "small Jew" because she was too prominent and a survivor.[105] Nor did American Jews, in all likelihood, picture someone like her when they thought of their relatives killed by Hitler in Europe. "The line-up was always before my eyes," wrote Alfred Kazin. "I could imagine my father and mother, my sister and myself, our original tenement family of 'small Jews,' all too clearly—fuel for the flames, dying by a single flame that burned us all up at once."[106] Arendt was probably not in this line-up despite her close call at Gurs.

At a time when many New York intellectuals were both learning more about the destruction of the European Jews in extermination camps and reflecting on and learning more about their own Jewish roots, Arendt struck many of them as more German than Jewish. Kazin depicts her as "more influenced by Christianity than by Jewish tradition. . . . Even her acquired taste for republican liberty rather than social meliorism reflected her basic conditioning in the profound sense of the self at the heart of German Protestantism and German philosophy." This portrait of a Jewish woman as a German Gentile prioritizes her identification as European to present her as quintessentially different from most Americans:

> The real drama of European exiled writers in America—I limit myself to Mann and Arendt—is the contrast between their instinctive European sense of history and the optimistic American belief—should I call it the old American optimism?—that the future is as real as the present. . . . The America that began to rearm in 1940, miraculously recovered from the Depression, had a bounce, a new faith in progress as its destiny, that contrasted with the exhaustion and fearfulness of many exiles.[107]

Thomas Mann was commonly seen as the very symbol of German *Kultur*—a new Goethe revered but clearly different from most Americans, intellectuals or not. Placed in the same category as Mann—an association that would not have pleased Arendt, who disliked Mann's novels and even more so his political writing—she becomes German by association and non-American by implied dissociation.

The perception of Arendt through the terministic screen of German culture occurred within the broader context of the reception of other German exiles, not all Jews, who had fled to America during the war.[108] Long after the war, the complaints that the exiles changed American culture for the worse came from some prominent academics, not merely uninformed xenophobes. In 1963, "exposing" the German contamination of American cultural life—from the thematic of films to the spread of psychoanalysis—Allan Bloom accused the inevitable clash, as he perceived it, between the American spirit and German thought:

> German thought [post-Hegel] tended not toward liberation from one's own culture, as did earlier thought, but toward reconstituting the rootedness in one's own, which has been shattered by cosmopolitanism, philosophical and political. . . . We chose a system of thought that, like some wines, does not travel; we chose a way of looking at things that could never be ours and had as its starting point dislike of ours and our goals.[109]

By contrast to what Arendt had written to her friend Jaspers in 1946, for people like Bloom there was an American *national* tradition, one that was incompatible with the German one. Such a condemnation may not have been shared by the sophisticated cosmopolitans among New York intellectuals but the premise was. Writers like Kazin, for example, would not have easily succumbed to such oversimplification. Nevertheless, the more they positioned Arendt as German (admiringly or not), the more she remained foreign, especially to the American intellectuals for whom Jewishness was not merely a common ethnic background but also a collective ethos, which extended even to those who were not Jews. Barrett, who was not Jewish, felt so much at home in the "pervasively Jewish" circle of the New York intellectuals that he was not completely surprised when told by Sydney Hook (who was Jewish) that he (Barrett) "had more of a New York Jewish intonation than he [Hook]."[110] Arendt not only had a thick German accent, but after the publication of *Eichmann in Jerusalem*, she was excommunicated by her own people.

Originally published as a series of reports written for the *New Yorker*, *Eichmann in Jerusalem* was released as a book in 1963. The deluge of criticism prompted Arendt to publish a revised second edition in 1964 in which she corrected some factual errors while leaving the controversial theses of the book unchanged. She had been accused of having offered an outrageously flawed historical account: one critic counted 665 mistakes, possibly an exaggeration, yet still indicative of the magnitude of the problems raised by the text. Jacob Robinson, one of the harshest critics, devoted an entire book to identifying Arendt's errors and meticulously refuting her arguments.[111] Yet disagreements over factual inaccuracy do not explain the proportions of the controversy. The criticism issued against *Eichmann in Jerusalem* was exceptional in intensity and scale. The book was controversial primarily because of how Arendt portrayed Adolph Eichmann, SS lieutenant colonel in charge with overseeing the deportation of Jews to extermination camps, as a common family man and a good employee in the Nazi bureaucracy. She portrayed him as someone who merely did his job without fully understanding or worrying about consequences. Also controversial were her claims that the Jewish Councils should have done more to prevent the extermination of their people. Even more problematic was her claim that the Jewish Councils had actually collaborated in some instances with the Nazis in implementing the Final Solution. Overall, the book shocked all the more because its author was a Jew.

Among her critics were lesser known and arguably opportunistic authors who profited from the controversy by using it as an occasion to lobby for interventions that otherwise would have gone unheard. Even so, these were joined by people who were once her friends and were prestigious scholars, such as Gershom Scholem, or by well-known American intellectuals and political commentators, such as Lionel Abel, Irving Howe, and even by her erstwhile political mentor Kurt Blumenfeld.[112] The Council of Jews from Germany and the Anti-Defamation League of B'nai B'rith both publicly denounced the book. Nonetheless, the book did have supporters, who comprised an equally diverse group, including prestigious intellectuals, such as Mary McCarthy, Stephen Spender, and Daniel Bell, and, perhaps most important among them, camp survivor Bruno Bettelheim.[113]

Eichmann in Jerusalem remains one of the fifty most influential books written after the war according to *Time* magazine. The phrase used in the subtitle, "banality of evil," has become almost a cliché in journalistic and political discourse. In more or less simplified form, some of Arendt's arguments in this book have become standard in conversations about the Holocaust. Regardless how vilified it was by its critics, the book has made a deep impact on political consciousness especially in America, not only because Holocaust survivors represented a significant number in this country, but also because of the political moral of Arendt's account: if a totalitarian regime like the one responsible for the Final Solution relied, not on monsters, but on an effective ideology and a bureaucracy, totalitarianism could take root in any advanced bureaucratic society—even in America (or especially here, Marcuse would argue). Similar to "Little Rock," the stranger persona in *Eichmann in Jerusalem* is a powerful epistemic tool that leads to striking conceptual originality. Unlike "Little Rock," *Eichmann in Jerusalem* did not deal with a specifically American matter so there seemed to be less risk for overstepping boundaries. But the implications of her main theses were deeply significant for American politics at a time of major turmoil when the Vietnam War had reached its escalation under President Lyndon B. Johnson's leadership and the increased violence in the conflict between Palestinians and U.S.-backed Israel. Irving Howe deplored the influence Arendt's depiction of the Jewish Councils would have on "hundreds of thousands of good middle-class Americans [who] will have learned from those articles that the Jewish leadership in Europe was cowardly, inept, and even collaborationist."[114] But so many more middle-class Americans were outraged by the book and offered not only full support to the Jewish victims but also to the Israeli state. A reviewer of Margarette von Trotha's 2013 cinematic rendition of the controversy complained that Arendt's portrayal of Eichmann as a small-minded bureaucrat turned many Americans against Vietnam veterans, who had also followed orders.[115]

I will not review in detail the objections marshaled against the book, or indeed the defense, as both have received comprehensive coverage elsewhere.[116] I will focus instead on Arendt's persona and its connections to the book's ideas and style, both of which so many of her critics found offensive. Her style was not just an expository choice among others possible but the hallmark of her stranger persona and indeed the key to her conception of evil, which was now modified from the notion of a "radical evil" she had advanced in her work on totalitarianism. Arendt's stranger persona in *Eichmann in Jerusalem* has been perceived by many of her American readers as a betrayal of her Jewish origins. Scholem deplored her "frequently almost sneering and malicious tone" and her "flippancy" and "overtones of malice."[117] She had written the book, he concluded, as though she was not really a daughter of her people, without any love for the Jews. Indeed, there are few indications in the entire book that the author is Jewish and no indication of any special compassion for or solidarity with the Jews qua *Jews*. Arendt distanced herself from her Jewish identity to create an analytic vantage point from which to report the Eichmann trial. This distancing relies on narrative omniscience and uses Eichmann's viewpoint to examine the Final Solution. Arendt deliberately spoke at times in Eichmann's voice—as she imagines it based on both historical documents and her observations during the trial—to narrate critical events in which he played a role, such as in the deportation of Jews to extermination camps, in organizing shooting campaigns, and in implementing the last stages of the Final Solution. That does not mean, however, that she also agreed with Eichmann's perspective.

In response to Scholem's criticism, Arendt explained, "If you missed the irony of the sentence—which was plainly in *oratio obliqua*, reporting Eichmann's own words—I really can't help it."[118] But it was precisely irony and other stylistic choices that contributed to the controversial nature of the book. According to Walter Lacquer, "Miss Arendt was attacked not so much for what she said, [as] for how she said it."[119] The expository techniques Arendt chose—the use of irony and indirect free speech, instead of, for example, a tragic tone combined with narrative techniques that would convey a distancing from Eichmann and emotional identification with the victims of the Holocaust—are the specific techniques associated in this case with her stranger persona. They can also be explained within the broader context of her political philosophy with its deep-seated suspicion of the tragic mode. [120]

Arendt's conception of tragedy is Aristotelian, in that it emphasizes the audiences' cathartic identification with the victims as a way of "understand[ing] and accept[ing] the existence of painful realities they cannot change."[121] But she also believed that cathartic identification leads to resignation rather than action and thus cannot help us really learn anything from a troubled past. She held that emotional involvement does not encourage lucid analysis. Instead, she argued that "those young German men and women who every once in a while—on the occasion of all the *Diary of Anne Frank* hubbub and of the Eichmann trial—treat us to hysterical outbreaks of guilt feelings are not staggering under the weight of the past, their father's guilt; rather, they are trying to escape from the pressure of very present and actual problems into a cheap sentimentality."[122]

Instead of a narrative technique that would clearly convey compassion for the victims, and condemn the murderers, Arendt muddled the very distinction, by using "the fiction of a non-partisan, distanced point of observation, and assumed the fictional voice of a mobile observer who was also concerned with the voice of the observed murderer."[123] This position of a mobile observer gives her stranger persona, which was already known to be that of an impartial observer, a new dimension of moral indifference equally distant and detached from both the victims and their killer.

Arendt was present for the court proceedings as an American reporter. Nevertheless, she observed alternatively as a Jew, a war survivor, an opponent of the Israeli state, and an objective journalist. The only two times when she refers specifically to herself in the entire book appear at the very beginning. In the first instance, she describes the entrance of the three judges presiding as the court usher shouted "at the top of his voice," "Beth Hamishpath—the House of Justice . . . making *us* jump to our feet." Here, she introduces herself as a member of the audience present in the courtroom but without clarifying to her readers that she herself was Jewish, a former inmate at an internment camp, and a political refugee. Presumably the readers of the

New Yorker would have known some of that and may even have been familiar with her work. Her decision not to make a discursive space for herself in
such terms is, nevertheless, interesting. By contrast, she describes the setting
of the trial very carefully, identifying all of the participants—the court ste-
nographers, the translators, the accused, the witnesses, the prosecutor with
his staff of four assistant attorneys, and the counsel for the defense (accompanied for the first weeks of the trial by an assistant). This careful reconstruction of the stage of the show and of its protagonists is issued from the
perspective of an impartial spectator whose observations are unobstructed
by any physical, psychological, or symbolic constraints. Indeed, when referring to the multi-language translations of the proceedings, Arendt sounds
as though *she* could hear all of them at once: "the radio transmission, which
is excellent in French, bearable in English, and sheer comedy, frequently
incomprehensible, in German."[124] Indeed, she spoke all three languages and
could make such an assessment, but the polyglot comes across as equally
detached from any of the languages (and communities) spoken at the trial.

The multilingual discourse of the trial was designed to acknowledge
its international significance, but this is precisely why Arendt saw it as a
staged political melodrama: "there they were, seated at the top of the raised
platform, facing the audience as from the stage in a play. The audience was
supposed to represent the whole world," united in its condemnation of the
Holocaust. But this goal, she thinks, was not achieved:

> If the audience at the trial was to be the world and the play the huge pan-
> orama of Jewish sufferings, the reality was falling short of expectations and
> purposes. The journalists remained faithful for not much more than two
> weeks, after which the audience changed drastically. It was now supposed
> to consist of Israelis, of those who were too young to know the story or, as
> in the case of Oriental Jews, had never been told it.[125]

With this shift, Arendt's own argument shifts toward a critique of Israel
rather than mere objective coverage of the trial. If the press is no longer the
audience, intended or real, where does Arendt herself fit?[126] She finally introduces herself in the story, not just as one of the few journalists who stayed

beyond the first weeks of the trial (obviously, not the entire journalists' camp had left), but as a Jew. In making such a self-identification, however, Arendt simultaneously distances herself from other Jews:

> The trial was supposed to show them [the intended young audience members] what it meant to live among non-Jews, to convince them that only in Israel could a Jew be safe and live an honorable life. . . . But in this audience there were hardly any young people, and it did not consist of Israelis as distinguished from Jews. It was filled with "survivors," with middle-aged and elderly people, immigrants from Europe, *like myself*, who knew by heart all there was to know, and who were in no mood to learn any lessons and certainly did not need this trial to draw their own conclusions.[127]

While Arendt does not mention explicitly the professional role in which she was attending the trial, as a journalist and reporter for the American media, references to other journalists place her in that category and attribute to her the associated ethic of objectivity and impartiality. Indeed, she identifies herself first as a sort of disembodied spectator who surveys the scene and the agents from a bird's eye view and then places herself in a position of moral and epistemic authority. She is one of the survivors, and as such, someone who already knows "all there was to know." Combined with what critics perceived as lack of compassion for the victims, this claim to omniscience could easily seem arrogant.

Much of the negative reaction to the book was caused by the confusion created by its narrative style, which alternates between recounting Eichmann's activities during the war as told by Eichmann himself, Arendt's assessment of that account, and historical evidence available at the time about Eichmann. The story is assembled from three sources that have different degrees of verisimilitude and epistemic authority: his own autobiographical version, which was obviously designed to exculpate him; a third-person view that reflects not only on events and facts but also on Eichmann's own perspective on them; and a historical view that places Eichmann in the broader context of the Nazi apparatus. These three perspectives are interwoven in a way that makes distinguishing one from the other difficult.

Consider the overlap of Eichmann's perspective and Arendt's, fusing in free indirect speech, in the following example, in which Eichmann is discussing his role as the official appointed with the handling of the paperwork for the Jews who were being deported from Germany:

> He and his men and the Jews were all "pulling together," and whenever there were any difficulties the Jewish functionaries would come running to him to "unburden their hearts," to tell him "all their grief and sorrow," and to ask for his help. The Jews "desired" to emigrate, and he, Eichmann, was there to help them, because it so happened that at the same time the Nazi authorities had expressed a desire to see their Reich *Judenrein*.[128]

The use of quotation marks is clearly designed to differentiate Eichmann's own words from Arendt's, but the citation is inserted in a third-person narrative where the scare quotes can be easily missed. It is Eichmann who believes that he helped the Jews, not Arendt. Arendt preserves and highlights the euphemisms Eichmann uses to describe the situation, as a mere coincidence between the Jews' own wish to leave Germany and the Nazi policy, precisely because she wants to focus readers' attention on Eichmann's point of view—to get them to see the Nazi's treatment of Jews as *he* saw it.

Arendt guides readers through narrative technique to a particular perception of reality. Usually, this narrative technique, focalization, can be character- or narrator-based. When we follow the logic of the story, we tend to associate the character-bound focalization with more authenticity because we assume that a perspective "from the inside" is more accurate and reliable.[129] Yet the question still remains—the question that upset Scholem and others to the point of repudiating their friend—why did she not report Eichmann's claims at the trial using only direct speech, thus preserving intact the first-person perspective and signaling a clear distance between her view and Eichmann's? Why blend third-person accounts with the first-person perspective?

The answer is that she wanted to guide the readers, through indirect free speech, into the mental universe of Eichmann. Her manner of reproducing Eichmann's comments functions as a strategy of defamiliarization because it allows Arendt to introduce a perspective that is radically different from the one her readers would have already known. She presents this perspective without explicitly qualifying it as perverse, precisely because Eichmann did not see himself as perverse. In fact, several times during the trial, he insisted that he had tried to help Jews.

To consider the possibility that a man accused of being responsible for the death of millions of Jews actually helped them requires, of course, a morally uncomfortable leap of imagination. But it was precisely this effort that interested Arendt because it allowed her to introduce the idea that the Nazi criminal was not a murderer in the common sense of the term—someone who sets out to kill and knows that he is killing—but a new historical character that no longer sees the murder for what it is. The psychological mechanism of such a character is not mere self-deception but a more complicated process of being detached from the world around him.

For Arendt, Eichmann is primarily a man incapable of perceiving reality accurately because he is unable to think for himself. Thus, he was the ideal candidate for serving a totalitarian regime that took over his consciousness and controlled his perceptions to the point where he could see deportations as emigrations, thinking in the language of euphemisms used by the Nazis. This is the discourse of a regime that deliberately veiled the meaning of its actions—such as deportations as a preliminary step to mass murder—in terms designed to allow avoidance of responsibility for such actions. Arendt explains, "those who were told explicitly of the Fuehrer's orders were no longer mere 'bearer of orders,' but were advanced to 'bearers of secrets,' and a special oath was administered to them." For the rest of the members of the Nazi apparatus, a special set of "language rules" were designed to replace "bald words as 'extermination,' 'liquidation,' or 'killing'" with "prescribed code names for killing [such as] 'final solution,' 'evacuation' (*Aussiedlung*), and 'special treatment' (*Sonderhandlung*)."[130]

According to Arendt, Eichmann had internalized these "languages rules" to the point where he could not see what they were hiding. Arendt shows the impact of "languages rules" on Eichmann by using direct speech, sometimes quite extensively, as in the case of one of Eichmann's stories featuring his relation with the Jewish Councils. In reporting the exchange he had with one of the representatives of the Vienna Jewish Council, an older man named Storfer, who had requested his help upon being sent to an extermination camp, Eichmann presents his response as the compassionate reaction of a helpless friend. Arendt introduces the narrative in her own voice and then shifts to Eichmann's voice:

> Eichmann had received a telegram from Rudolf Hoss, Commandant of Auschwitz, telling him that Storfer had arrived and had urgently requested to see Eichmann. "*I said to myself*: O.K., this man has always behaved well, that is worth my while . . . I'll go there myself and see what is the matter with him. And I go to Ebner [chief of the Gestapo in Vienna], and Ebner says—I remember it only vaguely—"If only he had not been so clumsy; he went into hiding and tried to escape," something of the sort. And the police arrested him and sent him to the concentration camp, and according to the orders of the Reichsführer [Himmler], no one could get out once he was in. Nothing could be done, neither Dr. Ebner nor I not anybody could do anything about it. I went to Auschwitz and asked Hoss to see Storfer, "Yes, yes [Hoss said], he is in one of the labor gangs." With Storfer afterward, well, it was normal and human, we had a normal, human encounter. He told me all his grief and sorrow: I said: "Well, my dear old friend [*Ja, mein lieber guter Storfer*], we certainly got it! What rotten luck!"[131]

Storfer, the narrative continues, asked Eichmann if he could at least be relieved of work at Auschwitz. That turned out to be impossible as well. Eichmann arranged to get a special task (an easier one, in his view) for Storfer, swiping the gravel paths with a broom. This, and the fact that he had had such a friendly exchange with him, gave Eichmann a "great inner joy." After quoting Eichmann's account in its entirety, Arendt reverted to her own voice to bring the story to closure: "Six weeks after this normal human encounter, Storfer was dead—not gassed, apparently, but shot."[132] Her tone is neutral, and it is up to the reader to be moved and outraged at the tragic fate of one of Eichmann's victims.

Arendt's use of character-bound focalization allows her to challenge the master plot of the pathologically cruel and demonic Nazi officer who takes pleasure in seeing his victims suffer. By letting Eichmann narrate the events, she introduces a radically different perspective on these events, stressing that it is *his* but making it nevertheless coherent. The events are emplotted as if they followed not just a chronological order but also a logical one. The order is such: as representative of the Jewish council in Vienna, Storfer had been cooperative, and Eichmann wanted to express his gratitude. It was not, however, possible to help him, especially as Storfer had put himself in a bad situation by trying to flee arrest. Unable to help, Eichmann conveyed his regret and arranged for a less demanding task for Storfer at Auschwitz. This sequence appears coherent only because Eichmann sees it as such. By recounting the events as Eichmann saw them following one another, Arendt forces the reader to adopt Eichmann's perspective, including the perspective of himself: a reasonable and even compassionate man who is doing his job, dutifully following orders while trying to be helpful.

Narrative coherence acts as a form of explanation—in this case, an explanation for Eichmann's behavior—for not saving Storfer's life. Usually, coherent stories are more likely to be deemed credible but only insofar as they are consistent with other, culturally shared plots. Narrative explanations not only justify the occurrences of certain events, but they can also function as scaffolding for anticipation, or "structures in terms of the reader, listener, or viewer's possession of a range of possibilities. We accept a narrative 'explanation' by reacting emotionally to the events recounted in a story. A narrative explanation is believable within the confines of the story-world created in the narrative."[133] Because Eichmann's story does not resonate with a culturally sanctioned master plot, its coherence becomes morally outrageous. The effect of retelling Eichmann's story using his own words is one of identifying the gulf between his first-person perspective and a third-person one, Arendt's, not in order to ratify one or the other as much as to use this difference for pedagogical purposes. Eichmann's story allows Arendt to offer an alternative portrait and with it an alternative explanation for what made crimes such as Eichmann's possible. To this end, entering Eichmann's mind becomes crucial. The reader also hears the voice of a Gestapo official called Dr. Ebner, quoted directly by Eichmann. In the narrative reproduced by Arendt, Eichmann quotes Ebner to support his own claims, hoping that they would seem more credible. By maintaining the quotes from Ebner, Arendt was trying to show that the only authority Eichmann recognized, and took to be universally valid, was that of Nazi officials. Through direct speech, Arendt recreates Eichmann's mental universe in which compassion is replaced by bureaucratic politeness and judgment by bureaucratic servitude. In such a mental universe, events lack a tragic dimension because there is no moral or emotional context in which they could be identified as tragic. Eichmann could only focus on events isolated from the sequence to which they belong—arrest-deportation-death. In using direct speech, Arendt can also show what is completely absent from the world of this consciousness: the victim. Missing from Eichmann's account is Storfer's voice. This is the voice that he never quoted, only paraphrased.

The defamiliarization offered by direct speech and character-bound focalization marks a clear departure from the mainstream explanation of the Nazi criminal as the radical embodiment of evil. Arendt conceptualized evil not in Kantian terms as violation of moral norms but in Augustinian ones as absence of moral norms, as a fracture in the moral bone of humanity.[134] Defamiliarization reveals an important characteristic of the world of the Nazi, which is devoid of pity or compassion, not because its people are diabolical but because they do not see or hear their victims.

The impartiality of Arendt's stranger persona is illustrated by the double estrangement working in the example analyzed above. On the one hand, she seeks to distance herself from the common plot of the Nazi madman. On the other hand, she also distances herself from Eichmann's perspective, not only by relegating it to him through the use of direct speech but also through the irony contained in the final, concluding sentence, which adopts Eichmann's own words—after this "normal human encounter"—only to signal their absurdity. The impartiality feature in *Eichmann in Jerusalem* works through irony, which was repeatedly identified as one of the most offensive qualities of the book, as revealing a cold, unsympathetic Arendt. Yet Arendt only used irony to express her attitude toward Eichmann, not toward his victims. Irony is an apt trope for estrangement because it is predicated on a double discourse, a literal one and its negation (saying one thing and meaning the opposite). Irony is also a figure of judgment because the negation of the literal discourse has an evaluative component.[135]

Arendt's impartial observer is an ironist who judges events and situations *after* she has recreated them from the perspective of their main characters and *after* she has entered these characters' mental universe. Irony defines a moral framework for her because it enables judgment and condemnation. However, it does not make her into what Richard Rorty would call an ironist, a moral relativist who can entertain several worldviews at the same time and subscribe to different vocabularies without strict preference for one of her own.[136] Rather, Arendt writes, to use Berel Lang's distinction, as a romantic ironist, "cast as a transcendent knower of ironic reversal from a position outside it . . . in principle outside any [and every] particular setting."[137]

Arendt's most irate critics pointed to the irony in *Eichmann in Jerusalem* as a sign of her being too willing to excuse Eichmann. Indeed, she had used irony to achieve proximity to Eichmann, yet not as a way of excusing his perspective but as a strategy for making this perspective appear banal, rather than extraordinary. Consider her analysis of Eichmann's use of euphemisms in describing the fate of Jews during the war:

> Eichmann's distortions of reality were horrible because of the horrors they dealt with, but in principle they were not very different from things current in post–Hitler Germany. There is, for instance, Franz-Josef Strauss, former minister of Defense. . . . Strauss asked a widely publicized and apparently very successful question of Mr. Brandt—"What were you doing those twelve years outside Germany? We know what we were doing here in Germany"—with complete impunity, without anybody's batting an eye, let alone reminding the member of the Bonn government that what Germans in Germany were doing during those years has become notorious indeed. The same "innocence" is to be found in a recent casual remark by a respected and respectable German literary critic . . . reviewing a study of literature in the Third Reich, he said that its author "belonged with those intellectuals who at the outbreak of barbarism deserted us without exception." This author was of course a Jew, and he was expelled by the Nazis and

himself deserted by Gentiles. . . . Incidentally, the word "barbarism," today frequently applied by Germans to the Hitler period, is a distortion of reality; it is as though Jewish and non-Jewish intellectuals had fled a country that was no longer "refined" enough for them.[138]

By reproducing statements made by prominent politicians of the day, and then commenting on them ironically, Arendt makes it possible to compare different perspectives on reality. Once established, the comparative mode can be carried beyond a discussion of Eichmann. It prompts readers to criticize not just Nazis, but Germans; not just acts committed during a war but in times of peace as well; not just Germans, but also Americans. The ironic stance thus becomes a platform for moral evaluation extended beyond the task at hand to a more general reflection and condemnation. The purpose of this condemnation is not to indict *all* Germans (a generalization Arendt considered, following Jaspers, untenable), but to show how responsibility can be shifted and guilt avoided.[139] The Jerusalem tribunal had sought to absolutize guilt to the point where it could not be attributed to anyone in particular. It was the trial itself that made arguments like Eichmann's possible, showcasing in its disturbing nuance the process through which evil can be justified. As Arendt pointed out, the purpose of the trial was not so much to establish whether Eichmann was guilty but to show the magnitude of his guilt. Arendt called it, for that reason, a show trial.

The relation between different perspectives compared within the framework of irony is a hierarchical one, as indicated by the following example: "What for Hitler . . . was among the war's main objectives, with its implementation given top priority, regardless of economic and military considerations, and what for Eichmann was a job, with its daily routine, its ups and downs, was for the Jews quite literally the end of the world."[140] Here, the first two designations of the Final Solution, as a military objective and as a bureaucratic assignment, acquire a tragic dimension because they contrast so powerfully with the third designation of an apocalypse. Using three different names for the same event is, in part, necessitated by the frame of the trial, which requires that words that convey judgment be avoided until the end. The conventions of the trial prescribe an avoidance of a clear-cut terminology that would reflect the legal and moral assessment available only *after* the verdict has been issued. Yet this was an unusual trial, and it was precisely such an avoidance that was impossible, indeed even undesirable for the Israeli officials. At the time Arendt was writing, the third designation of the Final Solution—the extermination of Jews—operates as the default term. Any other use functions as unexpected.

Arendt's technique of defamiliarization was to alternate perspectives, by using different naming devices, in order to create an awareness of the Nazi, or totalitarian, mind. Its cruelty and inhumanity lie not in criminal intention but in the very lack of recognizing criminal actions as such. Read in the inverse order—which is the actual order in which one makes sense of the depictions—the characterization of the Jewish genocide ("literally the end of the world" for Jews) as a job dutifully executed toward reaching a military objective sounds like an indictment. It brings out precisely what the Nazi regime did not have: a moral conscience that distinguished between criminals and their victims. Without such a distinction, pity or humane treatment becomes impossible. The Nazis, by this logic, did not just dehumanize their victims (as many regimes do) to gives themselves permission to annihilate; they did not even recognize the category of the victim. Why, then, judge the Nazi regime from the viewpoint of a victim?

Irony affords an avoidance of the victim-standpoint because it tips the scale: it is no longer the Nazi world represented as the ultimate power crushing the completely powerless. Instead, the ironist is now the one who asserts power by dominating the target of her ironic discourse. But such detachment and empowering through irony required avoiding being in the position of the Jew as victim. This was the position Arendt avoided in her own life and career—a position she argued against as morally and politically pernicious. She would have agreed on this issue with Edward Said. I will return to this issue in chapter5, where I discuss Said's criticism of Zionism as a politics of victimhood.

Arendt's depiction of Eichmann and of his victims had profound consequences for the understanding of political evil, especially in an age when confrontations between nuclear world powers required new entries in a rhetoric of blame. Removing evil from the moral realm (as thus from particular nations or individuals) into institutional and bureaucratic machinery made it possible to indict the Nazis rather than Germany, or Israel rather than the Jewish people, and it would make it possible for Marcuse to indict capitalism instead of just America. But in targeting totalitarianism as an amoral and super-individual entity, Arendt also de-emphasized, as Deborah Lipstadt has argued, the role played by individuals' beliefs and attitudes. These coalesced over centuries, Lipstadt claimed, into anti-Semitism. For Lipstadt, a Jewish American historian who faced in court Holocaust denier David Irving, anti-Semitism is, even now, the backdrop of her life, as it was for Arendt's. Both Lipstadt and Arendt worry, though at different historical moments, that the Holocaust could be repeated. Yet their worry has a different source. For Lipstadt, it is anti-Semitism, for Arendt, it was totalitarianism. How one resists anti-Semitism and how one resists totalitarianism differ widely, and here Arendt's commitment to the political potential of the pariah becomes again relevant. Resisting the total domination of totalitarianism requires an oppositional stance that can challenge the very mechanisms of that system, as she had done in *Eichmann in Jerusalem* by first identifying those mechanisms. While Arendt would have wanted the Jewish councils to act in such defiance, as pariahs, she outraged readers who only saw those Jews as victims, rather than potential, dead heroes. More importantly, this vision of resistance enforced, albeit indirectly, her perspective on the limits of resistance as presented in "Reflections on Little Rock, Arkansas." Both essays condemn accommodation and praise strategic rebellion.

Upon publication in *The New Yorker*, Arendt's reports on the Eichmann trial were compared to James Baldwin's article, "A Letter from the South," which had been published a little while before.[141] In contrast to Arendt, Baldwin employed a highly emotional rhetoric to describe the despair in the life of African Americans who felt in the South like strangers in their own country. As Anson Rabinbach puts it, "many (Jewish American intellectuals) were uncomfortable with how Arendt had attempted to tell the story of the Holocaust in a way that markedly departed from Baldwin's 'melodramatic' story of black victims and white perpetrators."[142] Baldwin made a dramatically clear distinction between the black victims and their white oppressors. By muddling that distinction, Arendt was also making it hard to understand what kind of redress was necessary. Furthermore, the Eichmann controversy unfolded at a time when American Jews represented a "model of ethnic assimilation" to be adopted by other minorities as well, including the African American. Arendt opposed assimilation by representing its extreme consequences in the alleged collaboration of the Jewish councils. Her arguments in "Reflections" amounted to a similar attitude; by identifying Elizabeth Eckford as a potential parvenue, Arendt was also ominously predicting the suffering the parvenu can never avoid completely. It was an unacceptable position to many Americans, not only because it threatened the moral stature of the victims of the Holocaust and ignored the struggles of African Americans but also because it questioned a key American principle of social integration.

Arendt's stranger persona came across as an oppositional stance that made her commitment to a shared polis often go unnoticed. After the publication of his devastating review of *Eichmann in Jerusalem*, Podhoretz went to visit Arendt in her small Morningside Heights apartment to discuss with her, point by point, his objections to the book. While insisting that he made good faith efforts to explain his position and convince her that she was wrong, Podhoretz presents an inflexible Arendt who does not offer counterarguments but merely dismissals.[143] Most telling, however, is a seemingly minor detail in the narrative: Arendt neglected to turn on the light as the conversation continued into the evening, which caused increasing discomfort to Podhoretz. Inflexible and surrounded by dark, Arendt comes across as an ominous force, invisible yet powerfully present, arguing in ample exposes accompanied by long periods of silence and becoming increasingly hostile. Podhoretz felt ambushed, even though he was the attacker and Arendt had been the target of his devastating criticism.

In von Trotha's cinematic account of the *Eichmann in Jerusalem* controversy, Arendt comes across as stubborn yet passionate about ideas, and more than anything, determined to understand a fundamental aspect of the human experience: the evil. Renounced by some of her closest friends and demonized by her critics, she is alone with her books, looking pensive and melancholy. The film ends with Arendt lying down next to her books and smoking with eyes half closed, engaged in the *vita contemplativa* she praised in her philosophy, Arendt strikes a pose that is an interesting variation on the visual trope of the thinker from Lorenzo de Medici's to Auguste Rodin's representations. This calm and self-confident, yet also concentrated and troubled, Arendt captures well the stranger persona that inspired the brilliant ideas presented in *Eichmann in Jerusalem*, as well as their detraction.

CONCLUSION: THE THINKER IN POLITICS

In the *Eichmann in Jerusalem* controversy, Scholem accused Arendt of lacking *ahavat Yisrael* (love of the Jewish people). Instead of protesting against the accusation, surprisingly, she agreed:

> How right you are that I have no such love. . . . I have never in my life "loved" some nation or collective—not the German, French or American nation, or the working class, or whatever else might exist. The fact is that I love only my friends and am quite incapable of any other sort of love. . . . We would both agree that patriotism is impossible without constant opposition and critique.[144]

It was a patriotism of "constant opposition and critique" that connected Arendt to America. She insisted that racism cannot be stopped through military intervention and that genocide is not the product of evil minds but that of bureaucratic machinery. These were two of the most disturbing forms of political evil of the twentieth century, but they remain a cause for alarm and vigilance. Her take on these subjects differed markedly from that of other American commentators, and Arendt realized the difficulty of taking on such a task. The very fact that she did it bespeaks a determination that is, more than intellectual confidence, civic courage.

If she did not "love" the American people, she was certainly enamored with the political idea of America, to which she remained committed, sometimes against Americans themselves. At odds with most all other scholars and intellectuals of her time, Arendt spoke from an "alienated consciousness," to use an apt phrase offered by Dana Villa.[145] In the interview granted to Günter Gaus, she insisted on presenting herself as a political thinker, and not a philosopher proper.[146] This is not mere rhetorical self-effacement for the well-established philosopher she already was. Taken seriously, it reveals her concern that philosophers do not belong in the polis. Some of her American critics thought the same, and indeed rejected her political insights as too steeped in the "great Western" tradition in philosophy, and therefore incompatible with the "moral distinctiveness of representative [American] democracy."[147] Arendt's distinction between a philosopher and a political thinker goes back, as she herself points out, to a founding moment not only in Western philosophy, but also in Western politics. "The gulf between philosophy and politics," she reminds us, "opened historically with the trial and condemnation of Socrates." Yet she felt no sympathy for Socrates because, in her view, "he was not only unable to persuade his judges but could also not convince his friends."[148]

Neither did Arendt convince all of her friends, but she impressed upon all her American readers the importance of a politics dedicated to human plurality.[149] Anthony Grafton remembers the conversations around his family dinner table, during the Eichmann controversy, and credits Arendt with inspiring the emergence of a public and political discourse in which intellectuals could play an important role.[150] Grafton does not think Arendt was right, nor did his father, who had tried to interview her for *Life* magazine. So the question always remains: were Arendt's views right or wrong? One of the legacies of Plato is a conception of truth as the opposite of mere opinion. Philosophical discourse (dialectic), in this view, is the opposite of political discourse, which can only aim at persuasion. Yet in contemplating whether to choose the side of politics or philosophy, Arendt refused to get caught in the opposition between truth and opinion, or dialectic and rhetoric. Instead, she revisited the Socratic notion of opinion, *doxa*, and tried to reinvigorate its moral value:

> To Socrates, as to his fellow citizens, *doxa* was the formulation in speech of what *dokei moi*, that is, of what appears to me. This *doxa* had as its topic not what Aristotle called the *eikos*, the probable, the many *verisimilia* (as

distinguished from the *unum verum*, the one truth, on one hand, and the limitless falsehoods, the *falsa infinita*, on the other), but comprehended the world as it opens itself to me. . . . The assumption was that the world opens up differently to every man, according to his position in it; and that the "sameness" of the world, its commonness . . . resides in the fact that the same world opens up to everyone and that despite all differences between men and their positions in the world—and consequently their *doxai* (opinions)—"both you and I are human."[151]

Arendt's political positions and arguments were shaped by the worlds that had opened up to her, from Königsberg to Berlin, Paris, and New York. Yet she also insisted that experiences and opinions must add up coherently in a compelling image of a shared world. The role of a political thinker is to distill the different opinions of a community into an articulation of their common world, "not to rule the city but to be its 'gadfly,' not to tell philosophical truths but to make citizens more truthful."[152] This was her version of the Socratic ideal, and she tried to emulate it in the figure of the pariah.

In "Reflections on Little Rock, Arkansas" and *Eichmann in Jerusalem*, Arendt questioned the American *doxa* of that time (which remains, in part, our *doxa* today). Her arguments came from observing the uncommon in the most familiar occurrences, of which the young Arendt wrote to Heidegger. She argued, as Villa aptly put it, with the originality of "a radically estranged theorist . . . whose work reflects the consciousness of the exile rather than of the connected critic."[153] She was politically engaged but also emotionally detached. To the "culture of sentiment" enveloping patriotic discourse in America, Arendt responded with theoretical abstractions, or with irony.[154] In her view, there was no room for the "heart in politics."[155] And this was the most important lesson she had learned from America's Founding Fathers as she explained in *On Revolution*. She was justified in reminding her critics that "in political matters I am as much a native as any other American."[156]

3

HERBERT MARCUSE'S GERMAN REVOLUTION IN AMERICA

I N THE fall of 2011, days after the scandal triggered by police arrests at protests held at the University of California, Davis, another American campus welcomed the Fourth Biennial Conference of the International Herbert Marcuse Society. Preparations for this event hosted by the University of Pennsylvania had begun long before, yet the celebration of a radical leftist philosopher while the Occupy movement was sweeping the country is a coincidence that did not go unnoticed. The conference organizers and participants took full advantage of this charged political context. In the words of leading Marcuse scholar, Douglas Kellner, "for those of us who have been doing Marcuse scholarship this is utopia."[1] "Is it Comeback Time for Herbert Marcuse?" asked *The Chronicle of Higher Education*.[2] The responses and comments posted on the journal's online forum triggered a controversy all too similar to those that surrounded Marcuse's work and reputation during his lifetime. Once again acclaimed as political guru of the New Left, accused of anti-Americanism, criticized for his philosophical work, lambasted for his Marxism as well as anti-Marxism, Marcuse emerges from the online exchange as capable of heating up a debate today as he was fifty years ago.

In the 1960s, Marcuse was better known to the general American public than his colleagues Theodor W. Adorno or Max Horkheimer. Like them,

Marcuse was originally a member of the exiled Frankfurt Institute for Social Research. In a 1987 interview published in Germany, Leo Löwenthal, another well-known member of the group, insisted that Marcuse was the most famous German scholar living in America.[3] By the time the 1990s rolled in, however, Marcuse's fame had waned. Today, his philosophical work has more of a cult following among a few scholars and surviving New Leftists than a broad academic reception. Even his reputation as philosophical inspirer of the New Left movement has started to receive different assessments, revealed in the subtle shifts in the choice of words used to depict Marcuse's role. From "guru" to "godfather," Marcuse's American career seems to have followed a downward spiral.[4] His reputation is a product of political conjuncture, a distinct philosophical program, and opportune encounters with other scholars as well as political activists who were trying to ground a political agenda so radical in scope that it required intellectual justification.

In 1949, Adorno and Horkheimer returned to Germany (along with other prominent members of the German intellectual exiles). Marcuse and a few others, such as Erich Fromm and Leo Löwenthal, stayed in America. Of those who stayed, some were deliberate misfits in the new country. Löwenthal described this condition as "not going along" (*nicht mitmachen*): not accepting the values and beliefs of the new environment just for the sake of fitting in. Many German exiles saw adjustment as compromise.[5] Marcuse did not simply adjust . Rather, he tried to reshape American politics and society in a way that would reflect his own vision and to some extent the German political tradition in which he was formed. If Hannah Arendt came to be seen as a member of the New York intellectuals, her status always remained rather ex officio as a European philosopher. In the 1960s, Marcuse, however, was wholeheartedly, at times even euphorically, embraced by American radicals—students, academics, and activists involved in the New Left movement. Although adopting a political stance of radical opposition to official U.S. politics and government, he emphasized participation in the polis. More than any other foreign intellectual transplanted to America, he was an organic part of American political and intellectual discourse of the time.

Yet while his political impact in America may have been the product of connections to the New Left, his political views, and the way Marcuse expressed them, reflect a stranger persona. To some of his American students, Marcuse always remained a German professor, even though he demonstrated at political marches, side by side with them. In a profile published in 1970 in *Playboy* magazine, one of his former students, Michael Horowitz, remembers Marcuse as "German first, Jewish second, and contemporary American hardly at all."[6] Even when deeply involved in the day-to-day of American politics, he maintained a broader awareness of the international political context. He had direct knowledge of the students' revolt in France. He could make salient comparisons and draw important lessons applicable on American campuses, just as in Berlin or in Munich; his comments on German politics were informed by his knowledge of marginal groups in America and their political potential. His stranger persona was shaped by a broad internationalist agenda rather than a commitment to one nation in particular. This became quite clear in London, at the 1967 Congress for the Dialectic of Liberation, where Marcuse was not present as a German or as an American but as a radical leftist intellectual. In London, what he shared with the other participants was an intellectual sensibility: a combination of nonconformism and a pathos for change, whether the change was in artistic expression, scientific reasoning, or in politics. Marcuse revolved around people who shared his passion for renewal. Their goal was ambitious and could pass for either naïve or heretic: to transform the very idea of a political order throughout the world. They spoke of an egalitarian, "liberated," society that could challenge state and regime apparatuses on both sides of the divide of that era, in the capitalist West and the Soviet-dominated socialist bloc. This far-reaching agenda was internationalist in a Marxist sense, insofar as it transcended the national order but also, more generally (though still related), in a humanist sense, as a commitment to the improvement of the human experience for people around the globe.

After World War II, although a naturalized American already, Marcuse was indeed a citizen of the world, traveling across the United States from New York to California, as well as frequently to Germany and France. On the one hand, as in Edward Said's case, Marcuse's cosmopolitanism was the mark of a rootless intellectual who crosses national borders easily and makes his home among books and other scholars, wherever or whoever these may be. On the other hand, the itinerant Marcuse was not only a German American scholar but also a Jew. Yet he had nothing comparable to Arendt's experience in the Gurs internment camp or other German Jews' experience of the Holocaust. He had never been arrested by the Gestapo. He was politically involved, but his politics were not influenced by his being Jewish and not focused on Jewish concerns. Never just an armchair revolutionary, Marcuse marched in the streets. He clashed both with academics who theorized about politics without participating and with the New Left radicals who found political reflection too abstract for their concrete purposes. For one group, he was too politicized and eventually too famous to be also a scholar interested in the objective pursuit of knowledge. For the other group, he was wise but impractical—a "smart Jew" with all the implied negative connotations this image had in postwar America as I described in the introduction.

Marcuse's academic career in the United States was mired in scandal and controversy. His departure at the age of sixty-five from Brandeis University (where he taught from 1958 to 1965) was shrouded in rumors that he had been forced to retire because his incendiary speeches and public interventions were becoming increasingly problematic for the university officials and Board of Trustees. At his next and last academic post, Marcuse was in the center of a major political scandal as the University of California at San Diego (UCSD) was pressured to fire him on account on his involvement in the students' movement. Controversy threatened his legal status in the United States and almost left him without income, but it made him famous. While his German colleagues in America worked on similar philosophical problems—such as the emergence of totalitarianism in modern society or mechanisms of oppression in the advanced liberal state—Marcuse took his theoretical reflection to the level of a visible practice. He made his lectures more accessible to a larger audience but also participated in marches, signed petitions, and even got involved in a case of spontaneous revolt that led to breaking into a UCSD building. He later paid for the broken door.[7] To Adorno and Horkheimer, such actions deviated from the philosopher's true mission in the polis: reflection and conceptual critique. Both accused Marcuse of populism and of oversimplifying complex ideas in his work for the sake of winning over large audiences. Regardless whether this was Marcuse's intention, his critique of the advanced capitalist-liberal state constitutes a philosophical justification for the political rejection of American capitalism proposed by the 1960s American radicals. Yet some of the New Left leaders claimed in their recollections of that turbulent era that they had never even read Marcuse, or if they read, they did not understand him. By some accounts, Marcuse's influence on the student radicals and the New Left movement was significantly smaller than that of American intellectuals, for example, sociologist C. Wright Mills.[8] Paul Goodman, one of the New Left leaders, snubbed Marcuse as someone who "just doesn't know the American scene at all," while James Weinstein, editor of *Studies on the Left*, never forgave Marcuse for ignoring his requests to publish in the flagship journal of the movement.[9] Yet Marcuse's name became forever ensconced in the American student radicals' slogan "Mao is our leader, Marx our philosopher, and Marcuse its interpreter." That his influence on the New Left is so disputed reveals the reluctance to accept that a foreign-born philosophy professor could be so central to one of the most effervescent political movements inside the United States in the twentieth century.

What I am interested in here is not whether Marcuse was truly the main intellectual leader of the New Left but in how his particular brand of leftism took shape in America and how he delivered his ideas to an American public. His stranger persona is the product of a progression from abstract (and often abstruse) theory to active political participation. This persona follows a political as well as intellectual trajectory, from the arrival in the United States as a member of the Frankfurt-based Institute for Social Research to the break-up with the group, involvement in the Office of Strategic Services (OSS), academic positions, and finally involvement in the events of the 1960s. His political glory, like his fall out of grace (as by the mid-1970s the New Left took its distance from him, and Marcuse, in turn, disavowed them), can be traced to a persona that combines intellectual justification for political action with the revolutionary pathos of an outsider who has come to save the polis.

GERMAN MANDARINS AND THE
AMERICAN UNIVERSITY

Born in 1898 as the son of a prosperous merchant, Marcuse's political and intellectual development in Germany was, as Davis Jones has argued, "symptomatic of the possibilities available to a young man of the bourgeoisie, and his growing cultural interests and politically oppositional stance showed themselves early."[10] Indeed, after spending his early formative years in Berlin's liberal environment—a haven for artistic innovators and the political reactionary—Marcuse served in the army during World War I and participated in the revolutionary fervor following the sailors' rebellion in Kiel. The short-lived experience "in the political storm-center of the country" as representative of the Soldiers' Council made Marcuse into a political radical, only to disappoint him all the more upon the failure of the Weimar Republic.[11] In 1919, no longer active in politics, Marcuse enrolled at Humboldt University in Berlin and two years later transferred to Albert-Ludwigs University in Freiburg. His intellectual identity was shaped by several encounters with key philosophical figures, whether the encounters were on the pages of a book, as was the case with Hegel and Marx, or in person at Freiburg, where Marcuse studied with Martin Heidegger.

Marcuse began his American life as a member of the Frankfurt Institute for Social Research, a rather eclectic group of German philosophers. Horkheimer, the group's co-leader along with Adorno, had appointed Marcuse to the institute while it still operated in Germany, in 1933, but sent him immediately to the Geneva office. In 1934, after several European relocations (including Switzerland and England) were deemed unsafe for the majority Jewish membership of the group, the institute moved to the United States. Marcuse and his family arrived in New York, symbolically, on July 4, 1934. According to Barry Katz, "he immediately took out American naturalization papers."[12] Whether because he had lost all hope for Germany or because he immediately liked America, Marcuse decided right away to stay. This instant commitment to America makes the harsh criticism of his later books all the more intriguing and all the more irritating to his critics.

Unlike Arendt and the other European luminaries rescued by Varian Fry at the request of the American Emergency Rescue Committee, the members of the Frankfurt Institute needed little help beyond affidavits of support, which were promptly and generously issued by the president of Columbia University. Marcuse and the rest of the group arrived in America with the mystique of an exclusivist intellectual coterie, rich enough to live a comfortable life even as refugees. In 1934, at the height of the Depression years in the United States, the institute's annual budget of $30,000 was an enviable luxury.[13] Freed of financial worries from the beginning by the generous endowment offered by its founder, Hermann Weil, the institute was formed as an independent community of scholars dedicated to the pursuit of research on social matters. Money made these men patricians, slightly detached from the worries of the everyday citizen, in Germany and even more so in America. Despite their socialist views, the members of the Frankfurt Institute were more easily identifiable, especially by their American hosts, as aristocrats rather than members of the proletarian. As Martin Jay puts it, "at no time did a member of the institute affect the life-style of the working class."[14] Marcuse was no exception.

He joined the Frankfurt Institute for intellectual, as well as political reasons. He shared their leftist orientation and was interested, like them, in developing a philosophically grounded critique of capitalism and bourgeois society. The ties that kept the group together even abroad were also more aesthetic than political, as most of these scholars were strongly drawn to the arts, and indeed several of them were artists (Adorno as a musician, Horkheimer as a writer). The Frankfurt Institute's "*distaste* for the bourgeois society"[15] informed its members' political philosophy as well as their aesthetic. In their shared rejection of the bourgeois, Marcuse and his colleagues reacted as German mandarins, a special category of intellectuals and academics whose "ideology was based . . . from the beginning, upon an idealization of pure and impractical learning."[16] Ironically, the Frankfurt Institute was created in part as a rejection of the German mandarin ideology, and its replacement with a form of knowledge that was socially relevant and politically emancipatory. Yet the group retained elements of the Mandarin mentality. For instance, although all its members were committed to a socialist agenda as a result of their experience in the Weimar Republic and in connection to the German Socialist Party and Communist Party, few were politically active themselves.[17] In part, this limited political involvement was the direct consequence of the intellectual agenda of the institute: to develop a theoretical reflection that could guide new forms of political practice, beyond what was already available. The intellectuals who joined the Frankfurt Institute espoused a radical form of sociopolitical reform but were also convinced that such reform needs first to be understood in conceptual terms. The institute sought to develop a blending of theory and practice, captured by the hybrid philosophical term of praxis: "a kind of self-creating action, which differed from the externally motivated behavior produced by forces outside man's control."[18]

In this regard, Marcuse was the exception all along in Germany and later in the United States. In Germany, he took part in the Berlin rising and was a member of the Soldiers' Council. He abandoned politics, disaffected, after the murders of communist figures Rosa Luxemburg and Karl Liebknecht and turned to academic life. As he turned to more abstract, academic interests, he discovered and became enthralled with Heidegger's work at a time when this was not yet politicized.[19] Nevertheless, the short-lived association with Heidegger would cost Marcuse a lot as it cast a cloud of suspicion on his philosophical views, both from his later mentors and employers, Adorno and Horkheimer, and from American commentators. The Nazis' imminent advent to power forced Marcuse to abandon any plans for an academic career in Germany.

In the United States, avoiding direct political involvement became the institute's rule. Adorno and Horkheimer enforced it strictly to avoid casting any suspicion on their work and presence in America. Their fears were justified, for the strong leftist agenda and Marxist orientation of the Frankfurt school could make them into an easy prey, especially during the McCarthy era. In the early days of their exile, the group was frequently "visited by German speaking New York police detectives searching for Nazi sympathizers within the German community."[20] The institute leaders' cautiousness reflects an acute awareness of their foreignness as likely to arouse suspicion and lead to accusations, which indeed happened. Marcuse and several other members of the Frankfurt Institute were placed under surveillance by the Federal Bureau for Investigation. Their files reveal that what the FBI found most suspicious about these exiled intellectuals was the very fact that they were foreign born. What began as a routine check required by his application for a position with the OSS continued for many years. Between 1943 and 1976, Marcuse was repeatedly under investigation "for his supposed connection to Communist countries, organizations, ideologies, and sympathizers."[21] He had no illusions regarding the impact of his OSS activity on American policy, as he later admitted in a conversation with Jürgen Habermas.[22] Yet the environment he found at OSS was markedly different from that of the institute and must have had a significant influence on Marcuse as on the other immigrant scholars employed by the U.S. federal government. It was here that Marcuse had more daily interactions with Americans and with the research methodologies American scholars preferred.[23]

In Germany, Marcuse withdrew from politics into academe because he felt disenchanted after the failed political reform of the Weimar Republic. Yet in America, disenchantment served the opposite purpose, leading Marcuse to some of the most trenchant critiques of capitalism and of American society in particular. His notoriety in America, by comparison to the other institute members, was first and foremost the consequence of his active involvement in American life. His German colleagues chose "to remain silent about the major political questions of the day," and had a significantly smaller impact on the American intellectual scene, even though they lived in New York at a time when the New York intellectuals were most active culturally and politically.[24]

In New York, the Frankfurt Institute was isolated not only because it did not get involved in the political conversation of the time but also for strictly intellectual reasons. The clash of theories and methodologies taking place at Columbia between the German critical theory, then in the making, and the far more empirically oriented American school of sociology has been well documented.[25] While their American colleagues despised the abstract, seemingly speculative approach of the Frankfurt School, the Germans in turn rejected the focus on empiricism as naïve and reductive. Adorno and Horkheimer had little interest in intellectual cross-pollination, even though they agreed to collaborate with American colleagues in a few projects, most notably the study on authoritarianism. In Frankfurt, the institute was created "as a community of scholars whose solidarity would serve as a microcosmic foretaste of the brotherly society of the future."[26] Yet this "brotherly society" was not a transnational one, at least not while in exile. At Columbia, the members of the Frankfurt Institute preferred to keep to themselves and did not mix much with their American colleagues. It mattered, perhaps, that these German scholars were not only financially comfortable but also acutely aware of their wealth, compared to the financial struggles of most Americans.[27]

The members of the Frankfurt Institute stood out in America in one more way, and Marcuse was no exception in this regard: they were Jews but not particularly focused on their own Jewishness.[28] Unlike many New York Jewish intellectuals coming to prominence in the period who articulated their own individual and intellectual identity in specific reference to their Jewish heritage, Adorno, Horkheimer, Marcuse, Löwenthal, and Fromm, all came from assimilated families (as did Arendt). Marcuse's son, Peter, remembers his upbringing in a relaxed Jewish household where Jewishness was *not* the focus of the family's life:

We were certainly Jewish; we would never have been in the U.S. otherwise. My father was bar mitzvah'd, and to my knowledge his parents were relatively observant. But he himself was strictly secular. I remember at home hearing Jewish jokes, a smattering of Yiddish, Jewish friends, a Jewish intellectual circle—no doubt we were Jewish; but I remember no religious observance, no going to *schul* or services, even on the High Holy Days. At least before we arrived in the U.S., I suspect he never felt any contradiction between being German and being Jewish.[29]

Expressed primarily in the domestic, private realm, Marcuse's Jewishness seems disconnected from his sociopolitical views. Jay argues that it was the same for the other members of the group, all "anxious to deny any significance at all to their ethnic roots, a position that has not been eroded with time in most of their cases."[30] This might seem surprising because in *The*

Dialectic of the Enlightenment, Adorno and Horkheimer's most important work written in America, the examination of anti-Semitism plays an important role.[31] Yet even in that book, the focus is not on Jewish identity as much as on the discrimination against Jews as a particular sociopolitical mechanism tied up with the logic of capitalism. This subtle difference results in what Jonathan Judaken refers to as the "anti-anti-Semitism" of the Frankfurt School, instead of a philo-Semitism that could have made them more interested in or attracted to American Jews *as Jews*.[32] In New York especially, being Jewish could have led to alliances with Jewish philosophers (or philosophically inclined intellectuals) like Sydney Hook and others. Instead, as was also Arendt's case, the German Jews and the American Jews were enemies more often than friends.

Marcuse and his colleagues encountered in America a form of anti-Semitism different from their German experience and one that they did not anticipate or understand.[33] This created a predicament that was worsened by the fact that they had no major supporters among Jewish American intellectuals. Being too Jewish for some and not sufficiently Jewish for others contributed to the isolation of Adorno and Horkheimer. It affected Marcuse much less. As his son, Peter, recounts, Marcuse "found the more informal and open atmosphere of the U.S. more congenial than the more rigid and hierarchical relationships found in Germany."[34] The informality that seduced Marcuse appalled Adorno and yet their willingness to become involved in American life is both more complicated and simpler than a matter of social etiquette. Interest in American society was shared by all members of the Frankfurt Institute at least insofar as America represented the most advanced form of the capitalist society their work set out to critique. Adorno and Horkheimer critiqued it from outside—both from the abstract perspective of the philosopher who sits above the citizenry and from the perspective of the *German* philosopher (by continuing to write in German and publishing the institute's journal with the Dutch publisher Felix Alcan).[35] By contrast, Marcuse gradually abandoned the position of the German philosopher only engaged in reflection and not in action to become the philosopher-teacher to the citizenry, and he came close to being an American activist though he never quite reached that point, as I show later in the chapter. The turning point for his transformation took place while he was working for the OSS where he was more often in the company of Americans than of fellow Germans. Soon after the family arrived in the United States, "there was no question (Marcuse) was American—although clearly of German extraction."[36]

The change he experienced while in the service of the OSS can be seen as part of an immigrant acculturation in the workplace. Yet it also captures the special effectiveness of Marcuse's stranger persona, which asserted itself early on as being as assimilated as it would seem plausible. Marcuse's fame in America as a public figure was unprecedented for a philosopher who also happened to be a person of foreign nationality. Even though he became famous in his late years—so famous that his name was routinely mentioned in daily newspapers and known even to people with little interest in or familiarity with academics—Marcuse was speaking and writing with the authority of an insider. Ironically, notoriety was his most American feature. As Katz aptly points out, "in a great American tradition, Herbert Marcuse moved to California and became a 'star.'"[37]

At the same time, the "German extraction" mentioned almost as an afterthought by his son, Peter, played a key role in bringing him to the attention of American figures active on the political scene of the time, thus making it possible for him to become famous. Foreignness, in other words, gave him visibility. In an interview with Bryan Magee in 1978, Marcuse exhibited modesty in response to a question that was often posed to him: how did he become so famous? Although clearly attempting to avoid self-aggrandizing depictions, Marcuse was aware of the implied impertinence in his response and prefaced it with an apology: "I appear only as such a figure because others seem even less deserving."[38] Yet rather than accept it as a value judgment, this claim challenges us to press further: how was Marcuse more deserving? Some of his German colleagues in America were, by his own accounts, more sophisticated and intellectually accomplished (in the same interview, Marcuse insisted that Horkheimer was nothing less than a genius). Some American academics who were also connected to the New Left were politically more active and more daring (such as Angela Davis, his former student). It must be that what made Marcuse more deserving was that he was more political than the other German exiles and more philosophical than the other American intellectuals involved in the political life of the time. Yet this was not merely a hyphenated identity as much as a mixture of German and American that he employed strategically in political discourse and action, variously emphasizing one part over another.

After Marcuse stopped receiving the financial backing of Horkheimer and Adorno, in 1943, he joined (like several other German exiled intellectuals) the Research and Analysis section of the OSS. Marcuse had more direct, daily contact with Americans than with his former German colleagues, and he became more and more like the Americans around him. Yet the surviving pictures and video footage of Marcuse present the image of a European who never adopted, at least in appearance, the American relaxed style he apparently appreciated: outfitted with a suit, cigar, and heavy accent, he embodied another world and another sensibility.

THE AMERICANIZATION OF HERBERT MARCUSE

Marcuse began his integration in American politics by taking his distance from the Frankfurt Institute. The separation was, to some extent, unavoidable. Adorno and Horkheimer were skeptical of Marcuse's philosophical abilities from the moment he joined their group. They distrusted his phenomenological training and especially the influence they feared Heidegger had exerted on Marcuse. In the United States, Marcuse's early research was done entirely under the auspices of the institute, and the topics he studied were commissioned by Horkheimer as part of a larger, collective research agenda. The correspondence between Horkheimer and Adorno reveals a certain degree of disapproval and condescendence vis-à-vis their younger colleague's philosophical inquiries. By 1941, as the Institute's financial resources started to dwindle and relationships with Columbia to grow tense, Horkheimer began considering a potential relocation. His move to Santa Monica, California was more than a change in décor: by the time the Institute had left New York, several of its original members were pursuing individual careers in the United States, whether academic or governmental ones.

Marcuse remained loyal to the institute longer than he could have been expected, given the increased financial difficulties he incurred with the decrease in his payments, as well as the smugness of his employees.[39] According to Wiggershaus, Horkheimer deliberately pushed him to leave by offering less and less money and encouraging him to accept the first job offer he received, which happened to be at the Office of Strategic Information. But the separation from the institute had mainly intellectual causes. Marcuse, on the one hand, and Adorno and Horkheimer on the other, had widely different views on American popular culture, for example.[40] Adorno's intense dislike of jazz contrasted with Marcuse's appreciation of the Beat generation. Their disagreement was both philosophical and aesthetic, a clash between Adorno's high modernism and adumbrations of postmodernism in Marcuse.[41] They also differed in their attitudes toward the linguistic form of philosophical arguments. Horkheimer and especially Adorno cultivated and theorized the need for a philosophical discourse that breaks off with ordinary language by way of restoring clarity to ideas that had become muddled in mundane connotations. For them, Marcuse's discourse was too direct and simple. And indeed, no matter how difficult his prose might still seem, it is easier to parse by comparison to Adorno's and Horkheimer's.

This difference in philosophical expression is a reflection of different stylistic personalities. Yet it is also more than that: a reflection of culturally, indeed nationally, inflected stylistic personalities. Adorno's style, especially, is a distinctly German one, as he himself acknowledged.[42] Adorno was notoriously proud to write in an "untranslatable language."[43] By comparison, Marcuse's is *less* German even while not in any particular way *more* English. Imponderable as they might be, and easy to essentialize, these national labels operated as stylistic marks, not in light of some particular linguistic feature—preferred syntactic structure or lexical choices—but in connection to an intellectual tradition chosen as a sign of distinction.

Jay notes the difference in philosophical style between Marcuse and his mentors, depicting him as more analytical in expression and attributing this difference to a more limited interest in aesthetics. In other words, by being less of an artist than Adorno the pianist and Horkheimer the novelist, Marcuse was less allusive and more precise in his philosophical writings. If such claims remain difficult to substantiate—after all, one can develop different styles in different types of discourse—they point in the same direction of a marked difference between Marcuse and the main protagonists of the institute. As Jay further maintains, "his style was perhaps also a reflection of his belief that writing in a systematic, nonaphoristic, linear way was an effective way of analyzing and representing reality."[44] Adorno, by contrast, cultivated the fragment as stylistic trope, partly by way of capturing his foreigner's status: his writings were to be "messages in a bottle" (*Flaschenposts*) sent from his American exile. Furthermore, Adorno's language, even when not translated into English, represents, as Fredric Jameson notes, "a conduct of intransigence: the bristling mass of abstractions and cross-references is precisely intended to be read in situation, against the cheap facility of what surrounds it, as a warning to the reader of the price he has to pay for genuine thinking."[45] If to many American readers Marcuse would always sound equally intransigent and even distinctly *foreign*—in ways that I detail further— for the taste of his German colleagues he was accessible to the point of risking to become facile. In turn, Marcuse claimed to be aware that his writing was easier to read than his colleagues' and that he wanted it to be so.[46]

It is tempting to speculate that Marcuse's "reality," as he tried to analyze and represent it in his philosophical works, was increasingly a different one than what interested Adorno and Horkheimer, at least in terms of a social ontology. Moreover, it seems likely that their respective social ontologies were culturally inflected. After the publication in America of *Eros and Civilization*, Marcuse's seminal study of the political significance of Freud and psychoanalysis, Adorno and Horkheimer considered the possibility of a German translation that would have been published under the aegis of the institute (by then back in Germany, with its two leaders). While interested in and convinced by the ideas, Adorno had reservations about the style of the book, as he informed Marcuse:

It's true that I felt uneasy with a certain directness and "immediacy" (in the tainted sense we now give to the concept of mediation) in your English Freud text, although this did not affect the basic positions taken. It was precisely for this reason that I wanted you to produce the German version. It is simply a question of the difference between the levels of language. You only need to formulate your ideas in German to notice the sort of thing that was disturbing me and you'll change them in such a way that all of us will be able to stand behind them fully.[47]

Marcuse seems to have ignored Adorno's request for stylistic revisions along the lines of less "directness and immediacy," and the book was translated and published independent of the institute. This was more than a gesture signaling emancipation. As he grew increasingly more detached from Adorno and Horkheimer—the "we" referenced in Adorno's letter—Marcuse became philosophically more independent and original but also more tuned to the society in which he lived, which was American. Arguably, "part of the reason for the differing trajectories of Marcuse and Horkheimer and Adorno is that Marcuse stayed in America and, in some sense, sought to apply the insights of critical theory to the reality around him."[48] Far from seeking to move beyond the "immediacy" of particular situations, as Adorno advocated, Marcuse praised more and more often the valuable lessons he had learned by going in the street, and he dedicated himself to translating philosophical ideas into concrete political action. This respect for the concrete world, against abstractions and theoretical speculation, captures the key intellectual difference between him and Adorno and Horkheimer. It was, to a large extent, Marcuse's declared philosophical interest in a direct and immediate rendition of the "real" and Adorno's emphatic avoidance of it that determined their political significance, making one a "guru" of the New Left and the other an Ivory Tower thinker intelligible only to a select few. Yet the difference was stylistic and rhetorical more than philosophical proper. Significantly, upon his return to Germany, Adorno addressed the key political and moral issues facing post–Nazi Germany. He spoke, however, "in his aristocratic style and from his elitist stance."[49] Later, when the 1960s German radical students discovered and read with enthusiasm his works, using them to support their anti-capitalism critique, Adorno wanted nothing to do with the young rebels. The American Angela Davis traveled to Frankfurt in the hope that she could study with Adorno but quickly returned home when the philosopher dismissed contemptuously her interest in political activism. To Adorno, Davis recounts, being a philosopher and an activist was comparable to becoming a radio technician because one had an interest in media theory.[50]

Marcuse's "Americanization"—and I use the scare quotes to point out that this was a rhetorical self-construction and not merely assimilation we can take at face value—was the result of his membership in an intellectual and political community, obtained through both real and symbolic associations with key American figures who recognized and embraced him as one of their own. Davis, already a famous activist in the 1960s, was one of the important makers of the American Marcuse. It is no coincidence or surprise that upon her return from Germany, Davis became Marcuse's student at Brandeis. If Marcuse was the mentor, Davis, the student, was the purveyor of a new cultural identity. In her evocation of Marcuse, Davis has described him by emphasizing how different he was from Adorno. Marcuse, as she depicts him, not only allowed but also encouraged what Adorno had specifically forbidden her: to be involved in politics while studying to become a political philosopher. That does not mean that Davis made her mentor seem American just by pointing out how different he was from a philosopher such as Adorno, with similar ideas yet a resolutely German identity. Rather, through his affiliation with Davis and more generally, the New Left, Marcuse expressed solidarity with, indeed empathy for, his American colleagues and students, which became the chief characteristic of his stranger persona.

In an open letter to Davis, published in *Rampart* at Berkeley in 1971, after her imprisonment and trial on charges of complicity to murder, Marcuse begins by admitting a degree of discomfort at having been asked to introduce the publication of her lectures on Frederick Douglass. As he put it, "they (the essays) deal with a world to which I am still an outsider. . . . The world in which you grew up, your world (which is not mine) was one of cruelty, misery, and persecution." Marcuse repeatedly signals in his letter the difference between his world and that of his former student, but his goal is to show that his ability to understand Davis's reasons for political action, as well as to declare his support of her, are not dependent on a common world or a shared particular experience. "I do not know whether you were involved at all in these tragic events," continues Marcuse, "but I do know that you were deeply involved in the fight for the black people, for the oppressed everywhere, and that you could not limit your work for them to the classroom and to writing. . . . But you also fought for us too, who need freedom and who want freedom for all who are still unfree. In this sense, your cause is our cause."[51]

Signing his letter with a salutation that had been implied all throughout the text, "in solidarity," Marcuse entered Davis's world, even though this was, as he pointed out, fundamentally different from his. To justify his place in it, he redefined it as not only shaped by racial divide and a national-cultural history but in broader terms as the world of the "unfree." The ambiguity of the plural first-person pronoun "our," merging with a direct, almost intimate (within the conventional genre of the letter) singular second-person pronoun "your," points simultaneously to a racial and internationalist harmony of those who dare to rise against oppression in their search for freedom. The solidarity between the white German professor and his former African American student renders Marcuse's foreignness—to which he emphatically admitted in the beginning of the letter—irrelevant. This alienness to African American culture was overstated for rhetorical purposes anyway. Marcuse had a sustained interest in Frederick Douglass, who could "serve simultaneously as a revolutionary figure for the black nationalist and the German émigré alike." He claimed that the "pure display of evil" manifested in the Holocaust had only one precedent: slavery.[52]

In the 1960s, the relationship between Marcuse and New Left leaders like Davis served both sides, intellectually as well as politically. By embracing the New Left cause, Marcuse presented himself not as a sympathetic foreigner but as a politically engaged American. By embracing him, the American New Left presented itself to the larger American public as intellectually sophisticated. Marcuse would seem less of a stiff foreign professor and the American student rebels less of a rowdy bunch. Such mutually benefiting associations can be easily suspected of inauthenticity and opportunism. Take, for instance, the arguments proposed by Richard Wolin and Thomas Wheatland: that Marcuse cared much less than he claimed about the student radicals and the New Left movement and that Marcuse played a minor role in shaping the New Left. For Wolin, the proof that Marcuse's real commitment was always elsewhere comes in the form of an anecdote: scheduled to appear in New York at the 1966 Socialist Scholars Conference, Marcuse cancelled at the last moment, opting instead to attend a Hegel conference in Prague. This occurrence epitomizes, in Wolin's view, "the ill-fated alliance between Marcuse and his youthful admirers."[53] This biographical detail can indeed challenge the idea of an "Americanized" Marcuse on two levels, political and national: Marcuse, in this portrayal, chose "esoteric philosophy" over "the political aims of the movement," and perhaps even more importantly, Europe (Prague) over New York. Indeed, Marcuse's American commitment never took precedence over his internationalist agenda. However, his correspondence shows that he was not only especially interested in the political movement unfolding in the United States but also hopeful about its chance of success.[54]

For Wheatland, the issue is not whether Marcuse was genuinely committed to an American political movement but whether the movement was truly interested in his ideas. In his view,

> Marcuse may have been an unintentional prophet of the student movement, but he was never its guru. . . . Despite Marcuse's association with the spring of 1968, neither he nor his ideas were the source of this spectacular demonstration of discontent and opposition. The popular press was mistaken in its characterizations of Marcuse, and contemporary observers and historians have been misled by the error.[55]

By insisting that those who thought Marcuse was influential were wrong, Wheatland skirts an important question: why would the press promote such an "extremely unlikely American hero"[56] as mentor of an indigenous movement? Furthermore, in questioning Marcuse's importance to the American 1960s political events, Wheatland stresses the incompatibilities between the German philosopher and his American audience. The skirted question thus becomes all the more intriguing. To deal with it properly requires more than a factual account. Reputations are symbolic goods. Marcuse acquired a considerable symbolic capital over the years of his American life, and his reputation is not an anachronistic projection by scholars, or the period's media manipulation, but the rhetorical achievement of his particular form of stranger persona.

Regardless of whether the members of the New Left Movement read or understood Marcuse's philosophy—an issue likely to remain disputed—many frequently invoked his name and were at least familiar with the general tenor of his ideas, even if they had encountered them in other thinkers' (often American) books. Why did they invoke Marcuse? The answer I find most convincing comes from Paul Breines, one of the influential participants in the movement, who was especially active on the campus of the University of Wisconsin at Madison. In his reminiscences about the troubled 1960s decade, when he came of age politically speaking, Breines insists that he was "at no point in the process . . . drawn to American models of Leftism" and found instead more compelling the ones of European import. Although himself puzzled by this preference, Breines offers the following explanation:

> Why, for example, was I drawn more deeply into the European cultural history course taught by the non-leftist German-Jewish émigré, George Mosse, than to the course on American foreign policy offered by the very American socialist historian, William Appleman Williams? Was this because of the differing styles of academic charisma of the two teachers, both of whose courses were vital experiences for so many students? Or was my leaning toward Europe an expression of some budding estrangement from things American; a sophomoric but critical sense that genuine *Geist* could be found anywhere but here?[57]

Marcuse and other German scholars offered a symbolic space for reflection different from what American students already knew. Breines and his close friends at Madison spent the first years of the 1960s "buried in

Marcuse, Adorno, Horkheimer and the Frankfurt School's critique of the culture industry." For these young Americans, Marcuse's *One-Dimensional Man* was "*the* book."[58] When Breines left Madison for Germany in 1968, he joined what he jokingly calls in his reminiscences the circle of "*Frankfurter-kinder*" (Frankfurt kids). A point of pride for Breines, the association with the Frankfurt Institute made him suspicious to other leftist intellectuals at home, such as Paul Buhle, who questioned the "aloof cosmopolitanism" he saw as a characteristic that had slipped into the American ethos from German mentors.[59]

Was Marcuse an "aloof cosmopolitan"? Even as he became more and more involved in American politics, he also continued to travel to Europe on lecture tours and follow political events in Germany and in France. However "de-Germanized" he may have emerged by becoming emancipated from the Adorno and Horkheimer group, American critics did not immediately—or some ever—hail him as a fellow national. The opposite happened as his American books were repeatedly described by critics as difficult to read and understand and more importantly as belonging to a foreign intellectual tradition.

STAGES OF RADICALISM

As Marcuse's independent philosophical career unfolded, he became more and more critical not just of capitalism but of American capitalism in particular. His first major American publication was *Reason and Revolution* (1940), written under the auspices of the Frankfurt Institute and dedicated to Max Horkheimer. The book was a study of Hegel focused on defending the philosopher against any possible charges of protofascism and establishing instead a strong Marxist subtext *avant la lettre*. *Reason and Revolution* was not received well. Sydney Hook wrote a scathing review in *The New Republic*, depicting the book as *Tendenzschfrift* (deliberately using the German word in sarcasm) and ridiculing the very idea that Hegel would have to be shown not to have had a fascist ideology. Hook was a critic of the Frankfurt Institute as a group, not just of Marcuse. His dislike of critical theory came from a commitment to American pragmatism and particularly to the philosophy of John Dewey, who insisted on the need to match philosophical ideas with real-life applications. Critical theory and its practitioners, by contrast, seemed disconnected from reality, or at least American reality. Instructively, Hook's criticism of Marcuse focused on issues of style even more than the substance of the argument. "The chief weakness of Mr. Marcuse's exposition," he charged, "is that it will be intelligible in the main only to professional students, who will prefer to struggle with the original text. To other readers the exposition will remain opaque." In addition to launching a complaint that would be frequently heard regarding the general difficulty of all of the Frankfurt Institute writings, Hook uses this stylistic fault to negate the very possibility of Marcuse even having an audience. For those few readers who could both understand the text and would choose to read it, Hook follows up with an equally devastating criticism of the substance of the book. After granting that the author's "interpretations are much clearer than his exposition," he proceeds to maintain that "Mr. Marcuse's interpretations are . . . wide off the mark."[60] Clarity, little as Hook saw in the book, is useless in the absence of valid ideas.

Unflattering as the entire review was, Hook left the harshest remarks for the end and only made them in a veiled manner. Claiming that Hegel was the first philosopher to develop a systematic technique for "taking over the phrases and slogans of democratic movements and fill[ing] them with completely opposite content," Hook made clear his dislike of philosophy gone into the street. In this regard, Hegel could indeed be connected to an antidemocratic politics and held accountable as an implicit ideologue of totalitarian movements, National Socialist as well as communist. "Debasing the coinage of the mind has worse consequences than debasing currency," Hook declared emphatically.[61] By striving to defend Hegel, Marcuse was either ignoring his linguistic liberties, or worse, embracing them. Written in 1940, years before Marcuse himself furnished the New Left political slogans like "repressive tolerance," Hook's criticism seemed to target more a poor political taste than philosophical ideas in the author of *Reason and Revolution*. He ended the review rather ominously: "But this is a theme for independent development." Did Hook anticipate that Marcuse, too, would become a master at rhetorically merging his philosophical ideas with the slogans of a political movement?

Reason and Revolution was published the same year as Hook's own book, *Reason, Social Myth, and Democracy*, in 1940. Hook dedicated the volume to "the memory of a Great Adversary, Leon Trotsky." The difference in the choice of dedications is significant. As John Patrick Diggins astutely observed, they "marked respectively the death of the Old Left and the unanticipated birth of the New Left."[62] The New Left, however, would only achieve political prominence at least a decade later. Until then, Marcuse's American career went through another important stage, marked by the publication of his *Eros and Civilization* in 1955, a book often seen as the counterpart to Adorno and Horkheimer's *Dialectic of the Enlightenment*. At least as difficult to understand, if not even more, than the previous work, *Eros and Civilization* is steeped in the psychoanalytical concepts and vocabulary that were taking hold of American social sciences, in large part due to the influence of German refugee scholars. The thesis of the book, inspired by Freud, is that civilization relies on the sublimation of erotic instincts. Marcuse argued that radical societal and political change requires a rethinking of erotic inhibitions, such that the loosening or elimination of taboos and prohibitions expressed through social customs and law makes room for reevaluation. In a sweeping critique of Freud from a Marxist perspective, Marcuse argued for the need to create a nonrepressive society "based on a fundamentally different experience of being, a fundamentally different relation between man and nature, and fundamentally different existential relations."[63] At the time of its publication, the book entered more specialized debates, such as the one with Norman Brown who had also written a study inspired by psychoanalysis, *Love's Body*, presenting a version of eros that was driven by biology and in Britain with ethologists attempting to ascertain scientifically whether erotic drives can be transcended non-compulsively.[64] In retrospect, however, *Eros and Civilization* became especially known for its author's interest in connecting social and political life to what seemed like a plea for uninhibited sexuality.[65] Radical feminists and proponents of the liberated sexuality associated with Woodstock had easy recourse to claiming the book as a source of inspiration, or at least intellectual confirmation of their practices. Using a conceptual framework and a vocabulary that had come to be seen as symbols of the German influence on American thought, Marcuse reached conclusions that were already endorsed, independently, by some Americans during the 1960s. The stranger and the natives thought alike.

While his first American books gave him visibility beyond that of his Frankfurt School masters, Marcuse's reputation was definitively shaped by the publication of *One-Dimensional Man* in 1959. The book presented a bold revision of orthodox Marxism, offering a critique of advanced capitalist society far darker than the one originally proposed by Marx. Marcuse's was also a critique directly focused on *American* capitalist society. The book argued that capitalism creates a new kind of human beings, defined by conformism and dependence on others for making choices and decisions, rather than autonomous, creative, and able to imagine the world as different from what is merely given to them. At the center of capitalist society, Marcuse places consumption and technical rationality, defining both as pernicious forces that gradually colonize the individual mind and inhibit freedom. Increased consumption in the capitalist society defined by abundance and choice only leads to more consumption, spurned by the false belief that one needs more simply because more is available. Technical rationality is the logic of scientific and technological progress, which instills the wrong belief that a better life is made possible by an increase in mechanization. While mechanization might ease daily mundane challenges (such as cooking a meal faster or communicating at a distance), it does not improve the experience of life; indeed, it frequently worsens it, in Marcuse's view, because technological progress ends up requiring more production and thus allowing human beings less free or leisure time.

"One-dimensional man," as Marcuse defined the concept, was the modern individual deprived of the ability to dissent and thus deprived of a future. If in an overtly totalitarian society, such as the Soviet one, dissent was denied to citizens as an opportunity, capitalism denied it more subtly through distractions and an invasion of the mind that would ultimately render citizens incapable of dissent. The conformism of one-dimensional man in capitalist society is worse than the oppression experienced by a citizen in a totalitarian regime, in Marcuse's view, because the former no longer even realizes that dissent is possible. Douglas Kellner has traced this view to the Hegelian influence in Marcuse's work, especially as reflected in his concept of the individual as subject and as explained in *Reason and Revolution*: "The self-conscious subject, aware of its nature and powers, is a 'being-for-itself' and contains the powers of objectification in which it appropriates and makes its own ideas, forms of behavior, objects and institutions."[66]

One-dimensional man has lost this self-awareness as an entity distinct from all others and is no longer capable to relate to the surrounding world in a unique way. The concept, then, described a state of affairs that combines conformism with the inability to imagine "alternatives and potentialities that transcend the existing society."[67] It is not an exaggeration to argue that American life was the inspiration behind this concept. America presented Marcuse and his fellow Frankfurt Institute members with what they most disliked: "the regimented world of a bourgeois society without alternatives."[68] Marcuse's examples help us to flesh out this idea of regimentation specifically in the American context and resemble closely those that would be offered by a very different critic, Solzhenitsyn at Harvard. These examples include: advertising leading to widespread consumption of the same product, whether a deodorant or a TV show; the degradation of high art into simplified versions intended for broader audiences; the uniformization of political opinion through the dominance of media conglomerates; and the preponderance of knowledge forms that seek only to capture the existing reality rather than critique it or imagine another. These examples paint a broad picture of American life, indeed so broad that the book could easily read as a critique of America rather than capitalism, a concern at the heart of many irritated responses. Marcuse seemed to be seeing in America something different from what most Americans saw, not a prosperous and free country but the very center of evil capitalism. *One-Dimensional Man* was criticized from opposite directions of the political spectrum by Marxists and anti-Marxists alike. While each camp focused on a particular aspect of the book, all were equally troubled by the pervasiveness of Marcuse's critique, which seemed to leave no room for the recognition of beneficial aspects of capitalism. Many critics were especially put off by the "totalizing" aspect of Marcuse's argument, his overall indictment of capitalism. However, as Kellner has pointed out, such a totalizing aspect does not exist (at least not explicitly) in the book. Marcuse used *one-dimensional* as an adjective, rather than the noun *one-dimensionality*. The choice was important, as there is no one-dimensionality but rather a "co-operation between the universities, media, government, corporations and social institutions to combat nonconformist thought and behaviour" that creates the one-dimensional man.[69]

The depiction of advanced capitalist society as a totalitarian society could only come as a shock in a Cold War political discourse that routinely contrasted the totalitarian communist bloc to the free democratic world iconically represented by the United States. The book prompted charges that only a foreigner who did not love America could think that way. More than wounded national pride, such responses suggest a profound discomfort with a foreigner's criticism. Marcuse, however, frequently relied on American sources, especially on authors like C. Wright Mills, who were equally critical of their own country. The comparison to totalitarianism continued to raise more than one eyebrow, even in the aftermath of the Cold War dichotomous logic. By some accounts, the recourse to such an idea, especially as Marcuse formulated it in later works, when he compared the United States to Nazi Germany, had merely a sensationalistic purpose, to incite audiences.[70] Such sensationalist effects notwithstanding, the comparison between America and totalitarian regimes was long in the making. Even when still in Germany, Marcuse belonged to a group of Marxist German intellectuals who saw the development of bourgeois capitalist society as inevitably leading to totalitarianism.[71] The linchpin of this argument was the presence of totalitarian tendencies in a democratic order—a counterintuitive and disturbing thesis that seemed to create a political aporia: how can a democratic society be democratic if it can never completely escape its totalitarian tendencies? Marcuse's book seemed to leave no room for a way out. His use of the term "totalitarianism" was a target of heavy criticism for its conceptual entanglements, especially the conflation of Nazism and communism. But with the publication of *One-Dimensional Man*, the use of the term instituted a stranger persona in dark key, presenting to the American public a pessimistic outsider who hardly anticipates the revolutionary and energizing figure of the involved citizen from a decade later. It was difficult for Marcuse to overcome this early image. *One-Dimensional Man* consecrated Marcuse's image as a virulent critic of capitalist society, who offered even harsher condemnation in subsequent works, especially in "Repressive Tolerance" (1965) and *Essay on Liberation* (1969).[72] By then, the author had lectured widely around the country and had acquired a public persona closely connected to controversy and scandal as Russell Jacoby would later put it.[73] "Repressive Tolerance" is Marcuse's most controversial essay. Inspired by the Third World liberation movements that had swept the international arena, he argued that violence is an appropriate reaction against oppression. He differentiated the violence of the capitalist society against its citizens, often committed through nonphysical means, from the more blatant violence of citizens reacting in a revolutionary manner by destroying public property, throwing Molotov cocktails at a protest, or even committing murder. This was treading on thin ice. Trying to advance a more nuanced understanding of violence as opposition and dissent, in contradistinction to violence as repression and suppression, he became embroiled in what many critics and readers saw as murky rhetorical artifices. Against the backdrop of campus unrest around the country and the rise of the Black Panther Party, Marcuse's abstruse reflections of the acceptable and unacceptable use of violence could easily be misunderstood or oversimplified to present him as a supporter of anarchism or downright criminality.

To make matters worse, the essay introduced the concept of "a repressive tolerance," a euphemism built out of antiphrasis to argue that freedom of speech should not be extended to everybody. Certain groups or discourses, Marcuse insisted, deserve repressive or liberating tolerance, or, in plain speech, intolerance. To some critics, his way of phrasing such ideas was off-putting:

> Liberating tolerance, then, would mean intolerance against movements from the Right, and toleration of movements from the Left. . . . Withdrawal of tolerance from repressive movements before they become active; intolerance even toward thought, opinion, and word, and finally intolerance in the opposite direction, that is, toward the self-styled conservatives, to

the political Right—these anti-democratic notions respond to the actual development of the democratic society which has destroyed the basis for universal tolerance.[74]

Such discourse, as well as the explicit and relentless targeting of the Right can seem "worthy of a Bolshevik commissar."[75] The persona of a supporter of violence and intolerance who unabashedly proclaimed "anti-democratic notions" haunted Marcuse for the rest of his career. It attracted hate mail, murder threats sufficiently convincing to lead him to flee his California residence, the termination of his tenured appointment at UCSD, and constant queries from both hostile and friendly journalists. What they all wanted to know was whether or not Marcuse hated America and why he had chosen to stay in a country he criticized so much.

By the second half of the 1960s, Marcuse's pessimism seemed to have turned into anger, an emotional overtone that was especially attractive to the equally angry New Left movement. But anger was also a step toward the optimism of the last, most utopian, phase of Marcuse's radicalism. This phase is best captured in *Essay on Liberation*, which expanded the themes and arguments presented in his previous works. Yet the work also adds the element of aesthetic consciousness, an older preoccupation for Marcuse, dating back to his philosophical apprenticeship in Germany and his doctoral dissertation on the artist novel (*Kunstlerroman*). This is the element of aesthetics. For Marcuse, to liberate means to release human beings from an "affluent society" that is ugly and stultifying. Liberation from the world of one-dimensional man requires an "aesthetic ethos," which can reimagine the world after the very power to imagine has been altered by the mechanisms of the "affluent society."

The essay sounded occasionally like a religious leaflet promising salvation: liberation will restore the original natural beauty of the world— "cleansing the earth"—and create social and political structures that will allow human beings to enjoy life. But Marcuse was fairly specific: he asked for social policies developed according to existential and aesthetic criteria, such as urban zoning regulations protecting citizens from the pollution and cacophony of highways. Marcuse was ready to admit that such regulations would not be cost-effective (as they would inhibit massive infrastructure developments of highways, along with automobile production and gas consumption) and would thus go against the logic of the advanced capitalist society. By closely matching his vision of a change with an obstacle inherent in capitalism, he offered a political program by necessity utopian. In other words, the world he envisioned did not yet exist but would also never exist without a radical change in Americans' understanding of what it means to live and to be a human being.

Marcuse was not shy of offering grandiose visions. Where *One-Dimensional Man* offered a dark image of capitalism, *Essay on Liberation* envisioned an optimistic universe of beauty and freedom, utopian in contrast to actual America, yet nevertheless achievable. The individual inhabiting this universe is a human being refashioned by a new sensibility, who has aesthetic needs in addition to purely biological ones. For Marcuse, the need for beauty is an important element of a political consciousness, whether beauty is experienced through nature or art. At times, Marcuse's aesthetic comes across equally as an environmentalist agenda and an avant-garde art manifesto. The avant-garde artist revolutionary, especially as illustrated by the French poet André Breton, was Marcuse's political idol, until replaced by local inspirations, the American hippie and Black Panther.

From Breton, Marcuse borrowed the concept of the "Great Refusal" to describe the radical breaking with the reality of bourgeois society and the rejection of its moral and political order. Those capable of such refusal were artists, insofar as art allowed them to imagine an alternative universe. They were also all sorts of marginal individuals, the misfits and the disenfranchised, or simply the young who had not yet been perverted by the conventions of society. Rather surprisingly for a Marxist thinker (and disturbing for many of his critics on the left), Marcuse did not privilege the working class as a revolutionary force. In his earlier works, such as *One-Dimensional Man*, he overtly expressed skepticism regarding the revolutionary capabilities of the proletariat. American workers, especially, struck Marcuse as already controlled by the capitalist order and as merely subjected to the logic of overproduction and overconsumption. For Marcuse, the revolutionary subject is a marginal or maladjusted *individual*, not a whole social class. In this regard, his conception is more compatible with Hannah Arendt's *pariah* than with the Marxist focus on the working class. Marcuse himself wanted to be understood as such a pariah, even though he was not young, Black, or a hippie. In his recollections about Marcuse, Carl Schorske recounts seeing the philosopher get involved in a student protest with no fear of being arrested or compromised by his action.[76] Similarly, Davis recounts the occupation by a small group of faculty and students at the University of California at Berkeley of campus buildings with Marcuse being the second person to enter the building after the door had been pulled down. As I mentioned before, he was also, by all accounts, the one who sent an anonymous check to the university for the repairs.[77]

By locating the revolutionary subject into the marginal or disenfranchised agent, Marcuse implicitly proposed a vision of political change that begins outside the existing society, and thus, outside actual America. His stranger persona benefited already from a highly visible authority that made audiences pay attention to his vision, whether they liked it or not. In his well-publicized and memorable appearance at the famous 1967 Congress for the Dialectic of Liberation, along with an impressive cast of characters that included Stokeley Carmichael, Gregory Bateson, Paul Sweezy, Lucien Goldmann, and R. D. Lang, Marcuse opened his speech, titled "Liberation from the Affluent Society," by noticing the flowers surrounding the lectern. "I want to remind you," he began, "that flowers, by themselves, have no power whatsoever, other than the power of men and women who protect them and take care of them against aggression and destruction."[78] The thesis of the speech was that human beings are at risk of "submitting completely and voluntarily to a socio-political system, but also have the power to break their servitude." In advanced capitalist society, individuals live surrounded by an affluence that only increases their vulnerability to servitude. They live, Marcuse explained, in a society in which

the material as well as cultural needs of the underlying population are satisfied on a scale larger than ever before—but they are satisfied in line with the requirements and interests of the apparatus and of the powers which control the apparatus. And it is a society growing on the condition of accelerating waste, planned obsolescence and destruction, while the substratum of the population continues to live in poverty and misery.[79]

Such a denouncement could be easily interpreted in the Cold War climate of the mid-twentieth century as an endorsement of Soviet-style socialism. However, in his 1957 book *Soviet Marxism*, he had made it clear that he was not a supporter of the Soviet Union. Marcuse was equally critical of the socialist practices in the Soviet Bloc, and he even predicted that over time capitalist and socialist societies would become increasingly alike. His stranger persona was defined by an ideological equidistance with regard to the main attitudes of the time. In the London speech, Marcuse denied again forcefully that liberation from the affluent society merely amounted to a communist takeover. Rather, in his view, to be liberated from the affluent society meant to "break in the continuum of repression, which reaches into the depth dimension of the organism itself. . . . [L]iberation, involves organic, instinctual, biological changes at the same time as political and social changes."[80] More than an agenda for regime change, his concept of liberation is a vision for self-transformation. Marcuse was not only asking for new policies, but also, and more importantly, for a new way of imagining life.

Daring because it demanded an existential change, Marcuse's vision was nevertheless compelling, due to its rebelliousness, to a significant segment of American readers. These readers were young, enthusiastic, and educated, many of them students and intellectuals involved in the emergence of the New Left Movement. What attracted them to Marcuse's message, more than to similar messages issued both by other academics and by consecrated American political figures? In part, it was Marcuse's emphasis on the visceral nature of change imagined as a radical biological transformation of humanity. Packaged in an impressive philosophical armature and sounding perhaps a bit sci-fi, his message was also rather simple: you have to *embody* the change in order to institute it. The "new sensibility" described in *Essay on Liberation* comes with a whole new set of biological "needs" rather than political rights in their traditional sense. Not only does Marcuse see the need for beauty as part of the "new sensibility," but he also deemed justice and freedom biological needs because all three shape a "sensibility which rebels against the dictates of repressive reason" and all three "invoke the sensuous powers of the imagination."[81]

It is to such "sensuous powers" that the London address had tried to appeal. Using the common metaphor of flowers as symbol of beauty and fragility, Marcuse hoped to create a moment of aesthetic awareness that could inspire political reflection. What may have simply been an impromptu remark inspired by the sheer number of flowers on the stage where he spoke became the starting point of his analysis of liberation as a form of rediscovering and experiencing life outside the norms and conventions imposed by the capitalist society. Marcuse revisited the image in his *Essay on Liberation* where he proposed the notion of "flower power" to capture "the ingression of the aesthetic into the political." He assumed that liberation from capitalist society could only be an utopian project insofar as it relied on escaping ways of thinking and experiencing that had become deeply entrenched in a collective mind—"habituated thought," as the Russian formalists had put it. Marcuse saw the insertion of the aesthetic sensitivity into political action as a strategy for contesting taken-for-granted assumptions and for reverting meanings: "giving flowers to the police, 'flower power'—the redefinition and very negation of the sense of 'power'; the erotic belligerency in the songs of protest; the sensuousness of long hair, of the body unsoiled by plastic cleanliness."[82] The political consciousness envisioned in *Essay on Liberation* is at the same time an artistic consciousness insofar as the artist can imagine and represent alternative worlds radically different from the ones we inhabit. Similar to Erich Auerbach, Marcuse saw art as a strategy of engagement rather than avoidance, as a way of reorganizing rather than escaping the social world.[83] But he also feared that in the capitalist society art had lost its ability to transform our vision of the world, because it has become adapted to the taste of a mass public interested, at best, in spectacle and at worst in drab reproductions of its daily life.[84] In surrealism and in all manifestations of contemporary art that interest Marcuse in *Essay on Liberation*, he finds the political potential of nonconformism but also a radical break from "thinking as usual," as Schutz would have put it: "non-objective, abstract painting and sculpture, stream-of-consciousness and formalist literature, twelve-tone composition, blues and jazz: there are not merely new modes of perception reorienting and intensifying the old ones; they rather dissolve the very structure of perception in order to make room for . . . [a] reality [that] has to be discovered and projected."[85]

Aimed at a reality "to be discovered," this political-aesthetic vision was utopian in a way that troubled many of Marcuse's American critics. Marcuse seemed to be advocating a republic of and for artists and other aesthetes, a modern Arcadia with no economic concerns. What to Americans seemed utopian and thus simply unrealistic was a common trope in the German political tradition. German leftist political thinkers used utopia as a trope for conveying social criticism because utopia was a pedagogically effective strategy of estrangement. As Karl Mannheim put it, utopian projections force readers to make the "world subject to doubt." Yet once the vision thus advocated emerges, "the hour of full experimentation strikes."[86]

The job of experimentation went to the New Left activists while Marcuse remained the theorist, both praising achieved utopias (especially among the Beatniks and hippies) and renewing his plea for the importance of the utopian impulse. Philosophically, however, the notion of "utopia" continued to cause trouble for him. If utopianism is the perpetual rejection of our familiar, given circumstances, is the search for utopia a way of constantly deferring reality and creating a limbo? Was Marcuse, then, an impassionate revolutionary or a hopeless dreamer whose political views, though incendiary, had no content? The paradox of utopia—as clamoring for change but inevitably postponing it—created an unexpected opportunity for critics who did not want to deal with such radicalism. I review two such critical reactions in the next section. In rejecting Marcuse and his utopian vision, critics threw the baby out with the bath water, dismissing his ideas as foreign to their own intellectual tradition and the potential change they advocated as unnecessary. Marcuse's philosophical utopianism was a plea for revolution. More than anything else, this revolutionary stance is what troubled his American public.

THE STRANGER: FROM PROPHET TO FOOL

Each of Marcuse's works received, upon their initial publication, mixed reviews. Praise for the complexity of his philosophical ideas or temerity of political opinion came hand-in-hand with dismissal, often of the same things. Among the reviews that introduced his work to the American public, two stand out for their comprehensiveness as well as for their systematic critique of Marcuse's intellectual foreignness. Both are devastating criticisms written with eloquence and sophistication for a general yet intellectual public by two respected philosophers, Alasdair MacIntyre and George Kateb. MacIntyre published a monograph dedicated to Marcuse in a series coordinated by Frank Kermode and titled "Masters." Far from paying Marcuse a compliment through the very inclusion in a prestigious series, the book is rumored to have been commissioned by Kermode as a sort of intellectual execution: the first and last on the subject.[87] Kateb published an unusually long article in the magazine *Commentary* mixing praise with criticism and issuing an overall verdict that could hardly have been more devastating: Marcuse as an "almost mad," philosophically inaccurate and politically ineffectual "darling" of the lunatic fringe.

MacIntyre and Kateb treated Marcuse seriously and offered careful readings of his work. If in the end they dismissed him, their conclusions rested on their own philosophical commitments (and the arguments entailed), which they obligingly explained but did not defend. Ultimately, both philosophers mainly rejected Marcuse's style or focused on it by way of justifying their disagreement with his ideas. MacIntyre depicts this style as that of the "professoriate in imperial Germany," thus stressing at once its foreignness, elitism, and anachronism. Although he conceded that such style sounds "less offensive in English" than in German, MacIntyre implicitly drew attention to the negative aspects of Marcuse's voice. "Its very strangeness lends to it a certain charm," MacIntyre submitted, and the condescension again only emphasizes his disapproval. This disapproval, detailed over several chapters dedicated to each of Marcuse's works, zooms in on the German philosopher's "magical rather than philosophical use of language" by way of suggesting the philosophical inconsistency—even vacuity at times—of the ideas under scrutiny. Not only did MacIntyre find very little to agree with in Marcuse's work, but he also found no coherent criteria of truth available in his work and thus no sign that Marcuse himself could justify his positions. This discovery made MacIntyre feel entitled to dismiss, from the beginning of his study, all of Marcuse's "key positions" as "false." Philosophically false, the work is also politically dangerous, in Mac-Intyre's estimation, for it "invites us to repeat . . . part of the experience of Stalinism."[88]

The continuity from philosophical to political errors—more or less assumed by MacIntyre—was the foundation of Kateb's critique. While apparently more sympathetic to Marcuse, to whom he dispensed several compliments ("a splendid mind," "a more sophisticated thinker than the usual strident New Left intellectual"[89]), Kateb indicted him on similar grounds: Marcuse's philosophy was based on false premises and led to a political cul-de-sac.[90] While MacIntyre pondered Marcuse's style to point both to its strangeness and lack of philosophical substance, Kateb focused on its emotional overtones, on Marcuse's pessimism and anger as signs of an inflamed and thus unreasonable mind. These critiques pinned Marcuse in an inferior position even while claiming to take him seriously. More importantly, the inferiority they attributed to him is that of a stranger. To prove that his positions were indefensible, both MacIntyre and Kateb contrasted them to philosophies they deemed—and expected their audience to deem—foolproof. Marcuse was not confronted with counter-arguments as much as held accountable to an intellectual tradition to which he did not belong, whether that tradition was John Stuart Mill's utilitarianism (in Kateb's critique) or analytical philosophy more broadly conceived (in MacIntyre's). His critique compared to Chinese anti-American propaganda at the height of the Cold War (Kateb) and his claims dismissed as incompatible with his refugee status (Kateb again), Marcuse came across as a hostile outsider, prone to exaggeration or misinformation.

Commentary's generous space allocation for Kateb's study suggests a commitment to discussing Marcuse's philosophy in a detailed and hence respectful manner. In such matters, length is a way of paying homage. But what did the editors and the author of the article respect in the German philosopher? Certainly, it was not his fame, depicted by Kateb as "noise" to which "we must close our ears." Nor did they respect his political views as by 1970 *Commentary* had become a conservative publication. In encouraging readers to "try to hear what Marcuse is saying," Kateb shows an interest in what was behind the fame and the political opinion: the critique of

American advanced capitalist society. His study detailed Marcuse's claims and arguments, ordering them judiciously so they could fall into five clear categories. Besides the philosophical substance captured in this division, it was Marcuse's rhetoric that concerned Kateb. Emphasizing the "condemnatory" and "pessimistic" tone of a philosopher who even when "indulgent to the young" remains "austere, complex and full of doubt" and "too desperate to believe the worst,"[91] Kateb seems interested in tracing the anatomy of an emotionally charged work. By pointing out this emotional overcharge, Kateb could dismiss Marcuse's critique as lacking objectivity and exaggerated. Philosophical disagreements aside, Kateb faulted Marcuse for making claims that were either inaccurate depictions of American society or exaggerated some isolated, minor tendencies.

If America was not as "affluent" as Marcuse deemed it, then it also could not deserve such condemnation. By challenging the premise, Kateb could attack the conclusion. But his disagreement with Marcuse turns out to be a question of degree: not whether the critique was valid, but the extent to which it was. "Does not Marcuse grossly exaggerate," wondered Kateb, "the quantities at the disposal of the large majority in the affluent society." The concession that "the society as a whole is affluent beyond the fantasies of early utopia" does not prevent Kateb from insisting that we "look at the daily life of the millions. How much really could be taken away without the return of a stingy bleakness? To such "stingy bleakness" Kateb opposes an image of America as "consumer's paradise," the "age long dream" of the generations of immigrants flocking to the promised land. For Kateb, the "consumer's paradise" is not only utopia achieved and indeed a palpable utopia against Marcuse's undefined, vague alternative world; this utopia also has its own aesthetic value, the beauty of decadence with "unimpeachable finesse."[92]

Shifting from a philosophical disagreement to registering a difference in aesthetic preferences, Kateb's study is not merely a defense of American capitalist society but also an argument for its superiority, however relative. On the one hand, he charged that Marcuse's criticism contained "too much plain assertion, too much easy pessimism, too many tenuous connections in the development of the argument." On the other hand, Kateb also insisted that "the American system has possibilities for good which Marcuse does not wish to see, or does not wish to explain as emanating from that system itself."[93] In defending American society, Kateb was not rejecting *any* criticism by default but implying that only complaints that also come with an answer can be taken seriously. American society, as he sees it, can benefit from reforming policies but does not require sweeping change. In such a society, those who try to be prophets of revolution can only be fools.

A RHETORIC FOR THE NEW (LEFT) REVOLUTION

Indeed, how could one argue for revolution in the "consumer's paradise?" Yet Marcuse's most important contribution to the New Left was precisely a philosophical and revolutionary rhetoric. The emotional overcharge of Marcuse's stranger persona was also its key rhetorical advantage. From the dark pessimism of his earlier works to the utopian optimism of his later essays, Marcuse drew an emotional trajectory that linked the need for radical change to possibility. The task was not an easy one. Even among those most disenchanted with their country, the revolutionary impulse was not easily aroused in America (unlike in Europe). American history began with one revolution, followed by none. By contrast to the French context (with had been shaped in a long revolutionary tradition familiar to Marcuse, all the more brought to life by the events of May 1968), revolution is not a common trope in American political discourse. Even in the Port Huron statement of the Students for a Democratic Society—the most revolutionary of the New Left activist groups—the term "revolution" is absent. This "revolutionary deficit" made Marcuse's claims seem devoid of any practical value.[94] Their dark despair could be taken to mean either that no improvement was ever possible or that an improvement meant destroying the America that Americans knew. Kateb's verdict was that Marcuse lacked political realism. Kateb also sensed a revolutionary pathos in Marcuse's writing, which he dismissed as tantamount to being un-American.

As late as 1999, long after the turmoil of the New Left heydays, Marcuse's revolutionary tone triggered suspicion even from sympathetic American critics. In an article published by *The New Republic* in February 1999, Jeffrey Herf states: "revolution as a desirable goal has long since [the 1940s in Nazi Germany] lost any appeal for most Western leftists and all Western liberals."[95] This pronouncement allows him to add:

> To the extent to which the Frankfurt School stills speaks to our political perplexities, it speaks less in the utopian Marcuse than in the sober and chastened Horkheimer. . . . Like the old Dylan records on our shelves, the well-thumbed copies of *One-Dimensional Man* retain a talismanic and sentimental effect; but their intellectual effect is over. The political illusions of Herbert Marcuse should justly be consigned to the past.[96]

While rejecting the political contribution of Marcuse, Hart at least places him in the same cultural category as an American icon, Bob Dylan. Marcuse's revolution, then, was not a political as much as a cultural one (and part of a larger collective American effort). Hart might be closer to a correct understanding of Marcuse than Kateb was. In the German political tradition, "revolution" was not only a specific political event, but also a discursive strategy, a "metaphor of creativity," as critical theorist Hans Joas has described it. According to Joas, "the idea of *revolution* assumes that there is a potential of human creativity relative to the social world, namely that we can fundamentally reorganize the social institutions that govern human coexistence." Against a religiously infused conception of revolution as providentially endorsed (as in the case of the American Revolution, arguably), the metaphor of revolution as primarily driven by a faith in "human beings themselves [as] the makers of this new beginning."[97]

Whether or not there was a revolution in 1960s America, the political movement most interested in organizing one, the New Left, found in Marcuse's philosophy an intellectual justification as well as rhetorical pathos. Marcuse urged change as an outburst of creativity and affirmation of human freedom. Yet to be politically usable, a rhetorical pathos needs to strike the right chord. It hardly did so with the pessimism of *One-Dimensional Man*, which not only bothered conservative critics but also sympathetic revolutionary spirits, including former Frankfurt Institute colleagues, such as Eric

Fromm. In the end of the book, Marcuse quoted Walter Benjamin's famous paradox of hope: "hope is only for those who are hopeless."[98] Seizing on this quote, Fromm charged that it showed how wrong those are who attack or admire Marcuse as a revolutionary leader, for revolution was never based on hopelessness, nor can it ever be. But Marcuse is not even concerned with politics; for if one is not concerned with steps between the present and the future, one does not deal with politics, radical or otherwise. Marcuse is essentially an example of an alienated intellectual, who presents his personal despair as a theory of radicalism.[99]

Fromm may have been right about Marcuse's initial political disinterestedness, but his political commitment can hardly be contested in the later works. Marcuse's revolutionary rhetoric underwent a transition from dark "despair" to the explosive activism that made him a speaker in much demand during the 1960s and 1970s. This rhetoric follows an ambitious emotional arc from the low notes of pessimism to the intense cry for change and self-transformation. The initial pessimism can be read as deliberate avoidance of what Walter Benjamin derisively called "leftwing melancholy": the abstruse, clever, ironic stance of a critique that comes as a wink to those in the know and ends up merely registering its own political impotence.[100] By choosing pessimism instead of cynicism, Marcuse already stated political commitment rather than abandonment. His critique aimed at action rather than overindulgent preaching to the choir.

The darkness of this early pessimism was overstated by critics like Fromm. Marcuse's is rather a strategic pessimism, as its political charge gets tempered by the philosophical abstraction of the "one-dimensional man." Part of a larger but also pointed critique of American capitalism, the phrase "one-dimensional man" is a metonymy: it refers to American citizens but identifies them through a more general category that contains properties that are primarily characteristic of Americans. Metonymy presupposes an easily recognizable relation between objects and is thus an "irresistibly and necessarily conventional" trope. Common metonymies like "the White House" (for the American executive branch) or "home" (for one's family or place of origin) become "closely knit into the fabric of language."[101] "One-dimensional man" had no such conventional, easily recognizable meaning when Marcuse introduced it. If anything, the phrase sounded abstract and technical. However, it had the advantage of allowing a deflection of the criticism. Marcuse did not appear directly as a critic of American society, just as American readers could, in principle, ignore the fact that it was their own portrait that "one-dimensional man" offered (and indeed, as I have said, the concept was broader in scope as it applied to all advanced capitalist societies). The metonymy also had the role of deflecting the pessimism, which seemed a consequence of a broader despair in the fate of democratic societies but not directly one vis-à-vis the United States.

By emptying the subject of his critique of national specificity, Marcuse was not only thinking within a traditional Marxist framework of internationalism but also prompting his readers to consider the idea of a social world in which creativity and autonomy are systematically stifled by the very functioning of that society. Once the depiction of such a world became sufficiently compelling, readers could start recognizing familiar contours and discover that world as their own. The metonymy of "one-dimensional man" demanded of American readers to confront their world and themselves by presenting them with an image they were expected to see as their own reflection. The metonymy, then, was a strategy of estrangement serving as mirroring technique: the "one-dimensional man" was the American citizen.

The metonymy of a "one-dimensional man," in its deliberate avoidance of a directly identified referent, drove a wedge between the harshness of the analysis and its object, American society, shielding it from the otherwise dismissive force of the criticism. Redemption is implicit in Marcuse's metonymy as American society is both critiqued and expected to act and change. Critics like Kateb accused Marcuse of indicting America without identifying any culprits. This was a political philosophy without any political agents on whom one could pin responsibility, both for what was wrong and what needed to be righted. The American C. Wright Mills had offered a political critique in his *Power Elite* that read almost like a detective novel by comparison to Marcuse.[102] Mill's whodunit approach identified specific agents who could be held accountable: the government, the professional politician, intellectuals, the military, or city dwellers. Yet by avoiding such specificity, Marcuse did not only leave the roster open. More importantly, he created a buffer between the abstract category and its possible referents—a hospitable space for the American New Left, who found in Marcuse the arguments of a powerful social and political critique, without feeling indicted themselves, as Americans.

"One-dimensional man" was not a common metonymy in the sense that it did not spring from everyday talk. Uncommon and unfamiliar metonymies became the hallmark of Marcuse's thinking and played a key role in shaping his most memorable phrases, which were adopted as slogans by the New Left movement. The most famous and enduring were "affluent society" and "repressive tolerance" although each of them worked differently. "Affluent society" came closer to capitalizing on the conventionality of metonymy as a trope. By contrast to the Great Depression, American prosperity during the Cold War was not only a comforting reality to an increasing number of citizens but also a distinguishing feature of a society increasingly more pleased with itself. Poverty, always worse on the other side of the ideological divide of the Iron Curtain, became a political weapon and proof that political orders other than capitalism were defective. The affluent society was an honorific in a political discourse that conflated ideological positions with material gain and moral value. How could one, then, wish for liberation from such a society? As I have already shown, this contradiction was a challenge for Marcuse but one that he may have welcomed. Contradiction, antithesis, and antiphrasis created a shock effect that was well suited for the New Left's slogans and the headlines that made it famous in the media. The logic of contradiction was a strategy of inversion and exposure, of giving negative force to phenomena commonly deemed positive, and vice versa. Marcuse's penchant for antinomy came against the backdrop of a public discourse in which, as he explained, "speech moves in synonyms and tautologies; actually, it never moves toward the qualitative difference. The analytic structure insulates the governing noun from those of its contents which would invalidate or at least disturb the accepted use of the noun in statements of policy and public opinion. The ritualized concept is made immune against contradiction." Marcuse restored the rhetorical value of contradiction, and through contradiction he challenged official political discourse with its "unified, functional language . . . an irreconcilably anti-critical and anti-dialectical language."[103]

The antiphrastic tenor of Marcuse's other famous metonymy, "repressive tolerance," allowed him to insert a sarcastic overtone in what had previously appeared as dark despair. In the context of the seriousness of Cold War official discourse with its black-and-white dichotomies, irony and sarcasm introduced a level of skepticism, a critical echo that questioned what was otherwise taken for granted. Marcuse deplored the language of the "one-dimensional man" as too authoritarian as reflected in the preferred grammatical patterns of official discourse in which "the noun governs the sentence in an authoritarian and totalitarian fashion, and the sentence becomes a declaration to be accepted—it repels demonstration, qualifications, negation of its codified and declared meaning."[104] Sarcasm was Marcuse's antidote to such linguistic totalitarianism because its double entendre forced readers to think beyond accepted phrases and shared meanings. Sarcasm, then, was a prompt for creativity, comparable in this respect to slang and colloquial speech. Marcuse, who had not grown up on the streets of Detroit or Harlem, had an aesthetic appreciation for African American idioms and slang in general. It is tempting to speculate that this interest in nonstandardized language and its elevation to an expression of freedom and creativity is the ultimate dream of the nonnative speaker liberated of the stigma of his own "deviant" linguistic identity. This was Marcuse's subtle way of positioning himself within American citizenry and among the people on the margins that he admired. Such alignment is a double naturalization, civic and moral simultaneously, for in Marcuse's view in slang and colloquial speech "it is as if the common man (or his anonymous spokesman) would in his speech assert his humanity against the powers that be, as if the rejection and revolt, subdued in the political sphere, would burst out in the vocabulary that calls things by their names: 'headshrinker' and 'egghead,' 'boob tube,' 'think tank,' 'beat it' and 'dig it,'" and 'gone, man, gone.'"[105]

Marcuse's own trademark metonymies have none of the visceral quality of the American slang that excited him so much. Yet his metonymies, too, form a discourse of euphemism, understatement, and indirection in order to challenge taken-for-granted meanings without being aggressive or confrontational. All of Marcuse's metonymies are a strategy of estrangement, as all of them demand reflection and can thus modify an existing understanding. The abstractness of his expressions, along with unabashed philosophizing even in rhetorical circumstances that could have benefited from a less specialized discourse (such as the London congress), represents another strategy of defamiliarization. Marcuse's style strains the audiences' attention to force them to see what would otherwise remain unnoticed. Recourse to abstraction was in all likelihood deliberate on the part of a philosopher (especially one who had also been accused by his German colleagues of too much concreteness in his style). Marcuse abhorred the political style of the time "of an overwhelming *concreteness*." In his view, "this language, which constantly imposes *images*, militates against the development and expression of *concepts*. In its immediacy and directness, it impedes conceptual thinking; thus, it impedes thinking."[106]

Was Marcuse's strategy of defamiliarization through metonymy effective within the official Cold War discourse? Marcuse's 1965 Syracuse lecture offers a sample of direct engagement with American presidential rhetoric and thus with official American Cold War discourse.[107] On November 12, 1965, he was invited to deliver the Arthur F. Bentley seminar on the Great Society, held at the Syracuse University Maxwell Graduate School of Citizenship and Public Affairs. The lecture offers a potpourri of Marcuse's favorite philosophical and political statements but places them carefully in response to claims made by American officials, specifically by President Lyndon Johnson. Marcuse summarized the concept of a "Great Society," as used by the president, focusing on its defining characteristics: unbridled growth, constantly renewed challenge, abundance and liberty for all, and progress subsumed to the citizens' needs. In response to what official propaganda (his term) envisions as an idyllic universe, Marcuse counters by turning the image of abundance on its head: "a society which couples abundance and liberty in the dynamic of unbridled growth and perpetual challenge is the ideal of a system based on the perpetuation of scarcity."[108]

Introducing scarcity in this vision of abundance is a rhetorical artifice made possible by stringing the features listed by Johnson and pointing out their incompatibility. How can one have perpetual growth without perpetual scarcity? The focus on scarcity creates a paradox but one that had its risks. The perpetuation of scarcity would mean that America's poor could never disappear. Therefore, the "affluent society" cannot exist as such, only affluent groups within society. Marcuse risked undermining his own conception of an affluent society by insisting on the existence of poverty in America. As we have seen, critics like Kateb seized this opportunity to accuse Marcuse of exaggerating or making no sense. Yet the logic of the metonymy is based on Marcuse's distinction between actual and feared scarcity: while the poor do exist in American capitalism, scarcity is what this society most dreads. The obsession with production and accumulation thus becomes the *flight from poverty*, the foundational trope of the Horatio Alger narrative in its Cold War revival.

Marcuse's critique of presidential sobriquets like the "Great Society" works by systematically subverting the president's claims: Johnson's vision of America was that of a place where "we will raise our families, free from the dark shadow of war and suspicion among nations." Marcuse's is that of "a society which wages war or is prepared to wage war all over the world." This emphasis on a militaristic complex of American society represents more than a Cold War reflex as it draws attention to the fact that the affluent society "calls for an Enemy against whom the aggressive energy can be released which cannot be channeled into the normal, daily struggle for existence." This "Enemy" imagined by the affluent society is not an ideology, like communism, or a country, like the Soviet Union, but the sheer irreducible existence of "have-nots, whether Communist or not." To overcome this logic of enmity required radical change not only within the U.S. but also in world politics and especially an elimination of "the established hierarchy of Master and Servant, Top and Bottom, a hierarchy which has created and sustained the have-nations, Capitalist *and* Communist."[109]

Marcuse found this type of hierarchical thinking everywhere in public discourse, from presidential speeches to newspapers headlines announcing U.S. victories in Vietnam, thus celebrating "one of the most shameful acts of civilization," worse even than Nazism. "I have lived through two World Wars," he maintained, "but I cannot recall any such brazen advertisement of slaughter. Nor can I remember—even in the Nazi press—a headline such as that which announces: 'U.S. Pleased Over Lack of Protests on Tear Gas.'"[110] While arguably minimizing the magnitude of the opposition to the war among Americans, Marcuse concluded the talk with a bleak prophesy of a violent society to come. "This sort of reporting," he insisted, "consumed daily by millions, appeals to killers and the need for killers."[111] The Great Society, in his view, was a world of fear, scarcity, and violence. Using apocalyptic imagery that radically reversed the presidential idyllic projection, Marcuse issued a call to *violent* action, with little room left in that particular speech to justify the potential violence of his own brand of radicalism. Indeed, he often had to respond to accusations that his philosophy preached violence.

As his philosophical views moved closer and closer toward espousing the need for an overthrow of the status quo by any means, it became rhetorically difficult for Marcuse to deny any support of violent means. In an interview for San Diego's KFMB-TV, Harold Keen put it bluntly: "one of the major problems of opposition to you by the American Legion and Assemblyman Stull of San Diego, is that you are a revolutionary who has asked the students to engage in guerilla warfare and sabotage as steps toward establishing a left-wing dictatorship."[112] Marcuse responded by trying to clarify his conceptual position, rather than denying the charge, as the interviewer and American audiences wanted. He expostulated on the difference between the illegitimate violence of a state or government against its people and the legitimate violent response of the victims. His metonymy of "repressive tolerance" was meant to drive home this distinction by pointing out the insidious forms of violence masquerading as freedom and tolerance: aggressive marketing, workplace policies focused on increased production, or the lack of leisure time. While not aggressive in a direct and concrete way, these were forms of repression, and dangerous no less. As an oxymoron, the metonymy of "repressive tolerance" referenced the violence as well as deception—the deceptive allure of policies and institutions that oppress while seeming to satisfy particular needs and functions. The oxymoron was an invitation to respond to deception with outrage. Such a rhetorical cliffhanger was meant to make a violent response appear justified.

More than any other of his key metonymies, "repressive violence" was confusing because it left an important question unanswered: who decides when violence is acceptable and when not? To malicious critics, the obvious answer seemed to be: Marcuse himself. The role of guru for the student activists seemed to confirm it, making Marcuse vulnerable to charges of implicit self-aggrandizement. Such charges made him uneasy, and he repeatedly rejected the role of "guru" of the New Left movement, insisting that "the students neither want a new father image, a new daddy, nor do they need one, and if I would tell them something, they would certainly have their own ideas about it and would not attempt it."[113]

Far from merely self-promoting, Marcuse articulated an overall vision of the intellectual as an agent of change and moral and political guardian. His vision included force and violence. He did not present his political agenda in the same way as the New Left leaders, and in key circumstances, he seemed rather ambivalent about its justifiability. Again, after all, he did volunteer to pay for the destroyed door on the Berkeley campus.

CONCLUSION: THE LEGACY OF MARCUSE

Marcuse's American rise and fall (and the brief revival with the Occupy movements) were unparalleled for a foreigner, regardless of whether he was the guru of the New Left or just another intellectual who lent credence to the movement. Does this mean that Marcuse was especially skilled, or that, after all, America is an inclusive and welcoming polity? The first answer seems more probable to me. The story of Marcuse's relation with the New Left does not have a happy ending. The relation gradually deteriorated as Marcuse was increasingly accused of elitism and intellectual arrogance. Several of Marcuse's American critics saw in him the German mandarin ideology, which had a reputation of having "always been elitist in character."[114] An article published in *Dissent* insisted that Marcuse's views were," though in reverse, the argument of Dostoevsky's Grand Inquisitor." In other words, he offered nothing short of a "dictatorship of the intellectuals."[115]

To charges of elitism, Marcuse responded with his own charges of anti-intellectualism. Already in a 1965 letter to New Left leader Mike Davis, he complained about detecting in the movement a strong anti-intellectual sentiment, almost an inferiority complex of being an intellectual and working *as* and with intellectuals. This may well be fatal to the whole movement, for this sentiment completely fails to understand the role of the intellectual today, in the one-dimensional society and totalitarian democracy. . . . Where it is first of all the question of *knowledge*, of developing the *consciousness* of what is going on and of the possible ways of getting out of the whole, the task is an intellectual one.[116]

Marcuse's break with the New Left was followed soon after by the collapse of the movement, which he explicitly attributed to its "contempt for theory as a directive for praxis."[117] He was no longer plugged in to the collective spirit of the movement, and he no longer claimed to speak on behalf of the American people, of those 99 percent of the American population, as decades later the Occupy movement would put it. Once he had turned into a solitary dissenter, Marcuse's stranger persona was left in a state of political nakedness. Frequently berated by extreme right groups as an ungrateful immigrant who should be deported, he found himself often in the position of having to justify his right to criticize American society. His justifications had an apologetic tone, different, for example, from the urgency and assertiveness of the native-born revolutionaries who had authored the Port Huron statement. Marcuse assured his readers that although he hated "the established power structure, [he] hate[d] by no means the people suffering under it." He found little to praise in contemporary America, but he had once known a better, mythical America: "I came to this country on the Fourth of July, 1934. When I saw the Statue of Liberty, I really felt like a human being. If I compare the country as it was, let's say, in 1934, when I came, and as it is now, I doubt sometimes that this is the same country."[118]

Whether or not 1930s America was better than it would become three decades later, or than it is now, is irrelevant (although Marcuse pressed the argument of a real deterioration). Marcuse's fated arrival in America on Independence Day, followed by his prompt naturalization, is its own political myth, reinforcing the immigrant origins of the nation. Tapping into the discourse of mythical America, Marcuse could appear as criticizing a temporary state of affairs. Why could he not be the one to start the revolution that would restore America's greatness (hypothesized or real)? To American ears, the criticism often sounded too defeatist. Too cosmopolitan in habits, too German in his rhetoric, and too theoretical in his writing for the practical goals of Americans interested in acting, his role was that of a catalyst. He offered Americans both a dystopian and an utopian portrait, but never stopped believing in the potential of the latter.

4

COLD WAR PROPHESIES

Alexander Solzhenitsyn and Mythological America

ALEXANDER SOLZHENITSYN arrived in America in 1974 after being expelled from the Soviet Union for his anticommunist dissident activity. The plane charged to execute the deportation took him to West Germany where he spent a short time before leaving for Switzerland. Europe impressed him with its institutions and especially the mechanisms of grass-roots democracy, but in the end he opted for the United States as the Tomi of his exile. Like Ovid, who spent his banishment complaining bitterly about the land to which he had been forced to go, Solzhenitsyn frequently expressed his disappointment in America. Yet, while the Roman poet was unhappy to be in a barbarian province that he perceived as inferior to his native empire, Solzhenitsyn had left behind a world of prison camps and food shortages. Many like him, struggling in the Eastern bloc countries, dreamed of reaching American shores. All America offered him, it would seem, was a familiar climate in Vermont and the opportunity to do research for his books in well-equipped libraries at major academic institutions. In 1992, excited to return to post-Soviet Russia, he thanked his Vermont neighbors for giving him peace to pursue his endeavors, in an abrupt and somewhat awkward farewell. He was satisfied: "I have done all that I wanted to do."[1] Indeed, he had managed to complete his work and lived to see the demise of communism. He might have also hoped that his presence in America had accomplished one more thing: to urge American intellectuals to restore the greatness of their nation—moral, political, and cultural—at a time of ideological crisis and power shifts throughout the world.

Solzhenitsyn had served as a Red Army commander during World War II and was twice decorated for his service. He was the son of a World War I widow and grew up in the provincial town of Rostov. Too poor to go to Moscow to pursue his dream of a literary education at the university, he graduated with a degree in mathematics and physics from the University of Rostov, a specialization that saved him later when he was sent to a work camp where he worked as a mathematician in a so-called *sharashia*.[2] In February 1945, he was arrested on the basis of critical comments about Stalin, which were found by the Soviet censorship in his correspondence and in his literary manuscripts. He was sentenced to eight years in a work camp. Upon completing his sentence, he received another one, "exiled for life." He was sent to southern Kazakhstan, but the second sentence was lifted in 1956. In his *samizdat* writing, Solzhenitsyn was an opponent of the entire Soviet system and of Marxism in general. His anticommunist views were well known to the KGB and eventually led to deportation. When he arrived in America, he had witnessed and survived the crimes of a totalitarian regime. Yet the United States did not seem to impress him much even just by comparison. Solzhenitsyn's negative view of America became the core of all of his public interventions in the United States. It came out more memorably and forcibly than anywhere else in his 1976 Harvard commencement address. The speech reached a wide audience, drew numerous responses from all corners of the political arena, and laid out a position that had major significance for the political order being reshaped as the Cold War was entering the détente phase, defined by efforts at collaboration and appeasement. His position seemed, in some ways, familiar to American audiences because it argued for the strict anti-Soviet containment policy of the early Cold War years. However, Solzhenitsyn's arguments were radically new because they no longer invoked the crimes committed by the Soviet Union or its violation of human rights, even though the author was famous for exposing those. This time, it was not the Soviet Union at the center of his diatribe but the United States. Solzhenitsyn criticized America and the West more generally for failing to oppose the growing threat of communism. Under his harsh accusations, though, was praise for America as the "land of the free," his vision of America similar to Arendt's but with a religious and moral spin. To the real America that was growing tired of Cold War political tensions, he held up the vision of a mythological nation that had once broken off with, only to redefine and dominate, Western civilization.

In the years before he delivered the Harvard address, Solzhenitsyn's novels documenting the harsh life of the citizens of the Soviet Union had reached Western audiences in French, English, and German translations, producing a splash that prompted an effusion of hyperboles from even the most restrained commentators. Solzhenitsyn's revelations about the repressive nature of the Soviet regime put a significant burden on leftist intellectuals in the West, who had been criticizing Western capitalism and who had been arguing for the advantages of socialism as a more egalitarian and humanitarian political alternative. The 1973 French publication of *The Gulag Archipelago* single-handedly marked the "symbolic moment" when Europe's political master narrative radically changed from a generally progressive and social-democratic to a more socially skeptical and conservative one.[3] In America, where the rise of corporatism had gone hand-in-hand with a decrease in social welfare programs and where the McCarthy era had left behind resentment among more than just intellectuals, Solzhenitsyn's depiction of socialist society as a place of death and horror made it difficult to complain about the alternative, regardless how imperfect it was.

The gruesome details, if not the main message, in Solzhenitsyn's denouncement of the Soviet Union were long awaited news for American anticommunists, who hailed him as a great hero of gigantic moral and artistic stature. Some of them had harshly criticized their own country for not mounting a stronger opposition to the communist bloc. Yet they probably did not expect Solzhenitsyn, also, to be critical of the United States. His comments on American politics and society echoed their arguments and even resembled their rhetoric, especially the "prophetic dualism" of the Eisenhower-Dulles era that opposed a benevolent America to a malevolent Soviet Union.[4] Solzhenitsyn, however, brought something new to the discussion. He criticized America as an outsider outraged by the nation's failure to oppose communism in the name of its ideals of freedom and democracy. Solzhenitsyn did not claim to be impartial, like Arendt, because he saw himself as a victim of America's indifference to the threats posed by the Soviet Union; his vision of the future, though bleak, was not merely pessimistic like Marcuse's, but downright apocalyptic. He argued with righteous indignation, trying to remind Americans of their moral responsibility to save the world and to shame them for faltering.

Ceremonial discourse such as a commencement address is a key practice in the rhetoric of citizenship: it implicitly socializes the young men and women to the requirements of a shared polity, by reminding them of what it means to be a good member of the community. Solzhenitsyn's speech was a hybrid of blame and praise, both identifying from different angles the behaviors and actions he was asking his audience to emulate. The mixing of praise and blame characterizes a uniquely American rhetorical genre, the jeremiad, a political sermon that "casts the rhetor into the role of a prophet, acting as a kind of intermediary between a god-like authoritative message source and the intended audience."[5] Unlike the strictly religious, European jeremiad, which played out as a moral lesson about the corruption of humanity in general, offering no advice and leaving little room for hope, the New World jeremiad was based on the premise that its audience was made of "people chosen not only for heaven but as instruments of a sacred historical design." The American jeremiad is "the ritual of a culture on an errand."[6]

Solzhenitsyn addressed Americans as a covenant people chosen by God for special purposes. Working within the conventions of the American genre, he berated but also flattered his audience by reminding them that they had a special responsibility because their nation was different from, and indeed superior to, any other. It was a time when America's exceptional status was coming into question abroad and at home. The year 1976 marked the height of détente, a period of relative relaxation in U.S.-Soviet Union relations, in stark contrast from previous head-on confrontations that sometimes made the possibility of nuclear war loom as a frightful possibility. Initially conceived by Harry Kissinger as a multileveled doctrine that tried to establish economic, military, and political links between the two countries by way of avoiding a military crisis caused by nuclear armament, détente had a mixed reception in the United States. To those who were tired of the international anxiety and tension imposed by the earlier confrontations between the Soviet Union and the United States, détente offered the promise of peace—all the more appealing as the specter of nuclear war had been constantly the focus of Cold War discourse. To those who had a fundamental mistrust in Russians, or who had been driven by a desire "to revitalize the American spirit through a crusade for Russian freedom," détente was an illusion (if not a lie) and an abandonment of a key mission.[7]

On both sides of the Iron Curtain, détente was a period of social fragmentation and protest. In the Soviet Union, détente made publication or circulation of antigovernment and anticommunist opinions in the form of *samizdat* literature possible. Subsequently, Solzhenitsyn was a key figure among other intellectuals who introduced in the Soviet Union a discourse of dissent. In the United States, the détente years were marked by local protests against domestic problems (such as racial segregation). Americans struggled with domestic problems that were unrelated to the confrontation with the Soviet Union. Yet détente foreign policy, with its emphasis on American-Soviet agreements, became a way of shifting attention away from the local scene. As Jeremy Suri argues, "détente ensured a safer status quo by discrediting domestic . . . challenges."[8] Anticommunist and even anti-Soviet sentiment in America waned compared to previous decades because official policy favored cooperation over opposition and because Americans were too worried about domestic problems.

Solzhenitsyn condemned the relaxation of American opposition to the Soviet Union and to communism yet disapproved of the word "anticommunism." "It is a very stupid word," he complained,

> badly put together. It makes it appear as though communism were something original, basic, and fundamental. Therefore it is taken as a point of departure, and anti-communism is defined in relation to communism. Here is why I say the word was poorly selected. . . . The primary, the eternal concept is humanity. And communism is anti-humanity. Whoever says "anti-communism" is saying, in effect, anti-anti-humanity. A poor construction.[9]

This was not mere stylistic quibbling. In the United States, the meaning of ideological labels like "anticommunism," "anti-Stalinism," "Trotskysm," "leftism," and "new leftism" tried to capture a diversity of political beliefs, both regarding American political players and institutions, and in response to international affairs. Solzhenitsyn brought back the black-and-white of the earlier Cold War arguments and pressed for a rendition of communism as the ultimate embodiment of evil. To him, communism was not an ideology but an offense against all human beings, and by raising against it, he was seeking to defend humanity, not just the victims of a particular state or political system. He had opposed this devil where it most mattered, in the Soviet Union. None of this, however, changed the fact that he was a Russian. Americans associated communism with Russians, not just with the Soviet Union. In America, Solzhenitsyn would have to reckon with the "widespread American tendency to view Russians as 'Oriental' and incapable of changing their national character."[10] In the early part of his stay in America, the balance between his universal prophet persona and his Russianness swayed the reception of his ideas in predictable ways. Those sympathetic to his views tended to ignore his nationality while the critics never forgot that these were the views of a Russian. Yet the Harvard address upset both these categories. American commentators on the left and on the right nearly unanimously rejected Solzhenitsyn's scathing criticism of the United States as the uninformed and unfounded beliefs of a foreigner who did not know or understand America. The "democratic consensus" in response to the 1976 Harvard address declared Solzhenitsyn wrong.

OUR COUNTRY, OUR CULTURE

During the early postwar years, efforts to reach some sort of political consensus had brought together intellectuals who, despite holding different ideological views, agreed on several issues, especially the need to maintain peace and to protect human rights across any political divide. These early attempts at finding a common ground often ended in conflict, with one side complaining that the other was unpatriotic, in the service of foreign interests, or trying to take control.[11] In his memoir, William Phillips discusses the political affiliations of the main representatives of his generation, placing

Sidney Hook, Elliot Cohen, Irving Kristol, and others on the "right," Diana Trilling and Merlyn Pitzele in the "middle" and gradually moving "left," and Daniel Bell, himself, and Norman Thomas among others decidedly on the "left." But what did such labels mean? "By 'right.'" Phillips explains, "I mean mostly the subordination of other issues to that of anti-Communism, the general support of the status-quo, and a hostility to most radical movements. By 'left' I mean a sympathy with the values and aims of liberalism (or socialism), as well as anti-Communism, and a critical attitude to all existing governments and institutions."[12]

Later, terms like "totalitarianism" or the "Occupied Zone," used in opposition to "unoccupied" or "the free world," replaced not only distinctions previously conveyed through labels such as "left" and "right," but also distinctions among nation-states.[13] As a confrontation between totalitarianism and freedom, the international world became, as Solzhenitsyn would put it in his Harvard speech, "split" between the West and its enemies. Such a clear-cut distinction shaped a worldview of two well-defined halves of the world, one evil and one good. In Cold War discourse, the evil half was the communist monolith, a term of "political shorthand [that] helped to shape popular and official conceptions of the Soviet Union and its allies, distilling the often messy realities of international relations into a neat, comprehensible formula. Its lesson was that all communists, regardless of their native land or political program, were first and foremost tools of Kremlin."[14]

Solzhenitsyn's Harvard address helped to shape a similar conception regarding the other side of the Iron Curtain. He posited another "monolith," the Western world as the enemy of communism, solely capable of stopping its international spread. Such reification of the Western world into an anticommunist enclave was no small feat in the ideologically turbulent years of the 1960s and 1970s, when the American intellectual elite was rocked by internal conflict. Debate in those circles concerned how to regard the threat of communism at home and whether it was serious enough to tolerate affiliations with McCarthyism, symbolic or concrete. The 1970s saw a split within the American intelligentsia, which went beyond political affiliation, into intellectual beliefs, attitudes toward Western civilization and America's relation to it, and perhaps most importantly, an understanding of the role of the United States in the international arena. Immediately after World War II, the United States had become a "liberal hegemonic agency" on the international arena. This hegemony was first of all economic rather than political as "the U.S. achieved investment, trade, and monetary gains based on an international liberal economic system it protected with a political and security order extended across the globe."[15] The cultural influence of America was a different matter: "the crassness of American culture, from films to beverages, and the self-interest and imperialist ambitions behind the American presence in Europe were commonplaces for many Europeans of Left or Right."[16] Europeans were reluctant to accept American domination. What became known as "the American question" referred to a near rejection of American values as anti-Western and European intellectuals' resentment of American domination. After the initial shock, American intellectuals' anxiety over what the Europeans thought diminished. This may have been the result of an increased conviction among Americans that "the world's cultural, not just geopolitical and economic, leadership had finally become theirs, with New York likely to replace Paris as the new center of cosmopolitanism."[17]

This view that America had become the world cultural center surfaces clearly in the proceedings of a symposium on "Our Country and Our Culture" organized in 1952 by the *Partisan Review*, which featured Norman Mailer, David Riesman, C. Wright Mills, Lionel Trilling, and Arthur Schlesinger Jr. The editors, William Phillips and William Rahv, prefaced the discussion with the suggestion that in the postwar era a radical change in the relation between America and Europe had taken place that placed America, for the first time in history, in a position of superiority: "America is no longer the raw and unformed land of promise from which men of superior gifts like James, Santayana, and Eliot departed, seeking in Europe what they found lacking in America. Europe is no longer regarded as a sanctuary. . . . The wheel has come full circle, and now America has become the protector of Western civilization, at least in a military and economic sense."[18]

To Williams and Rahv, this newly acquired power and prestige meant that "politically . . . [here was] a recognition that the kind of democracy which exists in America has an *intrinsic and positive value*; it is not merely a capitalist myth but a reality which must be defended against Russian totalitarianism."[19] Already during the war, many American intellectuals believed that America was "a repository of Western culture."[20] Ten years later, not all the respondents to the symposium agreed with this self-congratulatory assessment. Mailer, especially, seemed irritated by the self-righteousness and smug tone of the editors, reflected, in his view, in the overall profile of the journal. Riesman was also reluctant to accept the premise of American superiority, albeit his own evaluation of American society was also positive, as was, overall, that of the rest of the commentators. One thing that worried Phillips and Rahv, and which they deemed potentially dangerous for the superiority of America, was the advent of mass culture. One of the questions they addressed to the participants is more than a mere point of discussion as it reveals anxiety over what might be the undoing of the newly gained international domination of America: "Must the American intellectual and writer adapt himself to mass culture? If he must, what forms can this adaptation take? Or do you believe that a democratic society leads to a leveling of culture, to a mass culture which will overrun intellectual and aesthetic values traditional to Western civilization?"[21]

The respondents did not appear to view challenges posed by mass culture to intellectuals as a major concern, but they did acknowledge the issue. In the Harvard address, Solzhenitsyn would blame all the ills of American society on the consequences of mass culture, conformity, and the loss of morality. But in the symposium debate, Schlesinger offered an interesting qualification: to him, mass culture represented the natural consequence of the pluralism that had characterized American democracy from its inception. It was what had so impressed foreign visitors, such as Alexis de Tocqueville. Mass culture could only become a threat, Schlesinger argued, if cultural pluralism got stifled along with political pluralism. "Some have forgotten," he claimed,

> the wisdom of Tocqueville when a century ago he identified the antidote to the new power that democratic equality bestowed upon mass opinion. "Many people in France consider equality of conditions as one evil," he wrote, "and strive at least to escape from the latter." But I contend that in

order to combat the evils which equality may produce, there is only one effectual remedy—namely political freedom. . . . Tocqueville could not have been more right . . . [as] political freedom is the indispensable preliminary to any effective defense against the leveling of culture.[22]

What America claimed to have that was superior to the Soviet Union was political freedom. In defining political freedom, especially in ways that could strongly imply that it was absent in the communist bloc, American intellectuals relied on core principles of Western democracy: social pluralism, representative bodies, and the rule of law. In this definition, though, what is a global Western political model becomes distinctly American. For those who saw political freedom iconically represented by American society, its absence in other forms of political order only proved that the American model was synonymous with democracy. To this end, the testimony of dissidents such as Solzhenitsyn, who had firsthand experience of life in a totalitarian regime, was invaluable evidence. It was, however, evidence coming from a sullen foreigner who was reluctant to grant America any merit.

By the mid-1970s, the gap between the American "right" and "left" had widened, especially in the aftermath of the Vietnam and Korean wars and the McCarthy persecutions. By some accounts, "isolated elite politics and widespread disengagement . . . replaced the mass politics and public protests of the 1960s."[23] The political terrain, however, retained some of its original murkiness with respect to attitudes toward the very idea of American identity and the role that would best suit this identity in the international arena.

The politics of détente made it difficult to achieve a clear understanding of American identity and its international role. In an article published in February 1976 in the right-leaning, Jewish magazine *Commentary*, Theodore Draper, a former communist sympathizer and historian of socialist movements, complained that the term "détente" was "fluctuating and ambiguous . . . situated somewhere between cold war and rapprochement or even entente."[24] Draper believed that the concept lacked political substance. As such, it could not be used to articulate a new role for the United States in the international arena. Détente seemed to imply that America's policing over communist expansion was no longer necessary, and many Americans were reluctant to accept that. Critics of détente warned against the risk of a naive assumption that the improvements that had taken place in the Soviet Union under Leonid Brezhnev meant more than a temporary and limited opening of the totalitarian order. In 1972, former U.S. State Secretary George Kennan argued:

> The United States would do well not to indulge in unreal hopes for intimacy with either the Soviet regime or the Soviet population. There are deeply rooted traits in Soviet psychology—some of old Russian origin, some of more recent Soviet provenance—that would rule this out. Chief among these . . . are the congenital disregard of truth, the addiction to propagandistic exaggeration, distortion and falsehood, the habitual foulness of mouth in official utterance.[25]

Kennan's criticism of détente echoed that of dissidents from within the Soviet Union. Both Solzhenitsyn and Nobel laureate physicist, Andrei Sakharov, insisted on the importance of separating real détente from *pseudo-détente*, a distinction that caught the attention of anti-Soviet intellectual circles in the United States. With the publication in America of Sakharov's *My Country and the World* in 1975, Americans were presented with the image of a relaxation of tension among the two powers as a "cynical political game . . . serving temporary political and economic interests" rather than a genuine opening toward mutual recognition and collaboration. Sakharov, unlike Kennan, blamed Western leaders for trying to build political capital out of appeasing the Soviet regime, and he expressed indignation at the fact that the West, and the United States in particular, was "yielding one concession after another to its partner in détente," attributing it to "leftist-liberal faddishness."[26]

Critics on both sides questioned the sincerity and interests of those involved in implementing détente: the Soviet Union for obtaining economic advantages (such as the most favored nation clause) or the United States for curtailing the spread of communism and "freezing" the Soviet Union out of most Middle Eastern diplomacy?[27] More importantly, the détente years fostered a climate of mistrust within each of the superpowers—rather than vis-à-vis each other—as citizens became increasingly more suspicious of their own government's policies. Solzhenitsyn redirected the mistrust against the other, the foreigner.

A MOST WELCOME VISITOR

Shortly after Solzhenitsyn had been deported from the Soviet Union, Jesse Helms, Republican Senator of North Carolina, introduced a resolution to award him honorary American citizenship, which received broad political support. Helms's resolution was framed in the same language that had been used in 1963 to confer honorary citizenship on Winston Churchill. Despite being in such flattering company, Solzhenitsyn declined the invitation and invoked the inability to travel to the United States. Another invitation to visit the United States came from George Meany, president of the AFL-CIO. Solzhenitsyn declined again. Thus, John Dunlop argues, "Solzhenitsyn did not intrude into the political life of the United States. Rather, he was *asked in* by influential members of Congress and by the leader of the American trade union movement. . . . How is one to account . . . for this unusual interest in the opinions of an exiled Russian writer?"[28]

Dunlop believes that the answer lies in the significant political events taking place in America at that time, for example, the aftermath of the Vietnam War, the Watergate scandal, and the increased criticism of détente policy. But why would a foreigner be the source of enlightenment in such a time of domestic crisis? One answer could be that Solzhenitsyn was becoming the subject of attempts to manipulate his symbolic standing as a dissident, witness, and survivor. Those eager to greet him on American soil may already have held political convictions that they hoped to be reinforced by Solzhenitsyn's approval. Another possible, interrelated answer is that Solzhenitsyn's reputation made him especially credible to an American audience eager to learn more about life behind the Iron Curtain.

But in June 1975, when Solzhenitsyn finally agreed to visit the United States, his imminent visit became a cause of alarm to American officials. National Security Advisor Henry Kissinger sent a memo to President Gerald

Ford, anticipating pressure by Congress or Meany. Kissinger insisted that the president *not* receive Solzhenitsyn at the White House, because:

> Solzhenitsyn is a notable writer but his political views are an embarrassment even to his fellow dissidents. Not only would a meeting with the President offend the Soviets but it would raise some controversy about Solzhenitsyn's views of the United States and its allies. . . . Further, Solzhenitsyn has never before been received by a Chief of State and such a meeting would lend weight to his political views as opposed to literary talent.[29]

Indeed, the feared meeting did not take place, much to the indignation of some Americans. When the memo was leaked to the press, public sentiment blamed Kissinger's precautions on the duplicitous, immoral climate of détente. In the *Washington Post*, George Will wrote sarcastically: "The United States government may have to expel Aleksandr Solzhenitsyn from the republic, not only as a hands-across-the-barbed-wire gesture of solidarity with its détente partner, the Soviet government, but also to save the president and his attendants from nervous breakdowns."[30]

By the time he finally traveled to America, Solzhenitsyn had already established a following in the country through the translators and publishers who introduced his works to American audiences. Unlike his reception in Europe, especially in France and Great Britain, the early American response to his writing was not as enthusiastic as one might expect, especially given previous scandals such as that occasioned by the leaked Kissinger memo. *One Day in the Life of Ivan Denisovich*, Solzhenitsyn's first account of life in a Soviet prison camp, was published in America in 1962, with a cautionary editorial note: "This is not, of course, a work of art on the scale of Boris Pasternak's masterpiece, *Dr. Zhivago*, another Soviet novel to win a major audience in the United States."[31] The editors also distinguished the Gulag, about which Solzhenitsyn's book testified, from the Holocaust, according the latter more gravity and significance. The readers were thus instructed to read against a preconceived scale of values that did not give first rank to Solzhenitsyn or his experiences.

Public reception of the book in Europe was quite different from the cautious Knopf editorial comments. Biographer Michael Scammel describes the British reaction as "an orgy of masochistic euphoria," and in France, Bernard-Henri Lévy described the reaction to be of such intensity as "to immediately shake [the French] mental landscape and overturn . . . ideological guideposts."[32] France, of course, had long been dominated by a vocal, highly articulate, and prestigious, left-leaning intelligentsia. Intellectuals who were card-carrying members in the Communist Party were much more common than in the United States. Luminaries such as Jean-Paul Sartre had repeatedly declared their admiration for Lenin and Stalin. They had traveled to the Soviet Union and returned convinced that a communist society would be superior to that of capitalist and democratic Europe. In 1974, left-leaning *Le Monde* dismissed the revelations in *The Gulag Archipelago* as unreliable in that they came from "a declared enemy of socialism itself."[33] More moderate leftists, however, were duly impressed by Solzhenitsyn, calling him "triply unimpeachable in that he speaks from the triple depth of the people, the camps, and exile, Solzhenitsyn is the reincarnation of the great intellectual—Voltaire, Victor Hugo, Zola—who denounces the powers to be and shows how they can be resisted."[34]

Whether because Solzhenitsyn was too convincing to be easily dismissed or because the French Left was already approaching a crisis that would lead to its rupture, *The Gulag Archipelago* did force French intellectuals to reconsider the fundamental doctrine at the foundation of socialist state and communist regimes: Marxism. Those who proceeded most energetically to such reconsiderations came to be known as "Solzhenitsyn's children," among them, most famously, André Glucksmann, who argued that Marxism, not just Stalin, was directly responsible for the horrors of the Soviet Gulag.[35] In 1977, Lévy pronounced Marxism in France a compromised ideology, crediting Solzhenitsyn with its exposure:

All Solzhenitsyn had to do was to speak and we awoke from a dogmatic sleep. All he had to do was *appear*, and an all too long history finally came to an end: the history of those Marxists who for thirty years had been tracing the path of decadence in search of their guilty party, moving painfully from the "bureaucratic phenomenon" to the "Stalinist deviation," from "Stalin's crimes," to Lenin's "mistakes," finally from Leninism to the blunders of the earliest apostles, going through the Marxian soil one by one, sacrificing a scapegoat at each stage, but always preserving above suspicion the one he dares to denounce for the first time—the founding father in person, Karl Kapital and his holy scriptures.[36]

In lambasting Marxism and praising Solzhenitsyn as its lucid critic, Lévy creates a debatable equation between the exile of Soviet dissidents and a political awakening among Western intellectuals. In fact, the reception of Solzhenitsyn and other East European dissidents involved, even in Western Europe, a more complicated rapprochement between different agendas and discursive styles. In France, the denouncement of Marxism as the doctrine that led to the creation of the Gulag often became a strategy for promoting capitalism as the only feasible alternative, thus leading to what Pierre Nora calls a "new libertarianism" rather than a genuine reassessment of Marx.[37] By contrast, for Solzhenitsyn, repudiating Marxism was a way of questioning the political viability of communism: not to propose capitalism instead, but a nationalist (Russian) and religious (Orthodox) political order. Thus, while the strategy may have been the same, the goals were different.

Whether Solzhenitsyn helped French former communist intellectuals promote their political agenda or they helped him to promote his is hard to decide. What matters is that he came to the U.S. with the reputation of a truth-teller who had shaken the world and poured cold water on the leftist intelligentsia. In the United States, many of Solzhenitsyn's enthusiastic supporters already had an anticommunist agenda. An interesting example is that of Irving Howe, who published in the socialist magazine *Dissent* a review of Georg Lukács's 1971 study of Solzhenitsyn's literary technique as illustration of an aesthetic of social realism well used. Howe, a socialist who had become somewhat de-radicalized since his early days as a member of the Workers' Party, was critical of the Soviet Union and of standard Marxism. Lukács, an early member of the Hungarian Communist Party, imprisoned and deported, like Solzhenitsyn, during the Hungarian uprising, had outlined a Marxist theory of the novel, which was influential among many American left-leaning literary critics, including the editors of the *Partisan Review*. In his review, Howe compared Solzhenitsyn with Lukács to stress the first's courage and moral superiority. Howe concluded that Lukács had "chosen the role of the (at times) semi-dissident communist, but never an openly oppositionist communist, and certainly not a public opponent of the party-state dictatorship." Lukács, however, mostly expressed appreciation for Solzhenitsyn's literary style. To account for this discordance, Howe argued that the praise was just the psychological transference of Lukács's admiration for Solzhenitsyn as an implicit admission of his own moral inferiority: "At a number of points Lukács writes with approval of Solzhenitsyn's independence and courage. . . . A man as intelligent as Lukács could hardly have been unaware that he kept praising Solzhenitsyn for precisely the virtue he himself had rarely shown."[38]

We could question to what extent Howe's admiration for Solzhenitsyn's courage—a courage he deems "overwhelming"—might also be a psychological transference or a pretext for expressing his contempt for Lukacs.[39] He saw Lukács as the "semi-dissident" who not only would never become a dissident, but more importantly, would never renounce Marxism. In his endorsement of Solzhenitsyn's political and literary stance, Howe associates Lukács's Marxist aesthetic with cowardice and Solzhenitsyn's bourgeois realism with courage. The association is rather arbitrary and based on a positive assessment of Solzhenitsyn's literary achievements that can be debated but was then widely shared. Walter Kaufman said of that time, "In the early fifties Sartre and many others in France were arguing about two seemingly unrelated questions; whether it was permissible to admit that there were two camps in the Soviet Union, and whether the novel was dead. At one blow, Solzhenitsyn made these debates ridiculous."[40] This link between moral virtue and literary value went a long way toward building Solzhenitsyn's reputation in America. The equation also illustrates the conjoined work of the moral and stylistic dimensions of Solzhenitsyn's stranger persona. American critics who admired his literary style, a blend of nineteenth-century realism and journalistic reportage also became impressed with the moral stature of the writer. Or perhaps the reverse was true?

It is no surprise that in the United States, Solzhenitsyn excited especially conservative anticommunists. He fueled their "drive to revitalize the American spirit through a crusade for Russian freedom."[41] Yet his own vein of conservatism, as one American literary scholar astutely noticed, was different:

Solzhenitsyn's conservatism, like his moral stature, emerges from the experience of the Gulag. Ours, however, resembles more a failure of nerve. In our need for a moral hero who personifies and hallows a direction we seem anyway to be taking, we tend to overlook the authoritarianism of his stance, the degree to which it is in fact a response to Gulag and therefore in some sense still a part of Gulag. And while there is much appeal (even to non-Christians) in the Christian doctrine of redemption through suffering, the national form to which Solzhenitsyn seems ineluctably to attach that redemption certainly gives pause to a "rootless cosmopolitan" like myself.[42]

Although not all of them were "rootless cosmopolitans," American critics were irked by his brand of foreignness, which put them off not even as Americans but as intellectuals. Solzhenitsyn's often and emphatically expressed national allegiance to Russia not only stressed that he was not European and not American but also not an intellectual. His Slavophilism invoked the image of a cross-wearing, austere, somewhat grim, peasant. The austerity of his lifestyle in the Soviet Union was known to Western reporters who had been in contact with him and with his friends prior to his deportation. Solzhenitsyn liked to dress, eat, and act like a simple man. In his bedroom he kept a peasant pitchfork as a weapon he could use to defend himself against a possible intrusion from KGB agents.[43] For a Russian intellectual, this peasant persona was not uncommon or new. The Russian intelligentsia had had a long history of vacillating between a European identity and a non-European one, predicated upon inherently Slavic ideals and values such as unity and harmony in contradistinction to Western values such as individualism and competition. The proponents of a distinctly non-Western Russian identity included famous writers such as Dostoyevsky, but they remained, historically, a minority.[44]

To many Americans, the sullen, peasant-looking Solzhenitsyn was largely an enigma. His American residence in Cavendish, Vermont, magnified his mystique. Much was made about the 400-acre estate upon which Solzhenitsyn built his house, which included a small wooden Russian Orthodox chapel and was surrounded by an eight-foot high barbed wire fence with an electronically monitored entrance. The remoteness of the area, enshrined in an air of secrecy, with its harsh winters and bucolic landscape all seemed to create a Russian more than American setting. Even when he decided to settle in the United States, he did not adopt the culture, and when he returned to Russia after the collapse of the USSR, he seemed more concerned with saying goodbye to the surroundings rather than to his neighbors.[45]

About Solzhenitsyn's daily existence in Cavendish, Scammel writes that it had been "organized with a view to getting the maximum amount of work done, but also in such a way that they [were] ready to abandon everything and return to Russia at a moment's notice."[46] In 1976, Bernard Pivot, host of the French talk television show *Apostrophes* (and later the famous *Bouillon de culture*), visited Solzhenitsyn in Vermont. In his account that was translated and published in the *Boston Globe*, Pivot offered a simple, functional image, a "house built around a writer's literary project." But each time Pivot waxes poetic about the estate and its owner, he falls upon a Russian stock imagery, such as the tall birch, Solzhenitsyn's favorite tree, or the "small, pretty chapel filled with bright light at sunrise."[47] Pivot presents this conventional, rather inescapable Russianness of Solzhenitsyn as a mark of distinction systematically linked to his moral mission in exile: to chronicle the experiences of those who remained in the Gulag and make them known to the entire world, including people in the Soviet Union. In the America political arena, Solzhenitsyn could never escape his Russianness and did not even want to escape it. His Russianness was also cultivated by those around him at a time when being Russian was inextricably connected with the Cold War mythology of spies, adventurous escapes across barbed wire borders, and awe-inspiring achievements. The 1970s was the heyday of East European dissidents becoming visible in the West, among them famous writers, artists, and scientists from the Soviet Union: Andrei Sakharov, Oleg Bukovski, and Mihail Orlov. By some accounts, "magnified by the spotlight of superpower relations, their dramatic struggle against persecution frequently eclipsed the official rituals of détente."[48] The dissident persona of the opponent of the Soviet Union produced less sensation in America than in Europe, probably because Americans, accustomed to democratic regimes with no significant history of violently stifling criticism, had no corresponding tradition of, or respect for, dissidence as the practice of solitary, heroic individuals. Civil disobedience was the closest equivalent, but, while still in the process of emerging as a political process, it was also more centered on groups than individual agents.

What fired up Americans' imagination more than the persona of the dissident was that of an escapee from the mysterious world behind the Iron Curtain. Developed steadily over several decades from early news stories to Hollywood movies, memoirs, and novels depicting heroic flights from Eastern Europe, and featuring individuals willing to risk their lives rather than live under communism, the escapee emerged as a key entry in the Cold War cast of characters. As double survivor—of the tyranny left behind and of the dangerous trip to the free world, the escapee "anchored rhetorical figurations of a world rend between 'slave' and 'free,' making a metaphorical 'curtain' meaningful."[49]

Solzhenitsyn was not the traditional escapee because he had not freely chosen to leave the Soviet Union. But he had risked his life while in the Soviet Union, and his trip to the West was an adventure on its own terms, at least as it had been presented by Western media to their audiences.[50] Regardless how circumspect and sullen Solzhenitsyn appeared to the excited Western reporters at the Bonn airport, the man they greeted had escaped from behind the Iron Curtain. He and others like him who made the news in the United States were "assigned the task of advertising the desirability of United States citizenship."[51] Judging by his criticism of America, Solzhenitsyn was not the best candidate for such task. Against popular representations of the East European relieved to be finally in the free world, he performed the role of a reluctant sojourner. He was a survivor indeed but one who did not think his ordeal over and who was unwilling to celebrate the arrival and its location.

THE STRANGER TURNED PROPHET

Regardless of how Solzhenitsyn negotiated between the personae of a Russian dissident and that of escapee, he came to the United States as a survivor and a witness of the horrors committed by a totalitarian regime. This persona played the most significant part in his American reception because it spoke to a sense of wonder about life behind the Iron Curtain, which combined curiosity with fear and skepticism with anxiety. As witness and survivor, Solzhenitsyn's persona had symbolic value. In his writing, he claimed not to be seeking originality but to tell the story of people who could not do so themselves. He was not one of a kind, but one of many—a stance he strove to maintain throughout his interventions in the West, starting with the Nobel Prize acceptance speech in which he spoke on behalf of all of the writers who could not be present at the ceremony. This sense of representativeness is strongly present in Solzhenitsyn's literary work, especially in *The Gulag Archipelago*, which spoke, through design and form, with a collective voice, that of the many victims of Soviet communism. Yet his self-effacement may have been a bit disingenuous because his emphasis on the collective experience functions alongside a strong emphasis on Solzhenitsyn's own story. *The Gulag Archipelago* illustrates this paradox early on when the author warns: "This is not going to be a volume of memoirs about my own life. Therefore I am not going to recount the truly amusing details of my arrest, which was like no other."[52] What followed, however, was a detailed recounting of his unique story.

This coexistence of an individual's personal story and the story of many others, which presumably does not allow one to be more important than the others, marks the paradox of the survivor-witness. As a survivor, he is stronger than the others, but as a witness his task is to attest to the experience of the others precisely because they could not. In the United States, the response to Solzhenitsyn's survivor-witness persona was inflected by the publication of Holocaust survivors' memoirs. In their case, the paradox of witnessing was defined by the nature of the atrocities they had experienced. As Kelly Oliver points out, the witnesses' knowledge is both privileged and unreliable, insofar as witnesses of extreme experiences are in an unique, difficult position, both enriched by what they alone have seen and impoverished in their very humanity by the devastating experience in question. The paradox, then, comes down to the fact that, "to bear witness to their dehumanization is to repeat it by telling the world that they were reduced to worthless objects."[53]

The Gulag prisoners featured in Solzhenitsyn's book had been similarly subjected to dehumanizing experiences—humiliated, tortured, and stripped off of dignity and agency. Against that backdrop, Solzhenitsyn introduced elements of heroism throughout the book but heroism through elementary acts of resistance and defiance (such as refusing to squat and defecate at the order of a guard). In his stories, the protagonists retain their humanity because Solzhenitsyn systematically depicts them asserting their control over situations, no matter how trivial these situations were. Solzhenitsyn, then, performed an important moral task because "only by testifying, by witnessing objectification, can [survivors] reinscribe their subjectivity into situations that mutilated it to the point of annihilation."[54]

This was Solzhenitsyn's declared goal in collecting the stories of Gulag survivors and presenting them in his *Gulag Archipelago*. However, the American editors of *Ivan Denisovich* emphasized that, unlike Holocaust survivors who were tortured at the hands of a state that explicitly set out to annihilate them, those who escaped the Gulag were the isolated victims of a state acting on behalf of the people. Regardless of the amount of suffering endured by actual individuals, so long as Gulag prisoners were seen as individual cases of dissidence and disobedience, and not as generic exemplars in a politics of terror, Solzhenitsyn's stranger persona could not be symbolically effective. It was important for the success of his rhetoric of witnessing and survival that these citizens not be perceived primarily as political prisoners but mainly as people whose human rights had been violated. As political prisoners, the Gulag survivors were locked into a dynamic that legitimized violence as a means for authorizing and maintaining a state that was implementing the consensus of the population it represented. Regimes such as the Soviet communist one enjoyed the so-called revolutionary privilege, which made it seem acceptable to use violence for the purposes of social improvement. The acceptability of violence was grounded in the political discourse of the French Revolution: "The revolution is the war of liberty against its enemies . . . under the revolutionary regime the public authority is itself obliged to defend itself against all the factions which attack it. A revolutionary government owes good citizens all the protection of the nation; it owes enemies of the people only death."[55]

The French Revolution and the Russian Revolution are parallel in many ways, but the use of terror *as legitimate* is the most significant connection. The revolutionary experience came to be defined by a legitimation of terror exercised against those perceived as obstacles to social reform. Revolutionary privilege was at the center of Western support for communism as illustrated by Roger Baldwin, founder of the American Civil Liberties Union, in his chronicle of his 1927 trip to the Soviet Union: "Repressions in western democracies are violations of professed constitutional liberties, and I condemn them as such. Repressions in Soviet Russia are weapons of struggle in a transition period to socialism."[56]

The Moscow show trials struck the first blow to the revolutionary privilege, marking the beginning of concerns vis-à-vis the ferocity of Soviet violence. Yet some Western supporters remained firmly in favor of using any means necessary to maintain the Soviet order. Notably, French existential philosopher Maurice Merleau-Ponty argued that violence should only be condemned if it was not "authentic": genuinely subsumed to promoting the cause of communism and not the leadership's personal gains. This distinction between authentic (good) violence and illegitimate violence came to differentiate Leninism from Stalin's dictatorship. Still, Western supporters of communism and of the Soviet Union, such as Merleau-Ponty and Sartre in France or Dwight McDonald and Michael Harrington in the United States, remained reluctant to indict the Soviet Union—even less so communism—for its violent repressions.

Therefore, Solzhenitsyn's challenge in depicting the experience of forced labor camps was to present the prisoners as something other than enemies that needed to be crushed or than sacrificial victims. Instead, he insisted on their individuality and humanity by stressing the inhumanity of the regime that was persecuting them. This strategy was embedded in a more general approach, which involved questioning the distinction between Leninism and Stalinism—the first marking the positive pole, the second the negative one—and issuing a blanket accusation against the ideology at the center of the Soviet Union: communism. In his *Letters to Soviet Leaders*, as well as in his novels, he repeatedly argued for the necessity of repudiating Marxism.[57] Moreover, he emphasized the non-Russian origin of Marxism, calling it a "whirlwind from the West."[58]

Solzhenitsyn's portrayal of violence in the Gulag was especially compelling in the West as the political origin of the Gulag was linked to totalitarianism. Western scholars also linked the punitive system at the core of the Gulag to modernity writ large. In 1975 Michel Foucault published *Discipline and Punish*, in which he employed the metaphor of a carceral archipelago. In a 1976 interview, Foucault acknowledged the influence of Solzhenitsyn on his theory of power.[59] He also insisted that the conceptual foundation of the Gulag was neither Russian nor of Soviet origin but an import from the bourgeois nineteenth-century Western world. Thus, Foucault lent credence to Solzhenitsyn's claims that the human rights abuses taking place in the Soviet Union were the consequence of an originally Western ideology.

While Western scholars recognized the transnational dimension of totalitarianism and linked it to the emergence of a new form of power in modernity, Solzhenitsyn brought the conversation to a more concrete level and challenged the revolutionary privilege that had been used to justify the Soviet Union's uses of power. He insisted that violence is the annihilation of a person's agency and focused on the victim of revolutionary violence as a human being, rather than as a citizen of a particular state. Against the backdrop of an emerging human rights discourse—which was used increasingly more often by U.S. government officials to indict the Soviet Union—this approach was not only effective, but also conducive to a de-nationalization of the conflict.[60] The Cold War, as depicted by Solzhenitsyn, was no longer between nation-states (the United States against the Soviet Union) but between ideological and moral systems. This shift marked a new strategic phase in the Cold War, making the conflict more abstract than in earlier decades.

In the Harvard address, Solzhenitsyn invoked this abstract moral and ideological conflict but asked for a concrete confrontation between nation-states. If it avoided the confrontation, America would be the main culprit in the détente debacle, not only because the Soviet Union would win the war but because evil itself would prevail. Even at their vaguest, his accusations had a clear target: American citizens and their political complacency that had led to a softening of anti-Soviet policy and a betrayal of humanity.

THE PROPHET AT HARVARD

Solzhenitsyn delivered his Harvard commencement address through an interpreter on a rainy June day in front of a large audience that acted sympathetically throughout and in the end gave a standing ovation.[61] The overall reception far exceeded the immediate circumstances as the speech was broadcast live by CBS and reached an estimated 20,000 listeners. The genre of the commencement address falls squarely into the category of epideictic rhetoric, or ceremonial discourse. As such, certain conventions are expected—many of which Solzhenitsyn emphatically violated. Instead of a congratulatory, optimistic message, he offered a vehement criticism of Western society generally, illustrating his points with only American examples interspersed with ominous prophesies about an impending end of the humanity as long as the spread of communism continued. The speech was not only anti-détente but also struck some commentators as anti-Western and anti-American.

Despite the shockwaves sent by the Harvard address in the American media, the ideas presented in it had already been introduced to American audiences by Solzhenitsyn on previous occasions. In June and July 1975, in Washington, D.C., and New York City, at the invitation of the AFL-CIO, he spoke to audiences of labor union organizers, each time excoriating the Western nations for not intervening more forcefully against the Soviet Union. In 1976, he was invited to deliver a speech at the Hoover Institution at Stanford University upon being awarded the American Friendship Medal from the Freedom Foundation of the Valley Forge, Pennsylvania. Not only were the ideas presented in this speech identical to those included in the Harvard commencement address but so was the anti-Western rhetoric.[62] At Harvard, Solzhenitsyn's rhetoric was more restrained, and the figures and techniques less overstated than on some previous occasions. The message, however, harped on the same issues he had tackled in the past: the West is in a state of moral decay that makes its people unable to face courageously the imminent international danger posed by communism. Among the causes of the fall of the Western world, he listed the lack of spirituality, which he sometimes identified explicitly as secularism and at other times defined in broader terms such as the humanistic worldview that situates human beings in the center of the universe and does not recognize any superior force or entity. He posited that the West is morally and spiritually defunct. He bemoaned the West's obsession with happiness as shallow, materially derived satisfaction; the faddishness of Western intellectuals; the unlimited power and control exercised by the press in society; and the overall cowardice of Western societies. He concluded that Western civilization was not a viable model for humanity.

The speech consistently targeted the West as an all-encompassing totality. Yet audiences at Harvard and beyond knew beyond any doubt that Solzhenitsyn was speaking about America. After an early, isolated, and vague reference to Europe, the few examples he offered were all about America. His most irritated charge, against the power of the press, applied exclusively to the United States. The master trope of the address is the *totum pro parte* synecdoche, in this case using the whole to designate a part. This form of the device is seen less commonly than the use of the form wherein the part is named to function as the whole (e.g. fifty sail for fifty ships). Therefore, this peculiar use prompts examination. Why did Solzhenitsyn not identify the target of his criticism, the United States, directly? Practical reasons are not convincing. Regardless how applicable the criticism might have been to other countries (France paramount among them), a complete generalization was not possible. Nor can one hypothesize with any certainty that Solzhenitsyn was trying to avoid lodging direct insult for he had already made painfully explicit anti-American comments in public before.

Synecdoche is an apt trope for a prophetic vision for it reveals an omniscient mind that can penetrate straight to the core of a phenomenon, leaving aside incidental or marginal aspects. In his work on master tropes, Kenneth Burke finds a synecdochic pattern "in all theories of political representation, where some part of the social body . . . is held to be 'representative' of the society of the whole."[63] By employing the synecdoche that equates the West with America, Solzhenitsyn implicitly identified one country as representative of the entire civilization. This move has important consequences.

For one thing, it challenges the exceptional status of American culture and society. For another, the argument largely shifts to one country the responsibility that would normally befall several, indeed the entire Western civilization. Such a shift would have been meaningless unless accompanied by another move, also implicit in the logic of the synecdoche: the United States is seen as the best exemplar, indeed the model, of the Western world. The argument by model implies that the authority of the model is such as to constitute a guarantee. Solzhenitsyn, in other words, assumed that America would be recognized as the model for the entire Western world.

As I already mentioned, by 1976 America's ability to look like a model to the rest of the world was starting to come into question. The synecdochic logic of Solzhenitsyn's argument enforced the idea of a United States as dominating and representing the Western democratic world as leader of the free nations and main participant in the Cold War against the Soviet Union. The synecdoche created an iconic representation of a mythical America, carrier of all Western values, and thus responsible for its faith. The deemphasizing of American exceptionalism was replaced by a strong emphasis on America's hegemonic status. The synecdoche tapped into the rhetorical power of an "American mythology"—a distinct product of home-grown political rhetoric in Cold War America, "a mythical America whose business is the defense of freedom, . . . the last hope for the survival of peace and freedom in the world . . . a nation of destiny."[64]

Solzhenitsyn's arguments in the Harvard speech were original in that they offered an *indirect* exercise in American mythology, by contrasting and by chastising, not by praising. His complaint that America was not playing out its greatness becomes an implicit urging, and the criticism was as much a call to action as it was a reproach. Solzhenitsyn's explanation for America's decline contained a prescribed course for change and an implicit expression of faith in America's willingness and ability to change. Solzhenitsyn was no Oswald Spengler despite the suggestion made in his title. The moral decay he diagnosed in the West/America was not, for him, the inevitable end of a civilization but instead the consequence, both avoidable and correctable, of a Western worldview that had led to a loss of moral virtues and to ineffective institutions.

The synecdoche of America as the model for the entire West articulated this representation of a decayed society through strategies of defamiliarization used to shame Americans by showing to them how much the West and their own country have become like the evil communist monolith. The defamiliarization works through the way in which Solzhenitsyn interpreted the values and ideas at the very foundation of Western and American thought. He found the cause for the moral decay in the "humanistic consciousness," which originated, by his account, in the European Renaissance and found its full "political expression" during the Enlightenment. The humanistic consciousness is a source of much evil, in his view, precisely because it "did not admit the existence of intrinsic evil in man." Thus, it "started modern Western civilization on the dangerous trend of worshipping man and his material needs." The humanistic consciousness "proclaimed and practiced autonomy of man from any higher force above him."[65]

Solzhenitsyn made an important amendment to his indictment of the "humanistic consciousness": he stressed that it did not capture the original American spirit. American democracy, he claimed, was designed on the assumption that human beings are God's creatures. In his view, "two hundred or even fifty years ago, it would have seemed quite impossible, in America, that an individual be granted boundless freedom with no purpose, simply for the satisfaction of his whims. Subsequently, however, all such limitations were eroded everywhere in the West."[66]

The erosion, one assumes further, eventually also took place in America. Solzhenitsyn acknowledged his audience's exceptional character only to point out that this exceptionalism was fading away. This was more than a concession or a strategy for allowing hope in an argument with otherwise rather apocalyptic overtones. The difference he pointed out capitalizes on the logic of the jeremiad: once America abandoned its exceptional destiny and simply became more like any Western nation, it also became morally corrupt. The original "superiority" of America was obtained by breaking off with the West and dominating it both from within and without.

The most powerful use of defamiliarization in the Harvard address was to present the United States in its current state as displaying the same features as the Soviet Union, only even worse. He accused the Communist

Party and its leaders of frequent violations of the law, and, on this basis, he asserted that Soviet society was lawless. Then he charged that American society respected the law, but was far too dependent on it, and thus legalistic. To him, "legalism" is a worse fault because it marks the disappearance of a moral universe in which individuals can experience guilt and responsibility. Solzhenitsyn maintained that, instead of expecting a judge to decide whether a wrong has been committed, people should have their own moral consciousness to rely on in order to decide what is right. Solzhenitsyn believed that the legalism of Western and American society was evinced by a lack of moral values. In this society, legal sentences were pronounced to compensate for the lack of moral judgment. Solzhenitsyn held that legalism is not only morally vacuous but also politically unproductive: "after a certain level of the problem has been reached, legalistic thinking induces paralysis; it prevents one from seeing the scale and the meaning of events." This is the main reason "the West has great difficulty in finding its bearings amid contemporary events." Without a moral consciousness that knows good from evil, no apt political decisions can be made, Solzhenitsyn insisted ominously—the allusion to the misguided (in his view) policies of the détente all too transparent. The "soulless and smooth plane of legalism" is, for him, equally condemnable as the "abyss of lawlessness." Legalism appears just as bad, if not worse, than lawlessness because both represent a form of dehumanization: "I have spent all my life under a communist regime and I will tell you that a society without any objective legal scale is a terrible one indeed. But a society with no other scale but the legal one is also less than worthy of man. A society based on the letter of the law and never reaching any higher fails to take advantage of the full range of human possibilities."[67]

Solzhenitsyn was also very critical of the role played by the press in America. Soviet journalists were powerful because they were political potentates appointed by the state. He was outraged to discover that in the United States the press had just as much power by simply being able to control public opinion and that it had thus become "the greatest power within the Western countries." While Solzhenitsyn could have criticized, as others have done, the power acquired by media conglomerates in the United

States, he attacked it as reflecting a political phenomenon that is at the center of a totalitarian society. Feigning surprise, as "someone coming from the totalitarian East with is rigorously unified press," he expressed outrage upon discovering "a common trend of preferences within the Western press as a whole . . . generally accepted patterns of judgment, the sum effect being not competition but unification."[68]

Solzhenitsyn knew that his audience would not disagree with him about the lawlessness of the Soviet regime or its abuse of power in the press, but he was asking them to accept that similar phenomena exist in the United States. The opposition between lawful/lawless and legitimate/illegitimate (applied to the power of the press) is respun into an opposition between legal/legalistic, legitimate/illegitimate. The recurrence often ends up creating an overarching category, that of morality, which transcends, in Solzhenitsyn's view, the law, the state, or the media, and works in opposition to something else: communism. A country without a strong, well-defined, and well-functioning morality is doomed to become communist. Through his stranger eyes, America looked as communist (or at least on its way to becoming as communist) as Soviet Russia.

In Solzhenitsyn's depiction, America and the West were exclusively secular societies controlled by the press and corporate conglomerates and ruled by a technical legal system rather than shared moral precepts. By ignoring the presence of a strong religiously minded political and intellectual elite in the United States, the Harvard address tries to create a coherent sketch— and inevitably only a sketch—of American society, iconically defined by secularism, legalism, and materialism. Such a depiction is important in the logic of the argument because the features on which it rests also apply to a communist society. Throughout the speech, Solzhenitsyn alluded to this similarity often, finally bluntly stating: "This is the essence of the crisis: the split in the world is less terrifying than the similarity of the disease afflicting its main sections."[69]

Solzhenitsyn talked to his audience about an America that was the very epitome of the West yet he used strategies that enabled him to describe it as increasingly resembling the communist East. If the synecdoche of the West as America served as a strategy for invoking the American mythology of a chosen nation, his specific examples brought to life a people in decline. Through radical reversals of hierarchies of values, such as law-abiding turned into legalistic, or humanist into materialist, he located the cause of the "fall" before he could introduce a solution. The prophet could thus scold his covenant audience for straying away from their mission, which was to create a democratic society, and veering instead toward a totalitarian one. The claim and the reproach, put so bluntly, sounded absurd and dystopian in a Cold War context. They were likely to render a phrase like "a communist America" oxymoronic, both ideologically and historically. Of course, the specter of a communist America was not unheard of in this period, but Solzhenitsyn spoke in messianic terms and employed eschatological imagery. Even when willing to tone down his rhetoric for his young audience of Harvard graduates, he still sounded threatening: "If the world has not approached its end, it has reached a major watershed in history, equal in importance to the turn from the Middle Ages to the Renaissance." To rise to such ominous occasion, Solzhenitsyn demanded from his audience "a spiritual blaze . . . a new height of vision . . . a new level of life."[70]

Critics detected in this rhetoric of renewal and purification through fire echoes of the early Cold War militaristic rhetoric. Solzhenitsyn's images of renewal and transformation were suffused with their own revolutionary pathos, which was designed to replace the revolutionary privilege of communism. Was he merely proposing a change of regime in the Soviet Union? If so, by what means? In the context of détente arguments, images of rupture and fire suggested war, and for that reason could seem repellant. Indeed, those most critical of the speech repeatedly condemned his "crusade," admonishing against the implications of his arguments for intensifying the Cold War and encouraging open hostilities between the United States and the Soviet Union.

On the other hand, the genre of the jeremiad requires the construction of an image of impending disaster, making change appear imperative as a last chance granted to a "people on probation."[71] Against the meliorist pro-détente arguments, Solzhenitsyn offered the vision of an apocalypse that could be avoided only through violent transformation of the status quo. Although he did not explicitly invoke concrete violent acts, the symbolic violence of his rhetoric showed the wrath of a prophet scolding his sinful audience. Yet his angry rhetoric conflicted with the jeremiad's expectation of upcoming hope and relief, both of which he underplayed. Historically, the jeremiad has been an apt political intervention when its audience experienced some form of suffering or disaffection that could be described as punishment for their sin. Indeed, the social fragmentation and sociopolitical tensions this created in the years leading up to and during détente can hardly be overstated. Without an external enemy to use as a scapegoat,

> many Americans came to regard groups of fellow countrymen as enemies with whom they were engaged in a struggle for the nation's very soul. Whites versus blacks, liberals versus conservatives (as well as liberals versus radicals), young versus old, men versus women, hawks versus doves, rich versus poor, taxpayers versus welfare recipients, the religious versus the secular, the hip versus the straight, the gay versus the straight—everywhere one looked, new battalions took the field, in a spirit ranging from that of redemptive sacrifice to vengeful defiance.[72]

If America's sin was its failure to act as the great chosen nation it was (and thus fight against the communist monolith), then the punishment apparently was the national identity crisis that was consuming them. As a stranger, Solzhenitsyn could take on the prophet persona because he neither shared the sins of his audience nor feared their punishment. As a survivor and witness of extreme suffering, which rendered him wiser and more experienced than anyone else, he was justified in judging the West, Americans, and, indeed, human nature. James Darsey states that, in a jeremiad, the prophetic role is successfully enacted once the audience recognizes the speaker's "ultimate sacrifice of self to duty or commitment" and requires "willingness to suffer [as] the most compelling evidence of the abandonment of the self."[73] Even the critics readily authorized Solzhenitsyn's prophetic persona. Most of them acknowledged that at Harvard he "spoke with the authority of a man inspired, and with the even greater authority of a man of supreme intellectual and moral courage."[74] His "truly heroic figure" was undeniable because he had been shaped by "the intense moral experience of the gulag."[75] Michael Novak, a religious commentator, spoke for many when he claimed, "out of the long grayness of his own despair, out of the years in which surrender must have seemed attractive and hopelessness realistic, Solzhenitsyn was saved by faith in the power of simple truth."[76]

In addressing his American audience as a nation that had lost its bearings, Solzhenitsyn was probing an open wound. The success of the speech cannot be measured only by its immediate approbation, though even that was significant, but more by its subsequent impact. Insofar as it succeeded in connecting a domestic sense of disorientation to an international crisis, the speech played a key role in legitimizing interventionist political discourses that were pleading for American involvement in non-American conflicts. In an article published in *Foreign Affairs* two years later, Solzhenitsyn expressed satisfaction with the general reception of his speech. "The Harvard speech rewarded me with an outpouring of favorable responses from the American public at large (some of these found their way into newspapers). For that reason I was not perturbed by the outburst of reproaches which an angry press rained down upon me."[77]

However, responses published in the press in the aftermath of the speech tell a different story about its success. If a significant part of Solzhenitsyn's audience and the most audible rejected the message of his jeremiad, it was less because they disagreed with his depiction of the West/America and more because it came from a source they deemed to be unauthorized: a foreigner. In the *Washington Post* editorial published the day after the speech, Solzhenitsyn's views are described as "very Russian," arising from "particular religious and political strains *remote* from modern Western experience," which makes him into "an unreliable witness."[78] The *National Review*, one of the publications that endorsed some of Solzhenitsyn's comments, blamed the negative reception on misunderstandings produced by the fact that the speech had not been accurately translated. By drawing attention to the speech as a *translation*, the editors foregrounded the foreignness of the author. No surprise, then, that the article also maintained that, insofar as Solzhenitsyn was right, his arguments were already available to American audiences from American authors: "At his best, he can say with Walt Whitman, 'I am a man, I suffered, I was there.'"[79]

A common strategy employed by critics was to accept Solzhenitsyn's arguments but only insofar as they were comparable or even confirmed by the views of American or Western thinkers, especially when such thinkers had already made some of the same arguments. James Reston, a columnist for the *New York Times*, accepted some of Solzhenitsyn's points as "good questions" but was quick to point out that such questions had been asked and answered better by Archibald MacLeish and Oswald Spengler.[80] George Will, then a syndicated columnist with the Washington Post Writers Group, placed Solzhenitsyn in a "submerged but continuous tradition" that included Henry Adams, Irving Babbitt, Paul Elmer More, Peter Viereck, and Alexis de Tocqueville.[81] Critics on both sides of the debate all explicitly identified Solzhenitsyn as not American, which hardly needed to be pointed out. Solzhenitsyn himself reinforced that image, describing himself as an exile in the West to the Western audience he was about to criticize. He invited them to listen to him "as a friend" rather than "enemy." In response, a *Washington Star* editorial on June 11 hailed him as "the great Russian prophet in our midst," thus acknowledging his presence, that of the exiled dissident, only by way of signaling an absence—that of the citizen's right to make criticism of his community.[82] Olga Andreyev Carlisle, another exile but also a naturalized citizen, writing for *Newsweek*, informed American readers that Solzhenitsyn's "soul is still Russian" and at Harvard "he was really speaking to the Soviet leaders and to the Russian people."[83] Similarly focused on Solzhenitsyn's commitment to Russia was Mary McGrory, writing for the *Washington Star*, who argued that the Harvard address should be seen as "the personal statement of a conservative, religious, and terribly homesick Russian."[84] Perhaps most emphatic to claim the unreliability of an exile's assessment was MacLeish, who insisted, "Solzhenitsyn . . . knows little of our American lives or of ourselves. . . . He sees few Americans, speaks little English, and what he knows of the Republic he knows not from human witnesses but from television programs, which present their depressing parody of American life to him as they present it also to us but with this difference—that we know the parody for what it is."[85]

Whether MacLeish was right about Solzhenitsyn's knowledge of American society remains debatable.[86] To even distinguish between Solzhenitsyn's direct experience of American life versus indirect knowledge from external sources assumes that community membership, which living among Americans would have afforded Solzhenitsyn, is a precondition for speaking authoritatively about the affairs of that community. As a nonmember, he could not be taken seriously, regardless of how similar his criticisms were to charges issued by actual members.

From prophet to fool, Solzhenitsyn's fall in the eyes of American audiences was accompanied by an increased emphasis on his foreignness. Commenting on the Harvard address in 1980, after the immediate heated echoes had died out, Hook wrote, "Solzhenitsyn speaks in a foreign tongue," and stressed Solzhenitsyn's lack of intelligibility by adding, "[he] uses expressions that remain opaque in translation."[87] What the foreigner missed was America's greatness. As critics suggested which aspects of American society Solzhenitsyn misunderstood, they recreated the synecdochic image of a chosen nation that best represents the Western world and thus the one that carries responsibility for the West's future. In defending their country, the respondents accepted the terms of the assessment as established by Solzhenitsyn. In other words, they did not offer their own version of America or the West but changed the evaluation of the image proposed by Solzhenitsyn. This contrast between evaluations rather than depictions is illustrated by the *New York Times* article:

Where Mr. Solzhenitsyn sees only softness and indecision in this country, we see more—tolerance of many ideas, humility before the ultimate truths, a recognition of the responsibilities imposed by own awful power. . . . Perhaps now that he (Solzhenitsyn) is settled in America, he may come to learn that at least some of this nation's apparent weaknesses are precious and abiding strengths.[88]

Requiring that someone live in America to understand it or to have a positive evaluation of it dooms the stranger to inevitable misunderstanding. At the same time, this reasoning allows an important modification of the strategy used by Solzhenitsyn: the difference between being inside or outside America is converted into a difference between being on the side of the mighty or the weak.

To defend America against the accusations made by Solzhenitsyn was especially important to those smarting from the sting of a particular charge: America is not a model for the victims of communism in the Soviet Union. Solzhenitsyn had used the charge to increase the weight of his criticism. The implication of such a claim, which is that the United States is just as bad as a totalitarian society, echoed his claims about the Western origin of communism. To his critics, such a put-down was a de-mythologizing blow that prompted especially irritated protests. The sarcasm in the *Washington Star*'s version of the rebuttal is especially telling because it allowed the author to turn the criticism on its head:

> The West, says Mr. Solzhenitsyn, is not today an appealing model for the spiritual rebirth of the totalitarian nations. To which the right answer is: *Of course it isn't—and can't be.* Those who are regimented in an evil society and soul-destroying system will not find an alternative model of regimentation by looking west. They will find, however, a system that affords human nature the opportunity to declare itself freely, in all its glory and its sordidness.[89]

Challenging an approach that presumes any one nation can serve as a model for all others, the *Washington Star* editors dismissed Solzhenitsyn's accusations as reflecting a "regimented" mind only to reestablish the image of a model America. In other words, they took at face value and reclaimed the "model" status. James Reston, writing for the *New York Times* on June 11, 1978, reinforced America's model-status by reminding readers that Solzhenitsyn even being allowed to criticize America is a measure of American's superiority: "at least he was allowed to say all these things. On commencement day at Moscow University, if they have one, the 'spiritual superiority' of the Soviet Union probably wouldn't have allowed it."[90] Similarly seeing perhaps more the escapee than the exile in Solzhenitsyn,

MacLeish accused Solzhenitsyn of not understanding that the value Americans place on freedom is the defining feature of America as well as the measure of its greatness:

> if he could talk to us, he would realize that we put our freedom first before our responsibility because we are a free people—because a free people is a people that rules itself—because it must decide for itself what its responsibilities are—because there is no one else to decide this for us—neither the state police nor a state church not anyone. . . . [H]e would have learned that we have not lost our will as a people—that it is precisely our will as a people which makes us true believers in that human spirit for which he means to speak.[91]

By relying on the potential appeal of the apparent irony of the situation, Reston simultaneously resorts to a more traditional reading of the United States, defined through freedom of speech, available to anyone, including a critic like Solzhenitsyn, in contrast to its absence in the Soviet Union. By focusing on freedom and self-governance as the defining values of the American nation, MacLeish implicitly created an opposition between America and nation-states ruled by other values (singling out religion in response to Solzhenitsyn's emphasis on the need for religion in a secular West). The Americans envisioned by MacLeish, as mythically "free people," cannot be criticized by Solzhenitsyn because they are exemplary embodiments of the "human spirit." A similar strategy of rebuiliding mythical America appears in Schlesinger's article in which Americans are described as defined by the virtue of humility: "Knowing the crimes committed in the name of a single Truth, Americans prefer to keep their ears open to a multitude of competing lower-case truths. Ours has been a nation of skepticism, experiments, accommodation, self-criticism, piecemeal but constant reform—mixture of traits repugnant to the authoritarian and messianic personality, but perhaps not too bad for all that."[92]

The heaviest hit targets in the Harvard address were the legal system and the press. In their defense, Hook questioned—perhaps for the first and only time—the synecdochic representation of America and its institutions as emblematic for the West:

Solzhenitsyn fails to realize that many of the defects in the current American legal process are not rooted in the democratic system. In democratic countries like England and Canada . . . the law is far less egregiously an ass than in so many of our state and federal jurisdictions. This is even more obvious with respect to the press . . . professional standards of media reporting in England are superior to those in the United States, though even there they leave something to be desired.[93]

Hook's depiction of American institutions as inferior, but inferior to other *Western* institutions is an implicit defense of the West. Employing a moral vocabulary that talks about the "evils of a democracy" alongside medical terms like "cure," Hook not only makes the moral disaster described by Solzhenitsyn seem an exaggeration but also implies that the exaggeration misses an important point: if the West is not a model for the rest of the world through concrete institutions operating at a given moment, it does not mean that its foundations and principles cannot, over time and in perhaps different instantiations, have the value of a model.

Hook's essay gives clearer expression than other responses to an idea that was, nevertheless, central to all of them: the exemplary nature of American democracy and of its main institutions, including the press. Responding to Solzhenitsyn's criticism, American intellectuals were compelled to mount a defense of the country and the civilization they saw as under attack. In so doing, they validated the glorified image of America invoked by Solzhenitsyn himself before he proceeded to lament its decay. As in a sort of didactic reverse psychology, the "great Russian prophet"—as many tagged him—lured American intellectuals into accepting through defensive justification a mythological portrait of America as an emblematic illustration of the West at its best, struggling with its own demons, and, in the end, destined to overcome its challenges and be ready to rescue the rest of humanity. They were prompted to accept this mythology by protesting its contestation by a foreigner as well as by taking for granted the vision of a foreigner.

That Americans both listened to and dismissed Solzhenitsyn captures the paradoxical nature of the stranger persona. He was, in his critics' eyes, both a prophet and an outsider with flawed understanding. In his case, the paradox is explained by the ambivalence of his persona, caught between the transnational pathos of the moral witness and the deeply national, even nationalist image of a Russian peasant. Commentators who had, on different occasions, expressed similar if not harsher criticism of American society now subscribed to a glorification of America that left an important assumption unchallenged: that the United States was responsible for the fate of the entire world. What emerges intact from this confrontation between Solzhenitsyn and his American critics is the Cold War ideograph of America as "world policeman." Solzhenitsyn cannot be credited with the creation of the concept, which emerged from several directions at once, many entirely homegrown. Yet the exchange caused by the Harvard address was profoundly consequential insofar as it brought together, in their joint effort to defend America, conservatives and liberals, enthusiasts and skeptics.

CONCLUSION: ZHIVAGO'S SON AND SOLZHENITSYN'S AMERICAN CHILDREN

Let me return to the observation I made earlier in this chapter: the Knopf editors' instructions to American readers to keep in mind that the author of *Ivan Denisovich* was not as impressive as the author of *Doctor Zhivago*. What exactly were Americans assumed to have liked in Pasternak's novel that they would not also find in Solzhenitsyn? Could it have been the tragic tale of a man caught in the social and political chaos unleashed by the Russian Revolution; the intellectual's disillusionment with the ideals of the Russian Revolution; or simply the tragic love story centered on Yuri, a sensitive idealist in the tradition of the Western-influenced Russian intelligentsia? It may have been all of the above. Most importantly, Pasternak's story assured American audiences that the political ideals of communism were unsustainable and inhuman. The moral of Solzhenitsyn's literary work was exactly the same, albeit more bluntly stated. But while the tragic death of Pasternak's hero reminded American readers that they lived in a world where at least such tragedies do not happen, Solzhenitsyn offered no such assurance. He criticized Americans for their own ills and threatened them with an apocalyptic future.

How, then, could this foreigner play such a key role in American political rhetoric, both liberal and conservative? In the years following Solzhenitsyn's Harvard address, the synecdoche he used turned out to be the lynchpin of the Cold War political representation of the world. Even after the Cold War ended, whether America should police the world's trouble spots has remained a hot topic of debate. The assumption on which the question arises, however, has largely remained unquestioned. Why would a particular nation-state carry responsibility for all the other nation-states (as opposed to a transnational alliance, for instance)? The synecdoche manufactured by Solzhenitsyn offered a convenient, because seemingly benign, substitute for the image of a superior dominating Western civilization, which had clearly lost its currency in the postwar, postcolonial era. Where the West had colonized, the United States was merely trying to help. Yet insofar as the West came to mean the "free world" in Cold War discourse, the United States became the center of the free world. Such identifications enabled by the synecdochic logic offered reassurance in an environment loaded with apocalyptic predictions and suffused with the implicit anxiety.

Solzhenitsyn's synecdochic logic has continued to do its political work. Here is Michael Mandelbaum, a professor of American foreign policy at the Johns Hopkins University School of Advanced International Studies, making "the case for Goliath":

> The biblical Goliath served the Philistines but not the people of Israel. The twenty-first-century United States does both. It is not the lion of the international system, terrorizing and preying on smaller, weaker animals in order to survive itself. It is, rather, the elephant, which supports a wide variety of other creatures—smaller mammals, birds, and insects—by generating nourishment for them as it goes about the business of feeding itself. [94]

Translating Solzhenitsyn's Cold War claims into the morally inflected arguments of the war on terror, Max Boot, a fellow in national securities studies at the Council for Foreign Relations, has confidence in mythological America's moral mission to the point where its imperialism becomes necessary and justified as long as evil exists in the world: "If we want Iraq to avoid becoming a Somalia on steroids, we'd better get used to U.S. troops being deployed there for years, possibly decades, to come. If that raises hackles about American imperialism, so be it. We're going to be called an empire whatever we do. We might as well be a successful empire."[95]

It matters that Alexander Solzhenitsyn, a foreign intellectual, was a key participant in the ideological emergence and rhetorical justification of American imperialism. The responses to Solzhenitsyn's speech reveal that this ideology is more widely shared among American intellectuals than one would suspect and that it crosses political boundaries and comes out as a sui generis form of patriotism, as readiness to subscribe to a national self-image that is indeed so positive (perhaps even narcissistic) that it can easily lead to feelings of universal responsibility.

5

EDWARD SAID AND THE
CLASH OF IDENTITIES

E DWARD SAID, a Christian from West Jerusalem, raised in Cairo, and educated at British and American schools, is not an obvious fit in the panoply of foreign-born intellectuals discussed here. He inherited U.S. citizenship as the son of a Palestinian who had himself become an American citizen in 1930 after serving in the military for the United States during World War I. He first came to the U.S. to attend college, younger than any of the other intellectuals discussed here, and not forced to do so by a repressive state. If Arendt, Marcuse, and Solzhenitsyn were legally foreign as German or Russian nationals (even though the first two were naturalized) and culturally and linguistically foreign as their accent and behavior suggested it, Said appeared American. English was the household language of his bilingual childhood. He spoke it flawlessly and without accent. The adult Said showed in photos or portrayed in written evocations always appears as a strikingly handsome man, tall and impeccably dressed—vintage image for the New England intellectual, whether as the Harvard graduate he was or for the cultural icon Mary McCarthy called "the Yale man."[1] In his writing, he was the champion of those who had been systematically misrepresented by the Western tradition. His taste in books and music was not just that of an educated Western man but indeed almost of a traditionalist with marked preferences for the canonical figures in the pantheon of European high culture. As one critic put it, "much of Said's 'critical consciousness' was deeply 'American,' just as he was himself not just a scholar of American literature and culture but *personally, existentially, and legally American.*"[2]

Yet it is impossible to miss the consistent use of the plural first-person pronoun in his political commentary on the Palestinian effort at self-determination. There, Said spoke as a Palestinian. Moreover, he spoke in a political and intellectual climate defined by the "clash regime" that had been in the making since the Cold War (now with a different cast of characters), and that made it seem impossible that the same person could be Western *and* an Arab. The post–Cold War era continued to promote a political ontology centered on conflict. Said was one of the harshest critics of this worldview, which became all the more entrenched in the minds of many Americans after September 11, 2001. One month after the attacks, he criticized in the pages of the *Nation* Samuel P. Huntington's famous thesis of the clash of civilizations, trying to convince American readers of how disturbing and simplistic it was to make " 'civilizations' and 'identities' into what they are not: shut-down, sealed off entities that have been purged of the myriad currents and countercurrents that animate human history."[3]

Said's stranger persona was a product of multiple, even ambivalent, self-identifications as an intellectual, an exile, and a Palestinian. His reputation as author of *Orientalism*, key founder of postcolonialism, and professor at Columbia University was impressive enough but still not what made Tony Judt claim that Said was at the time of his death "the best known intellectual in the world."[4] It was not just the accolades and prestigious positions as chaired professor at Columbia University and president of the Modern Language Association but also the media bashing and hate mail that made him famous. As in Marcuse's case, Said's politics were controversial enough to place him in the attention of a public beyond academic audiences. He held unpopular views on highly sensitive topics, denouncing American imperialism in the Middle East and the Israeli destruction of Palestinians.

How did a comparative literature scholar come to take on such a difficult political mission? What is the relationship between his Palestinian origin and his intellectual production in the making of a stranger persona? I ask these questions because Said was not a Palestinian refugee in the common sense of the term, as Solzhenistyn had been an expelled Russian dissident. Yet toward the end of his career and life, Said identified increasingly as a Palestinian. I analyze the formation of his stranger persona by examining the arc traced from his academic self as exhibited in *Orientalism* and his influential BBC lectures on humanism, on Freud, and on intellectuals; to his journalistic and political self at the time he was a spokesperson for the Palestinian National Council and Yasser Arafat, while also publishing articles on Palestinian self-determination in major cultural media outlets; and finally to the protagonist of his memoir, *Out of Place*, presented as a Palestinian who overcomes adversity, learns from his misfortune, and becomes both intellectually and politically enlightened. The stranger persona that emerges from this trajectory is not the rootless cosmopolitan on a lecture tour, studying in a library, or playing piano in a concert hall or just an Arab struggling to defend the right to exist of a national entity—Palestine—but rather a stranger lamenting the loss of his nation and unwilling to join another one.

The apparent contradiction between his identification with the Palestinian people and the American consciousness his American colleagues especially appreciated in him was crucial to Said's stranger persona. According to Jeffrey Williams, Said was "granted a position to speak for Palestine by virtue of his cosmopolitan, Western persona—by virtue of *not* being an oriental, but a leading Western man of letters and professor."[5] We find a similar perception in the claim that "the principal reason why Said [has] served so effectively in America as a TV pitchman for the Palestinians is that his self-presentation is thoroughly Western; he comes off as the very model of a tolerant, liberal Western academic, his distinguished appearance and civilized manner serving to dispel any notion of Arabs as irrational, zealous, terror-prone."[6]

Said built his stranger persona by establishing that he was a foreigner, ironically enough by comparison to the other three intellectuals I have discussed in this book. Even as a foreigner, he was a "marvel of adjustment," to use a label he applied to his own intellectual heroes, who were exceptional individuals able to gain recognition from their new country while also enriching its cultural and intellectual tradition. At the same time, though, the term "adjustment," which made Said uneasy, might suggest compromise and lack of critical distance, resembling too much the art of "political trimming" he despised, as a strategy of success. Said preferred troublesome, maladjusted exiles, those who "remain outside the mainstream, unaccommodated, unco-opted, resistant" and adopted this stance in his political writing.[7]

In his criticism of U.S. foreign policy in the Middle East, Said spoke as someone who not only disagreed with, but felt removed from, American traditions and practices. Over the years, he wrote increasingly as a Palestinian. His critique had the pathos of an outraged outsider more than of a disappointed insider. In interviews, Said frequently described his interest in the Middle East as an awakening and as being "claimed by" Palestine.[8] Throughout his career, Said's persona gradually shifted from that of the intellectual as critic—a strongly epistemic stance focused on the task of investigating situations—to that of the critic as victim—a strongly emotional stance focused on eliciting compassion for all the other victims on whose behalf it argues.

In 1977, Said became a member of the Palestinian National Council (PNC), the equivalent of a parliament-in-exile for the stateless Palestinians. He began a political career committed to the ideals of moderation, avoidance of factional struggles, and strategic compromise. He rejected armed conflict and did not question the legitimacy of the Israeli state but asked for political recognition for Palestinians in the context of a binational state. This reconciliatory stance was equally ineffective with Arab and Israeli radicals and placed Said between two nationalisms that were not only competing political ideologies but also discourses that mobilized a different pathos of suffering and injustice. Although devotedly pro-Palestinian, Said was not always well liked in Arab countries, especially after his fallout with the PNC. Once seen as an advisor and even friend of Yasser Arafat, Said's strong criticism of the decisions made by Arab leaders at key political junctions, especially the Oslo accords, pushed him, in the eyes of many Arabs, on to the other side of the debate. Said complained that his work was not even known in the Arab world because of a boycott against his ideas.[9]

Said withdrew from the PNC in 1991 in protest over the Oslo accords, and his direct involvement with the Arab leadership gradually dwindled, until it disappeared completely. Yet his political activity continued beyond an official role in regular interventions in public and political discourse both in the United States and abroad, especially in Britain and in Egypt. His political mission, thus redefined, was to engage with what Luc Boltanski calls "the topic of denunciation."[10] His mission was to denounce the role played by the U.S. government in Israeli policies directed against Palestinians, and alongside, the complacency and even collaboration of influential American intellectuals. Beyond this concrete objective, Said's larger goal was denouncing the hypocrisy of Western liberalism and exposing its darker sides: colonialism and imperialism. He pursued this goal through regular interventions in major intellectual media outlets, in interviews, public lectures, keynote addresses, essays, and even in traditional academic papers. This forms a vast corpus that defies a comprehensive presentation or analysis within the confines of one chapter. I focus, therefore, on an intellectual and political course defined by three pivotal moments in his career as marked in *Orientalism*, *The Question of Palestine*, and *Out of Place*, while also drawing on several others, especially those written in the intervening decades.[11] These works are not only significant for Said's career; they also anchor a trajectory from scholar to political actor and from abstract thinking about the problem of representation to making himself into a representative example of Palestinian identity.

Said studied the discursive mechanisms of representation through literary analysis in *Orientalism*. He retraced these mechanisms in depictions of Palestinians in U.S. media and intellectual discourse in *The Question of Palestine*. In the later part of his career, he presented a strategy for political resistance by telling his own story as a Palestinian in an account of suffering and dispossession that became his memoir, *Out of Place*. This shift from literary criticism to political journalism and finally to memoir presents an interesting case of rhetorical scaffolding: all three texts shared a denunciatory purpose but were conceived differently. *Orientalism* was already political, even though written within the conventions of an academic genre. The book "breathed insurgence," by encouraging a radical rethinking of purportedly apolitical texts, novels, and poems.[12] *The Question of Palestine* used literary analysis as evidence for political claims while *Out of Place* blended political commentary with literary evocation. The understanding of representation as a discursive force, established by *Orientalism*, also constitutes the foundation of the later texts. But while *The Question of Palestine* justifies the accusation by using the analogy between Zionism and imperialism, the memoir reenacts the suffering of the victim, fashioning Said himself as a dispossessed and oppressed Palestinian.

Denunciation is a rhetorical task that presents several challenges. First, the accuser has to convince the audience to care about the alleged victims and be outraged at the purported wrongdoers. This becomes more difficult when the audience is physically and culturally distant in relation to the victims, as many Americans were to Palestinians, but closer in relation to the wrongdoers, as many Jewish-Americans were to the Israeli perspective. Thus, the accuser faces the challenge of representing the victims and the villains when, as Boltanski explains, "a clearly identified agent cannot be established for a sufficient length of time in place of the persecutor." The legacy of the Holocaust made it hard to represent Palestinians as victims to an American audience concerned with the victims of Nazism, the Jews, as the scandal surrounding *Eichmann in Jerusalem* had made clear. And because they saw Jews as victims, American audiences had a more difficult time shifting their representation to that of perpetrators, all the more so once the Palestinian Liberation Organization became involved in terrorist activity. This rapidly evolving and shifting dynamic of victimhood and villainy created a "crisis of the representation of the suffering." How to know who the victim is, and thus where the suffering lies? In response to this referential uncertainty, Said used "systems of accusation," which, in Boltanski's terms, proceed by "constructing stable chains so that the places in a particular situation can be filled by connecting different actors to large entities, to collective persons."[13] Said accused intellectual leaders and opinion makers of failing to promote particular representations of reality. Said also took issue with the philosophical traditions in which representations take shape, targeting Zionism as the ideology that had served as the foundation for the state of Israel and continues to legitimate Israeli politics in the Middle East, especially toward Palestinians. He understood Zionism as part of Western liberalism and as the legacy of the Enlightenment, but he was especially interested in the American version with its emphasis on the politics of national emancipation through the Puritan narrative of a chosen people, the narrative that had also been at the center of Solzhenitsyn's jeremiad.

Denunciation, as Said pursued it, is a pathos-driven discourse relying on tropes of indignation even in the midst of an objective and rigorous investigation. To strike the right balance between detached observation and outraged commentary is difficult. As Boltanski explains, "in a topic of denunciation . . . the statement is inserted within a structure of controversy. The speaker's words must be more than just invective. Meeting with resistance, the statement must equally appear in a *debatable* form. It must set out and argue its positions. The violence of accusation must be justified by proofs."[14] But denunciatory discourses also tend to split their addressees into a projected "universal audience" expected to share the outrage and respond with prompt compassion and an adversarial audience likely to challenge the representation and assignment of the roles of victims and perpetrators. Said's late reflections on humanism were designed to lend theoretical credence to the possibility of a universal audience who could understand the human experience in its manifold manifestations and thus be capable of compassion and sympathy across national, cultural, and religious divides. Yet his analyses of media depictions of Arabs in general and Palestinians in particular frequently presented a Said concerned especially with the making of adversarial audiences.

The denunciatory goal of Said's political writing gave it a distinctive emotional imprint. He wrote as an angry man, indeed appropriately so for someone denouncing oppression and wrongdoing. Yet the emotional and the investigative aspects of denunciation conflicted at times. The angry tone of his writing impacted the epistemic force of his arguments, rendering them less objective. Even a supporter like Homi Bhaba, while conceding that "there is much to agree with [in Said's arguments]," added that there is "much to question also. The high Saidian style speaks with a moral passion that sometimes sacrifices analytic precision to polemical outrage."[15]

In his review of *Covering Islam*, Clifford Geertz (who had already made it clear in his review of *Orientalism* that he was not a fan) grudgingly admitted that Said's exposure of the media demonization of Islam is justified and valid, yet he bemoaned the shrill, unattractive tone of the denunciation. In the *New Republic*, Leon Wieseltier (at the time a graduate student at

Harvard University and not yet the powerful editor he would later become) began his own review of *Covering Islam* by calling it an "angry book," and the overall negative assessment made it clear that such an adjective was not merely a neutral depiction. Peppered with phrases like "Said's philippic," "another apology for rejectionism," "his *jusq-auboutisme*" (fanaticism), and "morally pusillanimous," Wieseltier's analysis rejected Said's arguments consistently on the basis of their content as well as emotional tonality.[16]

Said's rhetoric of denunciation was that of an outsider who set out to provoke and to disturb. Anger is a fitting accompaniment for the unmasking of a wrong that has remained so far ignored. According to Boltanski, the display of outrage draws attention to the denouncer: "it is through indignation that he renders himself present in person, because indignation cannot be impersonal." Yet for Said the academic, such an emotional display was risky because it created a contrast with the ideal of the well-tempered scholar. As the denouncer is expected to move from an initial display of outrage to a dispassionate investigation, emotions are also expected to subside "because to gather proof [the denouncer] must direct reality."[17] The sociopolitical reality about which Said wrote was difficult to "direct" because the controversial nature of Palestinian-Israeli politics and U.S. involvement created a crisis of representation. Said intervened in this crisis by representing the *Palestinian* reality; therefore it makes sense that he would deemphasize his American identity. While it is hard to know if Said regarded the anger of the stranger more likely to be accepted in a denunciatory discourse, the rhetorical advantages of such a persona are clear. By positioning himself as a Palestinian, Said could also speak from the perspective of the victim. His anger was not the moral self-righteousness of a Western observer who at the end of the day falls asleep in a comfortable home but the authentic outrage of the harmed.

THE WISDOM OF THE EXILE

The very inclusion of Said in the cast of characters I discuss in this book requires some brief discussion. He was frequently called an exile, a term he often chose to identify himself, but is this "exile" comparable to Arendt,

Solzhenitsyn, and Marcuse who were forced to leave their country of origin and only came to the United States in an attempt to save their lives? Or was Said a cosmopolitan for whom national affiliations or attachment to a particular culturally defined lifestyle meant little? These two categories meld into a third one, which represents Said's most common characterization: as an intellectual whose mission is to "speak truth to power." Said's most sustained discussion of the role of intellectuals is featured in his 1993 Reith Lectures for the BBC. In these lectures, his conception of the intellectual is informed by the synthesis of two sources rarely used together: Julien Benda and Antonio Gramsci. From Benda's *Treason of the Clerks*, he took an idealized, heroic image of intellectuals as "thoroughgoing individuals with powerful personalities and, above all, . . . in a state of almost permanent opposition to the status quo." The "treason" referred to in Benda's title occurs when intellectuals abandon lofty ideals and become involved in "the organization of collective passions," especially class-related, or nationalist-driven conflicts. Despite the conservatism usually attributed to Benda (who saw intellectuals as superior agents situated above the rest of society), for Said this position "remains an attractive and compelling one." He was probably drawn precisely to the heroic requirement, which demands the intellectual be "someone able to speak the truth to power, a crusty, eloquent, fantastically courageous and angry individual for whom no worldly power is too big and imposing to be criticized and pointedly taken to task."[18] Because he stressed the political engagement of intellectuals, Said disliked specialization, critiquing it as a pernicious condition especially characteristic of American intellectuals. This idyllic return to the intellectual as a sage rather than mere professional reveals the underlying aesthetic motivation behind Said's conception of political engagement: "the aestheticized intellectual transcends the mire of worldly interest, in profession or state. . . . [T]he category of the amateur is precisely disinterested, without the same stakes or sheer economic need of the professional."[19] If Benda furnished a heroic ideal of the intellectual, Gramsci offered Said realism, especially in the sociological context of the twentieth-century West with its emphasis on, and diversification of, professional expertise from academics to journalists and policy experts to government officials—all with a possibly legitimate claim to intellectual authority. The Gramscian thrust of Said's conception of intellectuals is most evident in his interest in "organic intellectuals . . . who are actively engaged in society, that is, they constantly struggle to change minds and expand markets."[20]

The imperative of speaking from the margins and facing institutional powers at any risk is a well-established idea in the sociology of intellectuals. Yet for Said the mission of "speaking truth to power" aligns with a position of double eccentricity, different from a bohemian marginality and significantly more challenging. His message also focused on events and peoples outside of the United States—the Palestinians and the Israelis. Insofar as the meaning of these events and the actions of those involved in them could be familiar or even accessible to an American audience, it would likely be so in a Zionist perspective. Said's situational constraints were, as he himself described them, embedded in the Cold War and later its aftermath—a context equally shaped by "the United States' domination of the Western alliance, in which a consensus has emerged about resurgent or fundamentalist Islam being the new threat that has replaced Communism."[21] The Palestinian-born intellectual was speaking of the plight of millions of Palestinians to an audience whose country had played a key role in establishing Israel as the state that was now their main enemy. Second, but more important, Said's eccentricity is that of a critic who addressed a national polity within which his own status was ambiguous: a resident but not a native; a legal citizen but not a naturalized one who had desired himself, or asked to, acquire citizenship. This ambiguity led some critics to suggest that Said took advantage of his semi-outsider status to tackle the challenges of an intellectual climate ruled by an epistemic skepticism that could result in political sterility. By some accounts, "Said grafted Gramsci's organic intellectual with the modernist cosmopolitan in an effort to salvage an independent, often elite, metropolitan 'critical consciousness.'"[22] Yet Said was also the epitome of Simmel's cosmopolitan stranger, both detached from the American society he observes and immersed in it. He resembles the Arendtian pariah insofar as he could never, by his own admission, "understand what it means to love a country" just as she could never love a people.[23] Yet perhaps one reason Said could not love a country was precisely the political inexistence

EDWARD SAID AND THE CLASH OF IDENTITIES

of the country he could have called his: Palestine. While Arendt and Marcuse's Germany and Solzhenitsyn's Russia were inhospitable to their own citizens, these countries never lost their status as nation-states. Germany became again a democratic culture in the aftermath of World War II and the Cold War. Said's Palestine never gained a political existence during his lifetime. His pariah stranger persona, then, was a product of contingency as well as a credo.

That does not mean that Said simply accepted his status as an exile as the basis for his intellectual cosmopolitanism. At times he claimed his cosmopolitanism emphatically, critiquing the very idea of national ties and exhorting post-nationalism and exile as superior political attitudes conducive to peace and universal respect for others. American intellectuals liked him *as a cosmopolitan* rather than as a Palestinian. Fellow New York "exile" Tony Judt speaks for sympathetic readers of Said's work in insisting that "despite his identification with the Palestinian cause and his inexhaustible efforts to promote and explain it, Said quite lacked the sort of uninterrogated affiliation to a country or an idea that allows the activist or the ideologue to subsume any means to a single end."[24] Indeed, Said was often critical of Palestinian political leaders and was especially put off by their recourse to violence so much abhorred by most Westerners. Said condemned not only the violent acts but also what he called the "worship of fetishized military postures, guns, and slogans borrowed from theories of the people's war in Algeria and Vietnam."[25]

In his late political work, Said's "rootless cosmopolitanism" appears to be replaced by a concern with his origins, which become a major trope in his comments on Palestinian identity in *After the Last Sky* and even more so in his memoir. Said identified as an "exile" in part because exile corresponds, in ontological fashion, to a type of existence he cultivated, that of the intellectual who always situates himself outside and in opposition to the state. His ideal exile was Theodor W. Adorno. The two men had a lot in common: both were sons of wealthy parents, highly educated, artistic, passionately committed to high culture yet also discontent with the political status quo and committed to an intellectual reflection that could establish the grounds for political transformation. In Adorno, Said saw the "quintessential intellectual, hating *all* systems, whether on our side or theirs, with equal distaste." He shared Adorno's musical aesthetic with its emphasis on the discontinuous and the fragmentary as well as the deriving negative dialectics it inspired in Adorno's philosophy. Said embraced Adorno's exilic belief that "it is part of morality not to be at home in one's home."[26] And he was probably assured by Adorno's trajectory, from philosophical speculation to political reflection, all along taking delight in music while remaining focused on philosophy with all the earnestness of the expert. In Adorno, Said found the courage to be inopportune, both by living out of synch with one's own time, and in a political sense, by forcing contemporaries to face unpleasant realities.

In an interview published in the Israeli newspaper *Haaretz*, Said famously declared himself to be not only the sole surviving heir to Adorno but also "the last Jewish intellectual."[27] Besides the poignancy of this formulation coming from a Palestinian, the phrase is remarkable insofar as it reveals the main premise of Said's political ontology: once the historic condition of the Jewish people, exile is a privileged standpoint from which the intellectual can engage the nation-state. Said embraced an idyllic vision of exile, which transformed the political and existential crises facing exiles into a moral and epistemic superiority. The painful aspects of Schutz's stranger are missing from Said's early reflections on the intellectual as exile, always depicted as someone in a privileged position, doubly estranged and equally objective in relation to the homeland and to the adoptive country. This displacement—a topos to which Said devoted more attention in his memoir—becomes an observation stand from which the exile has a bird's-eye view on realities otherwise difficult to discern or to understand.

The Saidian exile is also different from Simmel's wandering stranger, who moves from one world to another. This distinction can be traced to Said's hesitation between Adorno and another model, Jean Genet, the French experimental writer who joined different national groups in search of a perpetual revolutionary mode, from the Algerian fighting for independence in his own country, France, to the Black Panthers in the United States, and finally to the Palestinian Liberation Organization. Said admired Genet's addiction to radical politics, reading it as the expression of the extraordinary freedom of "the outcast unconfined by ordinary social formality or 'human' norms." The victim of abuse as a young man, Genet sought out other kinds of victims, and his solidarity with the oppressed deliberately transcended cultural, national, and civilizational boundaries. Genet joined the Black Panthers at the height of the civil rights movement in the United States and the Palestinian Liberation Organization when each started organizing as a potentially revolutionary organization. It was precisely because he did not affiliate with a nation (not even his native France) that Genet was willing to join movements from North Africa to the United States and then the Middle East. Genet was, as Said aptly put it, "the other great modern dissolver of identity" after Adorno. Both rejected identity because they saw it as something thrown on an individual by someone more powerful. "Here is a man in love with 'the other,'" writes Said, "an outcast and a stranger himself, feeling the deepest sympathy for the Palestinian revolution as the 'metaphysical' uprising of outcasts and strangers . . . yet neither his 'total belief' nor 'the whole of myself' could be in it."[28] Said found Genet's attachment to Palestine to be more aesthetic than political, even to the detriment of the political. Much as he admired this French writer, the Palestinian-born Said wondered if Genet was not ultimately using other people's historic plight merely to stimulate his literary imagination.

Even though raised merely as an unlikely hypothetical, this question reveals Said's concern with the authenticity of political engagement, an authenticity he seemed to judge in connection to owning up to a particular national identity. In contrast to Genet, he presented his political engagement in the Palestinian cause as a consequence, even requirement, dictated by his Palestinian identity. His unfailing commitment to the Palestinian cause, in the context of his comparatively limited interest in other sites of political injustice, suggests that Said was not attracted to a political revolutionarism per se. He was interested, however, in the epistemic and moral foundation of revolutionary patriotism. While Genet's pursuit of revolutionary movements around the globe and Adorno's cultivation of the exile condition were both at root metaphysical (neither saw or sought an end to this state), Said's political commitment was focused on distinct, focused goals: self-determination for the Palestinians and the formation of a binational state in Israel. He was both less high-minded and more practically oriented than his idols to the point where he seemed unmistakably American: "In a sense the real model for Said was not the European theorists of high culture he so admired (whose own politics, especially in cold war afterlife, remained embarrassingly recessive at best) but the homegrown figure of Noam Chomsky.[29]

Yet Chomsky took a broader critical attitude toward American foreign policy that he deemed imperialist, whether applied in Bosnia or Indochina. Said acknowledged that "Palestinians are not alone . . . in being either misunderstood or ignored by the United States as it attempts to construct a foreign policy in Asia and Africa."[30] Yet he remained singularly concerned with U.S. foreign policy on the Israeli-Palestinian problem. This exclusive concern with Palestine inflected Said's stranger persona and required a careful elaboration of his own Palestinian identity. He had to position himself carefully as a Palestinian accusing the Western world, and especially America, for the plight of his people, without seeming like he only cared about the fate of Palestinians and not about the potential destructiveness of the West. This might seem strategic in a callous way, but it was rhetorically needed at a time when Western intellectuals concerned about global affairs might have cared about India or Algeria before they showed any interest in Palestine.

In an article published in his "Diary" column for the *London Review of Books*, Said recounts the disappointing encounter with several key French intellectuals (including Raymond Aron and Marcel Merleau-Ponty) at a meeting hosted by Jean-Paul Sartre in Michel Foucault's apartment and dedicated to the Palestinian problem. The actual occasion was a seminar on the Middle East organized by *Temps Modernes*, a liberal journal which played a major role in intellectual and political life in France and Europe and which had published articles on the Middle East, including the 1967 Israel-Egypt war. Recounting the trip, Said opened with a hyperbolical description of his surprise upon receiving the invitation from Sartre and Simone de Beauvoir themselves. The hyperbole he used was not merely tongue-in-cheek but also designed to give readers a measure of his original hope and the contrast with his later disillusionment:

> At first I thought the cable was a joke of some sort. It might just as well
> have been an invitation from Cosima and Richard Wagner to come to

Bayreuth, or from T. S. Eliot and Virginia Woolf to spend an afternoon at the offices of the *Dial*. It took me about two days to ascertain from various friends in New York and Paris that it was indeed genuine, and far less time than that to dispatch my unconditional acceptance.[31]

The luminaries Said joined in the discussion turned out to be primarily supporters of Israel, including Sartre himself. Said described the discussion as superficial, dominated either by a rehashing of well-known ideas and arguments or by extended socializing over long lunches. The contrast between the intellectual reputation of those present and the mediocrity or bias of their reflections on a thorny and urgent political problem is presented by Said with undisguised bitterness. Sartre's unflinching support for Algerian independence had inspired a veritable paean in Said's *Representations of the Intellectual*. The Sartre that Said met in Paris was old and frail, his only intervention a series of "the most banal platitudes imaginable."[32] Only a few days later, Sartre's pro-Israeli stance would garner praise from Bernard-Henri Lévy, the staunch conservative who had praised Solzhenitsyn and would have had every ideological reason to resent the once notoriously communist Sartre. The French Left and Right thus came together in their common support for Israel, confirming Said's worst fear: that the Palestinian cause is lost on Western intellectuals regardless of their ideological beliefs.

The indifference or downright hostility of liberal intellectuals regarding the Palestinian problem is a function of the "crisis of representation" in which it is mired. Not only does each side claim to be the other's victim, but the Israeli side fits no existent category of an oppressive power. On the contrary, Jews represent the iconic victim. To take this historic status into account, Said coined the phrase "victims of victims" to depict Palestinians. A state for the Jewish people was created in order to put an end to centuries of discrimination against the Jews by giving them an exit strategy from their oppressors and a safe political space. The legacy of the Holocaust was a morally unshakeable foundation for a bold political experiment: creating a state that would offer no political recognition to the population inhabiting its territory at the time of the founding. "It was the horrors of the Second World War that gave the Jewish people an unanswerable case," points out Jacqueline Rosen, adding: "the UN commissioners of 1947 who recommended partition of Palestine did so after visiting the displaced persons camps of Europe."[33]

The moral legacy of the Holocaust, a significant support for the Israeli state among Western liberal intellectuals who had previously shown support for colonized people around the world, and the special nature of the power dynamic in the Palestinian region—these were daunting constraints that defined Said's challenge as a political commentator. It took more than sheer relentlessness—a systematic and renewed effort at defending the Palestinian cause to Western audiences more likely to understand the Israeli position. Said was able to address these constraints by targeting the very "crisis of representation" that made denunciation such a difficult rhetorical task. He designed a theory of representation focused on exposing hidden oppression and unmasking the effects of power on the construction of identity. This theory, first laid out in *Orientalism*, had an explicit emancipatory mission, as its purpose was to provide a method for rethinking purposeful misrepresentations. The purpose of his approach was to articulate an epistemic indictment that could identify the sources of misrepresentation (authors, texts, and practices) as well as the techniques they had used. While the accusation targeted a broadly defined Western tradition of thought and pleaded for a rehabilitation of its victims, the accuser was not only Said the intellectual, but rather Said the stranger, the Palestinian speaking on behalf of a misrepresented culture.

DENUNCIATION AS INVESTIGATION

Despite his broad political notoriety as a supporter of Palestinian self-determination, Said's authority, as Timothy Brennan points out, "was always ultimately literary." At the same time, however, this literary authority shaped Said's political views by equipping him with a politically salient epistemology. As a theorist of representation, Said was concerned with the ways in which discourse depicts particular realities and thus makes them likely to withstand certain kinds of political, as well as moral, evaluations.

Said's understanding of literary representation had inconsistencies (as I show below) that carried over into his political representation of the Palestinian cause. At the same time, his recourse to "the tropes of literary criticism to express his political and social imagination" was more than a habit of mind.[34] It allowed him to wrestle with the complicated hermeneutics of political conflict between competing interpretations of the same historical events and circumstances. The shift from the relativist epistemology fashionable in literary theory to a rather foundationalist political epistemology focused on "speaking *truth* to power"—and inevitably assuming that there is such a thing as *truth*—was not easy.

That Said made this shift is a consequence of his own apprenticeship in a literary climate keener on dividing literature and politics rather than on blending them. His graduate education was less the product of, and more a reaction against, its academic environment at Harvard University. By his own account, he was dissatisfied from the beginning with the approach in vogue in literary studies at that time, which was rooted in the American New Criticism and demanded an exclusive focus on the text rather than on the authors or historical settings. Harvard shaped his intellectual sensibility in ways he was not always happy to acknowledge because it pinned him against his own political beliefs. Said described the humanistic education that emerged in the United States during the Cold War (which was partly what he learned at Harvard and a version of which he would later teach himself at Columbia) as centered on "the notion of nonpolitical analysis . . . meant as a barrier against the overt politicization of art that was said to be conspicuous of socialist realism."[35]

The ideal of the "disengaged humanist" had an even longer American genealogy, going back to the nineteenth-century New England literati and their preference for reflection over action. Yet by stressing the political origin of the nonpolitical stance he adopted as a student in the humanities in America, Said revealed the paradox on which his stranger persona was founded: attracted to the idea and inherent value of the disengaged humanist invested in high culture until the very end of his life its inherent value yet also repelled by the repressed political consciousness such disengagement involved. Said pondered the problematic consequences of structuralist (and later poststructuralist as well) thought. These schools of thought had left out the "world" of the text, the beliefs and values that had inspired it, and to which the text responded. Pleading for a rejoining of the *texte* with the *hors-texte*—the use of French itself a snide comment on the "fashionable nonsense" that had inspired it—Said aimed at a redefinition of the very mission of the literary critic, and by extension, of the intellectual. He opposed the "pernicious analytic of blind demarcation by which, for example, imagination is separated from thought, culture from power, history from form, texts from everything that is *hors texte*, and so forth."[36]

This analytic was the legacy of structuralism, which Said rejected. He recounted his disenchantment with structuralism as a political epiphany of sorts, focused on a concern with the disempowered:

> During the 1960s and 1970s the advent of French theory in the humanistic departments of American and English universities had brought about a severe if not crippling defeat of what was considered traditional humanism by the forces of structuralism and post-structuralism, both of which professed the death of man-the-author and asserted the preeminence of antihumanist systems such as those found in the work of Lévi-Strauss, Foucault himself, and Roland Barthes. . . . This group of pioneers showed, in effect, that the existence of systems of thinking and perceiving transcended the powers of individual subjects, individual humans who were inside those systems . . . and therefore had no power over them, only the choice to either use or be used by them.[37]

Yet in spite of his skepticism toward theory—especially in its French version—Said owed the conceptual inspiration for his most important work, *Orientalism*, to a key poststructuralist idea he had learned from Michel Foucault: that of epistemic power. As a study of representations of the Orient in the Western tradition, *Orientalism* bore the mark of Foucault's understanding of power as a discursive effect rather than a form of control exercised, often through explicit violence, by a state, nation, or individual over others. Said defined Orientalism as "a style of thought based upon an ontological and epistemological distinction made between "the Orient" and (most of the time) "the Occident."[38] The book revealed the host of negative representations of the Orient produced, maintained, and disseminated over the centuries in Western discourse, and it argued that these representations reflected a colonialist gaze more powerful and oppressive than the imperial armies that had been the agents of colonization on the ground. The epistemic power of Western discourse about the Orient resided in its ability to encapsulate an entire civilization and its people into a series of negative statements—about the slow, lazy, untrustworthy, lascivious, and cunning Arab—that would degrade Arab civilization to the status of the dark, uncivilized underworld.

Orientalism offered an indirect theory of representation by denouncing strategies of misrepresentation. Theoretically, the book kept notions like accuracy and validity at arm's length without fully discarding them. In Foucauldian terms, Orientalism acts as a gaze that seeks to capture disparate phenomena by imposing a fictive totality on them. The gaze is a form of epistemic capturing, as well as a violent act inasmuch as it erases or deceives in order to promote a particular representation at the expense of a competing one. Rather than examining the grounds on which the repressed representation can be deemed the *correct* one—which would have required answering how and who can establish its accuracy—Said was more concerned with how and who authorizes the misrepresentation. His depiction of the repressive (mis)representational act does not use the typical Foucauldian vocabulary but was still steeped in the rhetoric of surveillance:

> The Orientalist *surveys the Orient from above,* with the aim of getting hold of the whole sprawling panorama before him—culture, religion, mind, history, society. To do this he must see every detail through the device of a set of reductive categories (the Semite, the Muslim mind, the Orient, and so forth). Since these categories are schematic and efficient ones, and since it is more or less assumed that no Oriental can know himself the way a Orientalist can, any vision of the Orient comes to rely for its coherence and force on the person, institution, or discourse whose property it is.[39]

The popularity of the book—translated into several languages and reissued in several editions—was in part the result of the fact that the concept of Orientalism invited applications and extensions, along with critiques. Said's repertoire of Western texts scrutinizing and dehumanizing the Orient, inevitably incomplete, prompted repeated updates: not just the account of Napoleon's expedition to Egypt but also Gerard de Nerval's travelogue, Renaissance paintings depicting harem scenes, English Victorian novels chronicling the adventures of Bedouins, and even the French realism of an unlikely suspect, realist Gustave Flaubert, not only in his Egypt travelogue but also in the reveries of his famous heroine Emma Bovary. Yet the approach, starting with the geographical grounding of the Orient in the Arab world begged methodological questions: if the Orient was the discursive product of the colonizing Occident encountering its Other, should it not include other regions that suffered this epistemic assault: not just the Middle East but also Africa and Asia, not just the Arabs but also the Africans, the Indians, and the Chinese. Finally, "the kind of totalizing epistemological critique made by Said" raised some conceptual concerns about the author's assumptions regarding the issue of authenticity.[40] If the Orient was what the Occident saw, rather than what it *is*, how could the Occident ever discover the proper Orient?

Although the question of truth would acquire a special poignancy for Said later on, the book may not have intended to address the distinction between deceptive and accurate representations. Instead, as sympathetic critics have pointed out, *Orientalism* was primarily "committed to revealing how representational strategies were implicated in figuring colonial otherness, from teasing out the political unconscious of novels to showing the involvement of scholarly research in constructing images of the colonized that would serve the interests of policy and domination."[41] By other accounts, *Orientalism* rarely refers to Western knowledge production as ontological, preferring from his subject position to increasingly privilege the rhetoric of cultural and political domination.[42]

Since the book offered a sweeping indictment of colonialism as a form of intellectual oppression, it could not avoid questions about what the Orient *actually* was and how it related to the Occident. *Orientalism*, one critic astutely noticed, "did not arouse hostility only for its method or political critique, but also for the ontological anxiety it induced in Euro-American critics."[43] Said did not try to allay such anxieties and indeed may have preferred to encourage them by way of prompting more and deeper reflection on the realities of the Orient. At the same time, he gave little guidance on how such reflection might unfold. Hence, one of the criticisms against the book is that it "invites oppositional strategies of representation for the brute realities of Oriental life, but seems to ignore the task of finding more adequate ways to give accounts of, and for, the Orient." If one critiques representation while also admitting that representation can never aspire to the conditions of truth, then, as Nicholas Dirks put it, "why bother?"[44]

How to engage with the *reality* of the Orient?—this was a question anthropologists, more than any other professional group, complained that Said had left unanswered.[45] Geertz dismissed the book as an example of "ideological arguments cast as historiographic arguments."[46] The ideological implications of *Orientalism* were indeed undeniable. The denunciatory subtext of the book prompted methodological objections from those who saw the long-range capabilities of the critique: an attack on the orientalist policy of Israel. Robert Griffin, for instance, professor of English at Tel-Aviv University, accused Said of subscribing "to two conflicting epistemologies, a postmodernist one for his political enemies who are enmeshed in a web of historical determinations, and a classical one for himself, whose perspective is consonant with truth."[47] Also unanswered at this point was the question concerning the true value of any representational act. Can the Orient be depicted truthfully by anybody outside it? Can the native's perspective be accurately presented? Some postcolonial critics have insisted that Said himself vacillated "between the idea that true representation is theoretically possible and the opposite position that all representation is necessarily misrepresentation."[48] While primarily literary, such critiques also exposed the political vulnerability of Said's work, whose main thesis could be read as positing an ontological rift between self and other. Thus framed, the contribution could appear both intellectually banal and politically insolvable, prompting easy dismissal from hostile critics:

> Said's thesis amounts to a truism: that people look at the "other" through
> their own eyes, and tend to judge alien cultures by their own culture's stan-
> dards. A problem? Yes. But Said's take on it is problematic, too. Almost

consistently, he condemns any negative commentary by any Westerner on any aspect of the Orient. Often he seems to imply that the only proper Western posture toward the East is to suspend judgment entirely and bathe everything in sympathy.[49]

Said parted ways with postcolonial understandings of power that drew heavily on Foucault, emphasizing the discursive production of power—ironically what informed so many of his own analyses in *Orientalism*—at the expense of more concrete, brutal forms of coercion and the pessimism that makes political transformation seem utopian. If all the domains of knowledge that exist in a particular period enjoin a discursive complicity, forging together a "regime of truth" that makes particular characterizations appear valid no matter how flawed they might be if judged by other epistemic standards, how can statements and representations be challenged, contested, and eventually amended?[50] Said relied on Foucault's notion of epistemic power to indict the West on the level of its intellectual traditions rather than political institutions, but ultimately he saw the two, traditions and institutions, connected, just as Solzhenitsyn had attacked humanism for its creation of a legalistic materialist society. Said's own political stance, as opposed to his literary views, was based more on a traditional conception of power still mainly concerned with governments and policy makers. In Said's view, if the Occident relied on its scholars to construct a repulsive or terrifying image of the Orient, it was Western governments and politicians enforcing this representation as the basis of foreign policy decisions that had devastating consequences for the Arab world. Said's response was to denounce those scholars by analyzing their misrepresentations. He acknowledged traditional institutional power. He not only agreed to join the PNC and participate in diplomatic negotiations, but he even attempted to act as advisor to Yasser Arafat. He saw such work as necessary and as comparable to the intellectual's obligation to analyze and critique ideas.

As Said's political career took on an unprecedented visibility through televised appearances and participations in high-level negotiations, *The New York Review of Books* published a devastating critique of *Orientalism* not by a pundit or extreme right radical but by a professor of Middle

Eastern Studies at Princeton University. The critic, Bernard Lewis, was well known for his studies of Islam and modern Turkey. Controversial in his own right, he had served as former Foreign Office officer and leading advisor to the White House on Middle Eastern affairs under the Bush Sr. and Bush Jr. administrations. Lewis accused Said of maliciously politicizing a set of intellectual issues in a domain about which he was largely ignorant. Orientalists are, in Lewis's presentation, philologists and historians primarily, whose field of study deals with the languages and cultures of the Middle East. Yet once "students of the Orient . . . took to calling themselves philologists, historians, etc. dealing with Oriental topics . . . [they] began to use such terms as Sinologists and Indologists, Iranists and Arabists, to give a closer and more specific definition to the area and topic of their study." Insisting on the scholarly dimension of Orientalism in contrast to the political one stressed by Said, Lewis defended Orientalists by insisting upon their political disinterestedness. The Orientalists themselves had abandoned the term Orientalism once they realized it was "polluted beyond salvation." Respectable philologists and historians dedicated to the study of various geographic and cultural areas (including not just the Middle East but also Turkey, parts of Africa, southeast Asia, and Semitic culture) had thrown the term "Orientalism" into "the garbage heap of history." Unfortunately, Lewis lamented, "garbage heaps are not safe places. The words Orientalist and Orientalism, already discarded by scholars, were retrieved and reconditioned for a different purpose, as terms of polemical abuse."[51]

This metaphor of retrieval and recycling creates an image of uncleanliness to dismiss Said's work as not only politically biased but also repulsive to true scholars. Disturbed by both the content and the style of Said's book, especially by the language "with sexual overtones," Lewis took issue with several aspects of the arguments presented by *Orientalism*, from bibliographical gaps to sheer lack of expertise.[52] He alleged that Said had misspelled and mistranslated key terms, such as the Islamic term *tawhid* as "God's transcendental unity" instead of monotheism.

Lewis's critique puts into sharp contrast Said's Foucauldian assumption about knowledge as a form of power (possibly repressive) and the more traditional, Cartesian notion of the disinterested pursuit of knowledge through academic inquiry. To stress what he considered the absurdity of Said's approach, Lewis invited readers to consider an imaginary scenario featuring classicists instead of Orientalists:

> Imagine a situation in which a group of patriots and radicals from Greece decides that the profession of classical studies is insulting to the great heritage of Hellas, and that those engaged in these studies, known as classicists, are the latest manifestation of a deep and evil conspiracy, incubated for centuries, hatched in Europe, fledged in America, the purpose of which is to denigrate the Greek achievement and subjugate the Greek lands and peoples. . . . The poison has spread from Europe to the United States, where the teaching of Greek history, language, and literature in the universities is dominated by the evil race of classicists—men and women who are not of Greek origin, and who have no sympathy for Greek causes, and who, under a false mask of dispassionate scholarship, strive to keep the Greek people in a state of permanent subordination.[53]

The point of this scenario is to introduce the trope of political innocence, presenting scholarly inquiry as completely divorced from political interests. It could not matter to the current state of Greece, Lewis expects his audience to presume, what a Homer scholar from Princeton writes about the *Odyssey*. The analogy between classicists and Orientalists capitalizes on the academic specialization of both, waged against political relevance, which is assumed to involve less abstruseness and a focus on the present. For Lewis, scholars keep their eyes on distant lands and eras and that distance removes them from the ills of the present. Those who refuse to withdraw in the reclusiveness of intellectual pursuits are fools and manipulators. Lewis's sarcasm is a strategy of dismissing Said's claims without actually engaging with their substance but also a strategy of eliminating Said himself from the world of pure intellectual activity. Ridicule further dismisses Said as a commissar of political correctness who would want us "to save Greece from the classicists and bring the whole pernicious tradition of classical scholarship to an end. . . . [S]teps must be taken to ensure Greek or pro-Greek control of university centers and departments of Greek studies, and thus, by

EDWARD SAID AND THE CLASH OF IDENTITIES

a kind of academic prophylaxis, prevent the emergence of any further classical scholars or scholarship.[54] Whether Lewis intended the scenario to be read as a double dismissal, of the native's perspective and of a particular kind of political correctness, his criticism was an attack on Said as someone who does not belong in the world of ideas.

Yet *Orientalism* did not argue for the epistemic superiority or credibility of sources from inside the Orient. That Lewis read Said's critique as a self-promotion reveals his concern with the potential authority of the non-Western voice. A detailed and sophisticated reading of the Western canon, *Orientalism*, however, is not the work of a non-Western but, on the contrary, of an elite representative and connoisseur of the very tradition under discussion. The conceptual foundation of the book, with its indebtedness to Foucault, is also Western. Significantly, though, Said has often stressed the Arab inspiration of *Orientalism*. He frequently narrated the intellectual discovery marked by the book as inspired by a request he received from his friend Ibrahim Abu-Lughod, who invited him to deliver a paper about Western depictions of Arabs to a conference in Beirut.[55] Furthermore, Said often traced the intellectual gestation of the book directly to the emergence of his political interests in the Middle East. The vector of the influence also pointed the other way: while describing *Orientalism* as the intellectual response to a distinctly political problem, the writing of this book also marked his political awakening:

> I did not become politically engaged until 1967. Before then . . . there was a dissociation between my life in America during a time of extreme political quiescence and in the Middle East where I was aware of, but did not directly participate in, the major trends of the time. . . . [I]t was only with the publication of *Orientalism* in 1978 that I was forced to face the question . . . about the overlap between scholarship and politics.[56]

It is interesting that Said was not involved in politics at a time when many other Americans were also not very politically active. It was originally a period of postwar reconstruction followed by the early hype of the Cold War. In the years that followed, major military conflicts between Israel and neighboring Arab states took place, and unrest among the Palestinian population increasingly escalated into violent attacks and counterattacks. In the 1980s, the situation worsened markedly with the two Palestinian *intifadas* and the continuing expansion of Israel into former Palestinian territory. A pro-Israel stance became less tenable even for Jewish Americans, even for the sons and daughters of Holocaust survivors. How could they continue to support a state that was connected with the continuing violence in the Middle East? By wrestling with this question, Said put in the final elements of his system of accusation, identifying the key political strategy of legitimization used in the Israeli-Palestinian conflict: the discourse of Zionism. The conceptual breakthroughs of *Orientalism* informed the denunciation of Zionism as a theory of (mis)representation. Those who had criticized *Orientalism* had already positioned Said as an outsider (to the norms of Western scholarship) and contributed to the making of his stranger persona in its most politicized form.

DENUNCIATION AND ITS MASTER TROPES

In *The Question of Palestine*, published in 1979, only one year after *Orientalism*, Said's conception of representation was, by political necessity, a foundationalist one. Distinguishing sharply between hard facts and their ideologically motivated, distorted representation, the essays included in this book approach the task of denunciation as an epistemic investigation. "We must understand the struggle between Palestinians and Zionism," he insisted, "as a struggle between a presence and an interpretation, the former constantly appearing to be overpowered and eradicated by the latter." "What was this presence?"—he further asked. "No matter how backward, uncivilized, and silent they were, the Palestinian Arabs *were* on the land."[57] In Said's view, Zionism was responsible for the erasure of the Palestinian presence. Said's challenge, as he saw it, was to make "the case for a Palestinian presence in a world that tended to deny it."[58] Zionism provided Israel with a powerful mythology that allowed it to advance its territorial claims and unfold its state-building efforts. Palestinians had no comparable ideological advantage and often used the argument of physical presence to demand political rights.

American exceptionalism meant, among so many other things, no history of anti-Semitism in the sense that had stamped indelibly European history. American support for the new state of Israel did not stem from a guilty conscience about its treatment of Jews. From the beginning, the newly formed state of Israel had a tighter connection to the United States than to any other Western state. American Jewish organizations contributed heavily to the formation of the state of Israel through financial support and lobbying. After an initial and brief period of reservations, American high officials endorsed pro-Israeli policies. After the war, the ties of the Israeli state to the Jews living in America were especially important. In 1948, the Zionist Organization of America was "the largest single Zionist organization in the world with 250,000 members."[59] The link between Israel and the United States was not only a matter of political cooperation. Their deepest connection was the symbolic construction of their people as chosen nations. Furthermore, American Jews were able to reconcile their immigrant status with the postwar Zionist objective of ending the Jewish diaspora and bringing all of its children home to Israel. America, however, was itself a Promised Land, "not galut in the European sense [but] the country of economic opportunity and religious freedom." There was no contradiction between living as a Jew in America and supporting and lobbying for the state of Israel. On the contrary, the two tasks seemed continuous: "American cultural Zionism presented a blueprint for the development of American Jewry *in America*, parallel to and intimately connected with, the creation of a Jewish home in Palestine, both inspired by the same ideals of Jewish national renaissance."[60] The impressive success of Zionism in America led to more than initial support for Israel and continued to play out as lobbying for Israeli political decisions regarding relationships with the Arab countries. In his writings, Said went as far as to condemn American Zionism as the last tolerated form of racism and saw it as the source of anti-Palestinian sentiment in the United States.[61] American Zionism, then, was the focus point in Said's denunciation.

A Palestinian critiquing Zionism could easily appear biased, which could compromise the investigative purpose of the denunciation. To avoid such a pitfall, Said first framed the investigation as the analysis of a dissident-outsider, without identifying yet as an Arab. In standard Gramscian manner, he presented himself as a detached intellectual who is neither the Orientalist nor the Oriental but rather a mix of both, an Arab with a Western mind. This self-depiction is worth quoting at length:

> Most of my education, and certainly all of my basic intellectual formation, are Western; in what I have read, in what I write about, even in what I do politically, I am profoundly influenced by mainstream Western attitudes toward the history of the Jews, anti-Semitism, the destruction of European Jewry. Unlike most other Arab intellectuals, the majority of whom obviously have not had my kind of background, I have been directly exposed to those aspects of Jewish history and experience that have mattered singularly for Jews and for Western non-Jews reading and thinking about Jewish history. I know as well as any educated Western non-Jew can know, what anti-Semitism has meant for the Jews, especially in this century. Consequently I can understand the intertwined terror and exultation out of which Zionism has been nourished, and I think I can at least grasp the meaning of Israel for Jews, and even for the enlightened Western liberal. And yet, because I am an Arab Palestinian, I can also see and feel other things—and it is these things that complicate matters considerably, that cause me also to focus on Zionism's *other* aspects. The result it, I think, worth describing, not because what I think is so crucial, but because it is useful to see the same phenomenon in two complementary ways, not normally associated with each other.[62]

Such cautious self-positioning shows that Said understood the dangers involved in indicting an ideology widely assumed to have contributed in essential ways to ending anti-Semitic violence by giving Jews the safety of a land of their own. His criticism of Israel was often met with charges that he was an anti-Semite. He complained that "the refusal to accept the Zionist argument left anyone in the West with the poorest of alternatives: being simply negative, anti-Semitic, or an apologist for Islam and the Arabs."[63] His challenge was to design a stranger persona that could not be forced in the straightjacket of this dichotomy.

In *The Question of Palestine*, one of Said's strategies is to distinguish American Jews from promoters of Zionism—the latter a much broader category that became his target. In the decades after World War II, several prominent American intellectuals had traveled to the Middle East to report on the Israeli-Palestinian conflict, among them Catholic philosopher Ronald Niebuhr, writers Edmund Wilson and Saul Bellow, and others. The first three came under Said's attack not as American Jews (as indeed not all were) but as epistemic agents who have the ability and authority to shape public perceptions of the Palestinian problem. Said reads the articles published by these intellectuals as distorted Zionist misrepresentations. For example, criticizing Niebuhr's remarks in support of the partition of Israel in 1947, Said reads a Zionist erasure of the natives in the author's glossing over of the perspective of the Palestinians who have lost their land, their homes, and their political right to exist. Niebuhr had formulated a series of desiderata for the improvement of the situation in the region, issuing suggestions from a plural first-person perspective "we" in conjunction with verbs indicating a particular preference or desire: "We would like to see," or "we would want." The formulation not only strikes Said as condescending but also as based on an internalization of the Zionist perspective. He interprets Niebuhr as suggesting that the Palestinian viewpoint "is of little interest."[64]

Niebuhr, nonetheless, was making an argument for U.S. foreign policy, not claiming to represent the Palestinian or, for that matter, Israeli view. Granted, he showed no awareness of, or interest in, a Palestinian perspective and how it might be different from the Zionist perspective. Similarly, upon reading Edmund Wilson's *Black, Red, Blond, and Olive*, his account of his visit to Israel, Said bemoans the book's portrayal of the Arab population "as totally disgusting and unattractive."[65] Wilson had taken the precaution of stressing that he was conveying the Jewish perspective rather than offering his own: "In a large Arab town like Acre, the squalor of the swarming streets *inspires in an Israeli* the same distaste that it does in the visiting Westerner.

For the Jew, who takes family relations so seriously . . . the spectacle of flocks of urchins, dirty, untaught, diseased, bawling and shrieking and beginning in the narrow and dirty streets, inspires even moral horror."[66]

Said saw no difference between the Jewish perspective and Wilson's own. How could they have been different, given that, as Said lamented, in the region "Israel is the norm, Israelis are the presence, their ideas and institutions the authentically native ones; Arabs are a nuisance, Palestinians a quasi-mythical reality?"[67]

His critiques of Niebuhr and Wilson are two examples of Said's attempt to identify and take to task the way in which American political discourse was internalizing the Zionist perspective on Israel as its own. While his vast political journalism work tirelessly exposed book after book and author after author, such a piecemeal approach had obvious limitations. Besides making Said look like a watchdog, it was inevitably repetitive, as the exposé often revealed the same mechanism of misrepresentation. Said's political criticism was more effective and more consistent with his overall epistemological approach when he used techniques of estrangement to investigate the rhetorical mechanisms of Zionism, rather than just exposing it. He defined Zionism as "an avant-garde, redemptive Occidental movement" but hyperbolically emphasized its *Western* make-up by insisting that it "literally took over the typology employed by European culture." By insisting on the Western nature of Zionism, Said laid the foundation for advancing an analogy between Zionism and imperialism: in its impact on Palestinians, Zionism amounted to a "process of dispossession, displacement, and colonial de facto apartheid." Replete with the terms he had used to describe the mechanisms of Orientalism, his analysis depicted Israeli policies as imperialism writ large, as memorable phrases like "the Zionist colonial apparatus" suggest.[68] By reading Zionism in conjunction with an ideology he had already criticized in *Orientalism,* Said sought not just to track the source of the misrepresentation of Palestinians but also to explain its effectiveness.

The appropriateness of the analogy between Zionism and imperialism is subject to debate, and Said can be said to have privileged "the European, particularly British, imperial model."[69] Yet he drew even more on the analogy between Zionism and American liberalism, through a common trait:

the " 'pioneering' spirit, which Americans in particular have found it very easy to identify with." The analogy between Zionism and the American pioneering ethos is then turned on its head as Said points to the negative aspects of this ethos when used as justification for the destruction of natives and the claiming of a land already inhabited and owned. Zionism "occupied a place that made it possible to interpret Palestine and its realities to the West in terms that the West could understand and easily accept, specifically and generally."[70] The next step in the critique was to question Zionism as a story of national emancipation—the political making of the Jewish people.

As even his harshest critics admitted, Said tried to sympathize with the Jews' desire to find a land for their nation.[71] "In Jewish hearts," he conceded, "Israel had always been there, an actuality difficult for the natives to perceive. Zionism therefore reclaimed, redeemed, repeated, replanted, realized Palestine, and Jewish hegemony over it." Only an uninhabited territory can be a *terra nova* awaiting its pioneers. Palestinians had to be chased out to create "a place to be possessed *anew* and reconstructed." Said admitted that Jews saw Israel as a place they owned because they believed they had been the original inhabitants. For the Jews, "Israel was a return to a previous state of affairs." But such a view bore "a far greater resemblance to the methods and successes of nineteenth-century European colonialism than to some mysterious first-century forebears."[72]

That the pioneering enthusiasm promoted by Zionism resembles the pilgrim ethos at the center of American identity could explain the popularity of Zionism in the United States yet not necessarily (or precisely for this reason) justify its indictment. For this purpose, Said traced the pioneering ethos again back to European colonialism:

> *It is clear from Herzl's thinking* that [the international legitimization of Zionism] could not have been done unless there was a prior European inclination to view the natives as irrelevant *to begin with*. That is, those natives already fit a more or less acceptable classificatory grid, which made them sui generis inferior to Western or white men—and it is this grid that Zionists like Herzl appropriated, domesticating it from the general culture of their time to the unique needs of a developing Jewish nationalism.[73]

The reference to Theodor Herzl is important because his work was the foundational text of Zionism. But Said's reading of Herzl was challenged by Jewish scholars. It was indeed a simplified reading that left out complicated hermeneutical nuances to make an argument intended for a more general public. Critics dismissed it by claiming that it was grossly inaccurate. Israeli scholar Cameron Brown accused Said of changing Herzl's original language in order to make it sound more anti-Palestinian that it was. "Mangled quotations," Brown charged, helped Said depict Zionism as a colonialist ideology. Said's critique of Zionism was vulnerable to criticism of this sort, but a far bigger challenge was the very status of Zionists as the sons and daughters of the victims of anti-Semitism. Against the symbolic power of the Holocaust in legitimizing the Israeli perspective, Said needed an event of comparable proportions: he described Palestinians as prisoners of "the Arab *Gulag Archipelago.*"[74] When this phrase first appeared in print, the allusion to Solzhenitsyn could probably still resonate with some readers. In subsequent editions, terms like "Gulag" added historical specificity to the depiction of Palestinians as "victims of victims," rather than victims of a colonial power.

In *The Question of Palestine*, the process leading to this presumed "complete hegemonic coalescence between the liberal Western view of things and the Zionist-Israeli view" was discussed, rather briefly, with a passing reference to the common capitalist roots of liberalism and Zionism.[75] Without a careful genealogy that could have an explanatory purpose, attacking Zionism by comparing it to imperialism posed a significant rhetorical risk. To some extent, this risk is inherent in the trope of analogy, which requires, somewhat contradictorily, both sufficient similarity and difference between the terms of the comparison. Too similar, and the analogy becomes banal; too different, and the analogy is far-fetched. Was the analogy between Zionism and European imperialism an allusion to the assimilated Jews—the parvenus, using Arendt's term, who eagerly took on a European identity? On such a premise, the analogy was not only trite but also cheaply offensive. Or was Said overplaying the European dimension of the Jewish experience by comparing Zionist Jews to European imperial agents? If so, then the analogy was in part far-fetched. As critics complained, to emphasize the alliance between Zionism and the West amounted to an erasure of the non-European aspects of Jewish identity and to a glossing over of the historic significance to the state of Israel of those Jews who had lived in non-Western regions, the Arab Jews.[76]

Many of those who attacked Said's analogy between Zionism and imperialism took it too literally and missed its symbolic function. It was one of Said's most respectable opponents, philosopher Michael Walzer, who understood this symbolic function. Walzer had resorted to the trope of analogy himself from a radically revalorized perspective.[77] He proposed a rival account of Zionism, which compares it to anti-colonial political movements. In his reading of the Old Testament story of the Jewish exodus, Walzer finds the promise of salvation through national emancipation. His storyline was centered on events that remind the reader of the postcolonial, Third World, emancipatory revolutions: the departure of the Jews from Egypt is a response to political oppression; their exodus is a voyage of trials and tribulations and the arrival in Canaan is the reward for collective effort and commitment. Walzer's account is studded with trademark terms like "liberatory," "progressive," and "emancipatory," and the narrative he recounts is that of the Jews as similar to, indeed representatives of, oppressive peoples anywhere. Where Said compared Zionism to imperialism, Walzer compared it to national awakenings in the postcolonial world.

Walzer's analogy between Jewish emancipation and postcolonial liberation exposed the rhetorical flaws of Said's analogic argumentation but it was flawed itself. In response, Said challenged Walzer's interpretation of the Exodus story as a liberal progressive narrative that "moves from bondage and oppression in Egypt, through the wanderings in Sinai, to the Promised Land," featuring Moses as "not an Odysseus who returns home, but a popular leader—albeit an outsider—of a people undergoing both the travails and novel triumphs of national liberation."[78] Said argued that the liberal progressive narrative of Zionism as the story of political emancipation (especially powerful in the aftermath of World War II) replaced the actual historic events of violent confrontation, usurpation, and extermination constituting the "return" of the Israelis to the Promised Land. Walzer's conclusion makes sense only in a story that foregrounds events that depict the Israelis as an oppressed people yet backgrounds or omits contextual information that could place their oppression in a different perspective. For instance, Said reminded readers, once economic hardship hit, the Egyptians resented all foreigners, especially the affluent Jews. Walzer's strategic choice of events created a narrative in which religious and racial oppression obscured class and economic privilege making Zionism into a metaphor of liberation that could be applicable to any disenfranchised group.

Such contest between different kinds of estrangement techniques and the radically opposed political tropes they produced—domination versus emancipation—was difficult to sort out within the crisis of representation produced by the Israeli-Palestinian conflict. Jews were both victims of the Holocaust and heavily armed soldiers while Palestinians were refugees as well as suicide bombers. These competing analogies required referential clarification: who are the victims and who the wrongdoers? Said addressed this question through a broader critique of the representation of Israel as the final destination on a nation's road to salvation. Said understood Moses as Sigmund Freud had presented him in *Moses and Monotheism*, and Said relied on Freud's conception to challenge the assumption that Jewish identity is based on sameness, whether religious or racial. The recourse to a text by Freud, a Jewish thinker, was itself a technique of estrangement, a strategic choice for pressing the case of a binational Israeli state: if Jewish identity contained "foreign traces" from its very inception, in the very figure of the Egyptian leader, why could a state for the Jews not also recognize the presence of non-Jews in it? The figure of the Egyptian Moses evoked by Freud was not only a non-Jew but also a non-European, and therefore all the more open to an Arab co-nationality:

> For Freud, writing and thinking in the mid-1930s, the actuality of the non-European was its constitutive presence as a sort of fissure in the figure of Moses—founder of Judaism but an unreconstructed non-Jewish Egyptian none the less. . . . [O]ut of the travails of specifically European anti-Semitism, the establishment of Jewish identity politically in a state that took very specific legal and political positions effectively to seal off that identity from anything that was non-Jewish.[79]

Said presented his reading of Freud's *Moses and Monotheism* in 2001 in a BBC lecture that had originally been scheduled as a talk to be delivered in Vienna during the 1999 centennial anniversary of Freud's birth. Yet because of a highly controversial photograph that had just been published, which showed Said throwing a rock at an Israeli compound, the Freud Institute in Vienna withdrew the invitation. Some commentators have explained the decision as an attempt to avoid the complications that could have arisen in the midst of anti-Semitism charges leveled against Said in a Vienna dealing with its own scandals triggered by extreme right political candidate Peter Haider.[80] Said delivered the lecture later in London where Freud had spent his own exile. The controversy turned out to be rhetorically fortunate because it allowed Said to draw attention to his own status as an exile. Boldly comparing himself to Freud, as both had been forced into exile by racism and political discrimination, Said staged his reflections as a dialogue with Freud, the Jew, addressing him as an alter ego. Both Said and Freud were exiles: one had been exiled from Jerusalem by the Israelis, and the other, from a European land by Nazis—their common fate forging a symbolic brotherhood.

The Egyptian figure of Moses was politically rich for the argument for a binational Israel, and Said drew on it emphatically. Some responses to the lecture challenged the politicization of Freud's arguments and ignored the overdrawn comparison between Said and Freud. Those who openly supported Israel were not concerned about hermeneutic details, such as the accuracy or appropriateness of the analogy between the two authors. Instead, they challenged Said's exile persona. In the *New Republic*, editor Leon Wieseltier began his refutation by accusing Said of denying Jews the right to have a distinctly Jewish identity.[81] A New York Jew deeply committed to Judaism, Wieseltier charged that Said's claims regarding the central role of the non-Jewish element in Jewish history were both misconceived and offensive. Such a reading of Freud amounted, in Wieseltier's view, to nothing but "intellectual violence." Wieseltier argued that Jewishness is a distinct identity, "neither European, nor non-European." What seemed to incriminate Said in Wieseltier's eyes included seemingly minor details, such as the misspelling of the first name of a Jewish historian as Josef (Yerushalmi) instead of Yosef. " 'Josef' has a fine exilic ring, whereas 'Yosef' is so Hebrew, so housed." Yet Wieseltier's insistence on such detail, especially as steeped in sarcasm as it was, points to a deeper political subtext focused squarely on the national bounds of identity. In his view, the hybridity of Jewish identity does not mean that a Jewish state should allow other nationals in it (in other words, it does not constitute an argument for a binational state that would grant Palestinians political rights). "What matters, after all, is what a culture does with its heterogeneous material," which to Wieseltier meant containing it within the bounds of a distinct identity. For Wieseltier, to be exiled is to abandon your identity. The sarcastic tone accompanying references to Saidian trademark expressions like "exilic" and "cosmopolitan" marks the dismissal of Said's key point: the dissociation of the nation from the state. Yet the sarcasm is not merely a strategy of dismissing Said's arguments—as in Lewis's case—but also a dismissal of the authenticity of Said's status as an exile:

> And if the non-Jewish Jew, then why not the non-Palestinian Palestinian? Surely the blessing of cosmopolitanism, of all blessings, must be a universal one. If the Jews have been raised up by the spiritual blandishments of statelessness, then the Palestinians, too, should aspire to them. But Said likes it both ways. He enjoys the glamour of diasporism and the rectitude of nationalism.[82]

The absurd categories of the "non-Jewish Jew" and the "non-Palestinian Palestinian" are Wieseltier's way of deriding the territorial claims of Palestinians, as well as an implied affirmation of the one-nation state, as opposed to a binational state. It is also significant that Wieseltier did not acknowledge Said as a Palestinian but only as a promoter of Palestinian interests. For Wieseltier, Said was the stranger lurking on the margins of the nation, just as Brecht had once been in his FBI file.[83] For Wieseltier, Said was too much of a cosmopolitan to belong to a nation but too politically involved in Palestinian nationalist politics to be an authentic cosmopolitan. Forcing the paradox becomes a form of double negation and thus a way of dismissing not simply a particular author, Edward Said, but also the exile persona he had used and the political claims this persona implicitly supported.

The critique echoes an earlier attack published by the journal *Commentary*. Describing Said's prose as the "verbal equivalent of the weapons wielded by his colleagues on the Palestinian National Council" and his writing as "spill[ing] ink to justify their spilling of blood," Eugene Alexander had drawn the image of an Arab Said as violent, uncivilized, and incapable of engaging in intellectual argument.[84] Between this rendition of Said's Arab origin as an inferior status and its contestation as being merely political pretense, Said is depicted in these criticisms according to the same logic he had analyzed in the Zionist account of the Palestinian: first "an inconsequential native; then . . . an absent one; then . . . a less real person than any individual person belonging to the 'Jewish people,' whether that person was present in Israel or not."[85]

ESTRANGEMENT AND EMOTIONAL INVOLVEMENT: BEING PALESTINIAN

In *The Question of Palestine*, Said's strategy for creating presence for the Palestinian had sometimes proceeded as a rather desperate litany of assertions:

> There *is* a Palestinian people, there *is* an Israeli occupation of Palestinian lands, there *are* Palestinians under Israeli military occupation, there *are* Palestinians—650,000 of them—who are Israeli citizens and who constitute 15 percent of the population of Israel, there *is* a large Palestinian population in exile: these are actualities which the United States and most of the world have directly or indirectly acknowledged, which Israel too has acknowledged, if only in the forms of denial, rejection, threats of war, and punishment.[86]

These statements, however, did more than just repeat the same idea—the existence of Palestinians as an autonomous people. Repetition creates presence because with each statement the reality invoked gains more weight, more concreteness, and more detail.[87] The most concrete form of presence for Palestinians comes in *After the Last Sky*, the volume coauthored by Said and photographer Jean Mohr. Here, the reader can see the faces of Palestinians, the landscapes of their land, and the houses in which they live. Such direct presentation taps into the commonplace assumption that what we see in a photograph must exist. Even then, however, Said confronts the ambiguity of presentation as inevitably a representation. One of the most moving photos in the book (Said's own favorite) features a couple and a child in a terraced landscape with dense bushes and trees against the contours of houses and buildings in the foreground. The image is very hard to read: is it a family? Are they happy or sad? The multilayered structure of the setting suggests the multiplicity of meanings and the difficulty to arrange them in a coherent account. The image ends up confusing (to provoke and inspire) rather than merely describing.

To be politically effective, presence is not only what we can see but also what we understand, and an epistemic and moral, not just visual, display. In Said's memoir, *Out of Place*, on display is the author himself, as his own life's story is offered to readers as an analogic representation of Palestinian identity. Yet the memoir, too, treaded a difficult rhetorical ground. By the time it was published, Said was completely committed to politics and had become impatient with philosophical accounts that pontificated on political matters without showing a real solution and with philosophers who cared too much about their own welfare to be concerned about others. Said disliked what he deemed Foucault's "shift from the political to the personal [which] was, among other things, the effect of some disenchantment with the public sphere, more particularly perhaps because he [Foucault] felt that there was little he could do to affect it."[88] Yet such an inward turn echoes uncannily Said's own trajectory, revealing at the same time all its deep political significance.

Said had already experienced great disappointment in his official political activity. In 1982, he participated in the United Nations convention on the question of Palestine and was commissioned to produce a "Profile of the Palestinian People." The document, which outlined the history and identity of Palestinians, was eventually rejected by the UN. "Palestine yes, Palestinians no"—was Said's bitter reflection on what he deemed a silencing of the Palestinian narrative.[89] In *After the Last Sky*, he had complained that "the Palestinian story cannot be told smoothly" because it is too intertwined with discourses that negate the very existence of Palestinians and rendered them discontinuous by the experience of dislocation and dispossession.[90] What Mohr's moving photographs and Said's lyrical commentary tried to do in *After the Last Sky*, the memoir attempts in a more literary tradition and thus potentially more effective way: to tell the story of a Palestinian. *Out of Place* asserted the Palestinians' "permission to narrate" as a strategy for bringing into public discourse the Palestinian perspective, confiscated by Zionist ideology and its supporters in the West.[91] Retracing origins becomes Said's strategy of representing the Palestinians in a way that connects this people now scattered across several Arab countries back to the land of Palestine. The recovery of origins is an act of symbolic grounding with political relevance. The trope of origins frames the narrative vignettes accompanying Mohr's photographs, and Said insists on finding origins even when they are hard to uncover. In *After the Last* Sky, Said recounts his experience on a trip to Amman, Jordan—a key destination for Palestinian refugees—with his then thirteen-year-old son, Wadie, who made it a point of asking everyone they met whether they were Jordanian or Palestinian. When "one bearded taxi driver" answered that he was Jordanian, the boy pressed for the exact place of origin: where in Jordan, exactly? The father recounts what came next:

> Predictably the answer was Tul-Karm—a West Bank town—followed by a verbose disquisition on how "today" . . . there was no difference between Jordanians and Palestinians. Wadie, perhaps sensing my sullen disapproval of the driver's waffling and reacting to my unusual reluctance to press the point, insisted otherwise. 'There *is* a difference,' he said, only at his age he couldn't quite articulate it. For our pains the man drove us at least five miles out of our way, and then dumped us at the edge of the city.[92]

The *difference* between Palestinians and any other Arab nation has political consequences for the Palestinian claim to self-determination. This is why Said's memoir, which is largely a story about national awareness, centers on difference in the most personal, and possibly most politically effective, terms possible. It is the story of a Palestinian—Said himself—who was forced to leave his birthplace, to endure humiliation and rejection in his encounters with the colonizers (be they teachers or Israeli police officers), and who overcame these challenges. Said does not lecture the reader on Palestinian-Israeli politics but focuses instead mainly on his own childhood and youth, ending with the death of his parents and the protagonist's graduation from Harvard. Yet the political message is clearly conveyed through a careful juxtaposition of the child's innocence and his gradual discovery of the injustices and oppression afflicting the Palestinian people. The story of an unhappy childhood marked by encounters with cruel teachers, mean schoolmates, and strict cold parents, *Out of Place* reads like a novel by Charles Dickens. It is first and foremost a story of victimization, all the more moving as the victim is a child and the aggressors are all adults. Said's strategy of defamiliarization in the memoir is the Victorian trope of the "critical child," whose pure and thus accurate perception of the world demystifies and reveals a hidden political reality: the repression of Palestinians.[93]

As he recounts in this memoir, Said discovered he was an Arab much in the same way Arendt once discovered she was a Jew: at school, from other children, or from the English or American adults or children who rejected him. Yet the Said family was made of prosperous business owners who could afford servants and were able to finance their son's education at elite schools all the way into graduate studies. How could he recount his childhood as the story of a victim in the face of such obvious privilege? Said's strategy was to emphasize psychological victimhood. He also made some (rather unconvincing) attempts at invoking concrete material suffering and dispossession, such as the loss of the family home in Talbyia, the West Jerusalem neighborhood where Said was born. This particular narrative detail, which he had mentioned in interviews as well, created a stir in the media.

In 2000, *Commentary* featured an article by Justus Weiner, a Jewish American lawyer and researcher at the Jerusalem Center for Public Affairs, who charged that Said had fabricated his Palestinian past by lying about the years spent in West Jerusalem.[94] Weiner had spent a considerable amount of time and effort tracing down possible neighbors and schoolmates who could have confirmed Said's presence in Talbyia. His research indicated, he claimed, that nobody in that neighborhood had ever known Edward Said or a member of his family and that they could not have resided there but had lived in Egypt all along. Contesting the veracity of Said's autobiographical claims, Weiner explicitly aimed at more than discrediting him, or disputing the authenticity of this particular individual's claims. The overarching argument of Weiner's article is that Palestinian claims to a territory that belongs officially to Israel are spurious. The article outraged some of Said's longtime allies, such as Alexander Cockburn, who defended Said publicly.[95] Said himself offered biographical clarification, all the more needed as the attack was not merely personal. At the same time, precisely because the issue at stake was not merely factual but symbolic, an effective response required more than a denial of charges. The memoir legitimized Said's claims of being a dispossessed Palestinian. In this regard, the book offered, more than a personal story, the political tale of Palestinians. It is a story of origin conceived both spatially and temporally. By identifying Jerusalem as his place of birth, Said is anchoring his life story, and by extension that of other Palestinian refugees, to the territory from which their presence had been erased by Zionism. By making this place a point of origin in the sense of what Hannah Arendt called natality—the beginning of life as a fundamental beginning—Said was claiming historical and not just physical presence.[96]

> Our family home was in Talbiyah, a part of West Jerusalem that was sparsely inhabited but had been built and lived in exclusively by Palestinian Christians like us: the house was an imposing two-story stone villa with lots of rooms and a handsome garden in which my two youngest cousins, my sisters, and I would play. There was no neighborhood to speak of, although we knew everyone else in the as yet not clearly defined district. There were no immediate neighbors, although about five hundred yards away sat a row of similar villas where my cousins' friends lived. Today, the empty space has become a park, and the area around the house a lush, densely inhabited upper-class Jewish neighborhood.[97]

This description contrasts starkly with Wilson's report of dirty refugee camps crawling with filthy children. The house is a symbolic configuration designed to suggest, through its sheer size, social respectability and prosperity. The family residence is located in a kind of natural paradise, beyond any borders, outside a political space marked by the bureaucratic practices of a nation-state. The house (and by extension the family inhabiting it) relates to others in the community as neighbors and friends rather than fellow nationals or citizens. Indeed, the memoir emphasizes the different nature of the social life the author and his family lived even in multinational Cairo— a life defined not by bonds of citizenship (as not many of their immediate friends or acquaintances were Palestinian) but by deeper ties formed by a common subjection to colonial domination. Nationality is not assumed, as much as discovered throughout the experiences recounted as the protagonist gradually learns what it means to be an Arab and a Palestinian.

Throughout the book, the story faces the rhetorical difficulty of sustaining the analogy between millions of dispossessed Palestinians and the story of the Said family, seen by some as "an extreme case of an urban Palestinian whose relationship to the land is basically metaphorical."[98] An effective strategy appears in the opening scene, which centers on the image of the stately family house left behind in a territory forbidden to Palestinians. The house is a symbol of concrete, verifiable, origin against the mythical origin of Zionist Israel. It is all the more a sad irony that the house claimed by the Said family in West Jerusalem was later the residence of Martin Buber, who was not only a Jew arriving in Israel in his flight from Nazism but also an ardent proponent of Zionism as a philosophy of peacefulness and reconciliation and a supporter of Palestinian rights. Insisting upon the falsity of Said's claims, Weiner presents the Jews, in this case Buber and his family, as the true dispossessed victims of a lawsuit brought against them by the Said family to deprive them of their residence. The reader of the *Commentary* article is expected to feel outrage not only at the very act of evicting the aging philosopher and his family but also because this old man happened to be the author of *Zion*, which was first a lecture delivered in 1948 and most likely known to the primarily Jewish audience of the newspaper. In this lecture, Buber described Zionism as a philosophy grounded in the idea of a sacred space to which the Jewish people belong so organically that to live outside it would lead to their spiritual death.[99] In Buber's rendition of Zionism, Israel still features as the sacred land; for those Jews who do not inhabit it, life will be unhappy. This equation between living and being happy in the land is exactly how Said depicts his own family life, thus co-opting the Zionist trope of a life fulfilled through its roots and destroyed by uprootedness.

Weiner's entire investigation into the veracity of Said's autobiographical claims was staked on property and ownership as the main anchors that can legitimately ground identity. Was the house owned by the Said family or not? Is the land the property of Palestinians or the Israelis? As Amahl Bishara has shown, "The pairing of homeland and homes may seem transparent at first," because "the house is idealized as stable and unchanging." However, "domestic presence can exceed [it] in important and underrecognized ways."[100] While Weiner was looking for documents attesting to legal ownership of the house—and ignoring, of course, the dependence of such documents on the legitimacy of the authority that would have issued them—for Said inhabiting is created rhetorically through evocations of domesticity. The memoir did not include photocopies of property certificates, only evocations of everyday life: drinking tea on the balcony, running in the backyard, or a teenager locking himself up in his room to indulge in long periods of undisturbed reading. Said had already used this technique in his BBC documentary *In Search of Palestine*, which included a home movie of him and his sisters playing outside their Jerusalem family home with piano music in the background. The scene does not constitute hard proof that the family owned the house and the yard in which the children play as what the viewers see is just a home, not property documentation. But we also see the experience of being at home, which is what the Saids and the Palestinians lost. This distinction reveals a fundamental clash between different understandings of what counts as legitimate ownership, a clash that was relevant beyond Said's experience. One of the letters published in *Commentary* in response to Weiner's article echoed this conflict.[101] The writer, Robert Werman, recounts his own shock at receiving an unexpected call from an Arab man who claimed to have lived in his house and requested permission to show it to his son and daughter. Werman was shocked because, as he repeatedly insists, his house was in a neighborhood that never had Arab homeowners. Yet the visitor, once allowed inside, was clearly familiar with the house. How could this be?—puzzles Werman, at a loss for how to account for the perfect match between his property purchase document and a stranger's description of the property.

Stories like this put in stark contrast Said's representation of the Palestinian at home in his land with the legal category of the citizen authorized by official state documents to issue claims of residence ownership. From the perspective of the citizen, a native like Said and the Arab man who visited Werman have to be illegitimate or mendacious, otherwise they remain a mystery. For Werman, the Arab man's familiarity with his property is inexplicable because he would not accept the only possible (and rather obvious) explanation: that an Arab might have owned his house before any official documentation could even be available. While the discourse of legality and ownership behind such rejection is the discourse of the State (which issues property documents, street surveys, etc.), it is Zionism that gave it rhetorical power by representing the laws and rules issued by the state of Israel as divinely ordained rather than bureaucratic traces of a political power.

Zionism is centered on the trope of the Promised Land, the foundational myth of a sacred place left behind in a remote past and found again after centuries spent in diaspora. Said counteracted this myth with another foundational narrative: the Palestinians' fall from their own paradise, symbolized by his own exile from the place of his birth. In his memoir, Palestine is the land of a content and peaceful family life and happy childhood. Said wrote *Out of Place* after being diagnosed with chronic leukemia. The time of the writing of this book is significant. The heightened awareness of mortality sets a tragic tone to the recollections and infuses the experiences narrated with an emotional significance beyond their concrete content. The dying Said writes as someone who no longer has anything to lose and has thus nothing to hide. After the exile, the family is unhappy: the father has a nervous breakdown, the mother struggles with loneliness and anxiety, and later both parents fight terminal diseases. More important, the child becomes unhappy, losing his innocence, and discovering fear before experiencing his ultimate political awakening.

Most of Said's memoir presents the experience of colonization as a child's encounter with hostile British and Americans teachers. The official agents of empire are teachers in the expensive imperial schools attended by young Edward, from the cruel Mr. Bullen at the Gezira Preparatory School, who beats him for an infringement so insignificant that the narrator Said cannot even remember to Miss Clark at Victoria College, who singles him out in veritable "ontological condemnation." Said depicts his experience in an expensive exclusive school in a Dickensian manner, directing the reader's attention to the school as the cold repressive environment. Yet despite a strong emphasis on registering painful experiences he had in school, it is at home, and in relation to his own parents, that the protagonist develops the identity of a victim: in his father's constantly disappointed eyes, in the confusion created by his mother's alternate outbursts of love and anger, and in both parents' harsh rebukes for his minor "delinquencies" as well as for how he looks or speaks. It is the Westernized parents' gaze that sees in the handsome man readers know from photographs the very opposite of someone presentable (or indeed even acceptable). Young Said's body is judged by his parents as not just "imperfect" but also "morally flawed"—his face, too "weak," especially the mouth; his tongue, "aggressive, unpleasant, uncontrolled"; his hands compared to "hammers, pliers, clubs, steel wires"; and his posture deemed so poor that it had to be corrected by "metal chest expanders" that his father forced him to wear well into Edward's college years.[102]

The depiction of the pain inflicted by his parents on him psychologically and physically is far more moving than the narration of a scene in which a stiff, typically Victorian spinster teacher berates Said for being unruly during a school trip. Between the more conventional trope of the schoolteachers' cruelty and that of his father (the memoir reports several beatings administered by a strong man who could inflict serious pain as well as systematic moral disapproval) the contrast heavily indicts Said's own family over the English or American teachers. The teachers are placed in explicitly "colonialist" positions, which are fundamentally normative—judging the young Said and determining his "worth" as a student. Yet the parents' confirmation of the judgment is what ultimately seals the "ontological condemnation" and creates the colonized victim. Edward's mother, for instance, not only agrees with Miss Clark's rebuke but continues to agree with it by repeatedly referencing it to express discontent with her son's behavior.

In *After the Last Sky*, Said depicted the Palestinian family as united in grief for their stolen nation-land. He tried to address the contradiction created by depictions of his own family by insisting that, no matter what his parents said or did to him, he felt nothing but love for them. While such a statement can seem disingenuous, it need not have been so. Wadie Said, the father, embodied the paradox of the victim of colonization: he had accepted the demands of the imperial West to the point where he imposed them more strictly and more violently than Westerners themselves. The ideal posture he seeks to force on his son is, significantly, the posture of an idealized American body he had studied in a magazine. The cruel father is the colonized who, by being deprived of the life he could have had inside his nation, loses his very humanity and not just a nationality. He offers his son a life of economic comfort, financing his studies, paying for expensive trips to Europe but no affection. He supports him financially but not emotionally.

It is not a stretch to see in this representation of Wadie Said a political allegory in which the father stands in for a state that is willing and able to care for certain residents but will constantly look down on them. One of the arguments used by Israel against Palestinian claims to self-determination has positioned the state of Israel as economically more powerful than a Palestinian state could be and thus more capable of supporting Palestinians. The economic argument against the Palestinian presence, thus presented, is that it is not self-sustainable—just as the young Said could not amount to much, in his father's view, without his constant assessment, condemnation, and forceful correction. Said came to America in 1951 on what he calls his "banishment" to enroll in a college preparatory school after which he would attend Princeton and Harvard. He and his parents made the trip on a luxury ocean liner—hardly the immigrant voyage to Ellis Island. Yet Said succeeds in depicting the arrival as nevertheless a crossing of borders into a new universe. It was a universe he did not find attractive, much like his mother who disliked America and never agreed to live here (only to die in an American hospital). Coming to America was a coming of age: away from his parents, the young Said was free to find himself. Yet he recounts his formative experiences in the United States and the rising of his political consciousness, carefully avoiding the plot of an immigrant story in which America is the final destination on the road to self-discovery. He was already an American citizen. The memoir emphatically presents his alienation from an American identity as a child, from statements of non-belonging among Americans— "it was as an American businessman's son who hadn't the slightest feeling of being American I entered the Cairo School for American Children"— to frequent reflections on his unusual name, which not only straddled the Western identity desired by his parents and the Arab genealogy of the family, but also lent itself, phonetically, to adoptions and rejections. Edward could become "Ed" (as it happened in America). Said could be pronounced "Sigheed." At the same time, however, the amusement park in the vicinity of the school had an airplane ride called "Saida." For the other children, that name became a way of reminding Edward that he was not really Sigheed, and not really American. Yet he was also discouraged (mostly by his parents) to see himself as an Arab. Said acknowledges candidly throughout the book the difficulty he experienced as a child feeling anywhere like a native, trapped instead in an "impossible subjectivity."[103]

Said repeatedly said in interviews that he had written the memoir as a self-exploration, "laying open all the contradictions and irreconcilabilities," probably not just his own but also those of Palestinians in general.[104] The reception of *Out of Place* was mixed. While most reviewers acknowledged the powerful personal narrative recounted in the book, several questioned the representativeness of this story for Palestinian identity and dismissed the political relevance of Said's personal destiny. Some even ridiculed the attempt at finding political meaning in childhood experiences with strict teachers and camp counselors. In the *New York Times*, Ian Buruma sarcastically dismissed Said's suffering as equivalent to political oppression. Said's ill-at-ease with his European surname (which prompts a meditation on the European standard by which the Arab child is measured, mainly to be scolded for failing to meet it) and his disappointments caused by not being valedictorian, a table head, or a floor officer while in boarding school, which Said explains as discrimination against an Arab—such events and their *interpretation* strike Buruma as "rather grand political parallels and conclusions (drawn) from his personal experience of alienation and loneliness."[105] Buruma discredits the analogy at the center of the memoir between the "private troubles" of such a socially privileged man and "the troubles of all the dispossessed, and of the dispossessed Palestinians in particular." Dismissing the memoir as politically unconvincing, Buruma also challenged its literary merit, criticizing "the pompous tone." He did acknowledge, however, that Said's was powerful *personal* story:

> The hero emerging from his memoir is not the Palestinian activist so much as the alienated intellectual. The modern image of the heroic intellectual is that of a marginal figure, the deconstructionist of the official "narratives," the "exile." One finishes his book with the strong impression that Said presses the suffering of the Palestinian people into the service of his own credentials as an intellectual hero.[106]

This dismissal of the political significance of the book appeared in other analyses, including academic reviews that were less sarcastic and more reflective than Buruma's. Alan Confino, an Israeli-born historian, offered in the context of an overall positive review of the book, the same criticism as Buruma: "As long as Said keeps his focus on the personal, his narrative is touching and riveting. But he tends to leap from the personal and subjective to the political and impersonal in a way that challenges his credibility. . . . Sometimes a scolding is only a scolding, and a hot dog is only a hot dog." Confino had literary objections to the story, which he found too much in the style of a grand narrative set around the classical themes of vulnerability, heroism, and uprootedness. He objected most strongly to a conflation of two plots, one that is a "parable of modern—or, better, post-modern—life" and the other "a unique story of a specific individual."[107] Insofar as it was more than just one man's autobiography, the story could appeal to various kinds of readers, including Confino himself, a Jew who recognized in the book many of his own experiences as an Israeli living in the United States.

Writing for the *American Spectator*, Edward Grossman faulted Said for failing to represent the experience of those closest to sharing his fate: Christian Arabs in the Middle East. For that reason, the political claims staked by Said on his own childhood experiences struck Grossman as "unconvincing," unleashing his own analysis of the role played by Christian Arabs in the region. The memoir's silence on the situation of Arab Christians is indeed surprising given Said's own family background. But Grossman was not simply critical of an omission. He was also critical of what the memoir did cover and went as far as to suggest that the Palestinian plight has been rather convenient for people like Said—foreigners who come to the United States and invent strategic autobiographies. To support his claim, Grossman lists, among others, "the woman posing as Czar Nicholas II's daughter" and a lot of "naturalized Jews: nineteenth century investor and climber August Belmont, the director Josef von Sternberg, the tycoon Menachem Riklis, the diplomat Madeleine Albright. Compared to their lies, the gap between the facts of Said's life and the version he cultivated for so long is easily forgiven."[108] How could Said belong on this roster, other than as a target of nativist xenophobic rejection directed against *all* immigrants?

Meron Benvenisti, a former deputy mayor of Jerusalem and himself an author, reviewed Said's memoir in the *SAIS Review of International Affairs*, which is published by the Foreign Policy Institute at Johns Hopkins University. Benvenisti stresses repeatedly that his response to the memoir was that of a native of Jerusalem reading the account of another native. From this authoritative perspective, Benvenisti confirmed the emotional truth of Said's narrative and insisted that it did not matter whether the story was also factually true. He recognized the political subtext of a moving personal story and attacked by focusing directly on Said's victim persona, and by extension, on the victimization claimed by Palestinians. Benvenisti found *Out of Place* "a fascinating portrait of a privileged family and a pampered youth in the midst of great suffering and destruction." While willing to acknowledge Said's Palestinian origin, Benvenisti also dismissed it by reading it in terms of class. The Saids were "the educated, affluent, urban, and Westernized Palestinians who inhabited the elegant houses of Talbiyah." The contrast between the Jewish resident, Benvenisti, son of a teacher and nurse, raised in a two-bedroom apartment on the same street in Talbiyah, and the Palestinian native, Said, son of a wealthy businessman with a personal driver and numerous domestics, becomes a class conflict rather than one based on nationality. Palestinians like the Saids are not refugees but exiles, leaving behind a political mess they simply preferred to avoid. They abandoned "the

Palestinian masses, both in the cities and the villages" to an Israeli force not only militarily superior but also more determined to win and more broadly supported by the Jewish population. "I do not think," writes Benvenisti, "the likes of Edward Said were able to understand the desperate force that animated David and Leah Benvenisti. In the world of the Gezira Club or the garden parties of Mandatory Jerusalem, they did not count."[109] By reframing the conflict in terms of class, Benvenisti created a different interpretive context in which suffering and affluence are incompatible and thus reversed the roles: the Palestinians (at least those represented by Said) are not victims but privileged bourgeois without a national consciousness. The Israelis are not oppressors but merely fighters determined to win their land.

This response, compelling to some extent, does not take into account the Palestinians who had a different class background than the Saids. It can be an effective challenge to Said's story but not to the Palestinian national narrative. All it did was to join a choir of critical voices clamoring that Said's personal story cannot be taken as representative for the Palestinian experience. How to understand, then, Confino's claim, that "as a Palestinian, Said has written a testimony more eloquent than all his political writing; the personal is often more powerful than the purely political." Then what was the memoir a testimony to? Toward the end of his review, Confino revealed that he lives in the same neighborhood as Said's family, a "bow shot" from their house. "For Said, Talbiyah is a home lost, for me it is home, even as I also recognize that it is Said's lost home."[110] This unexpected affinity between the Palestinian author and his Israeli critic, nonetheless, is a subtle way to reject the political relevance of the memoir, an overemphasizing of its *human* (not national or state) dimension. Furthermore, the situation has changed now, Confino insists, as many Israelis like himself are not oblivious to the tragic fate of their Palestinian neighbors. By making Said's childhood experience seem merely historical, Confino also implied that an anti-Palestinian Israel was anachronistic.

The critics who attacked *Out of Place* held Said's privileged class status against him and charged that his experiences were not representative for the lives of most Palestinians. But the rhetorical function of the memoir was not to create an iconic timeless Palestinian identity, but to enact Palestinian identity in the particulars of a life. As Bishara notes, the memoir revealed "habits of emplacement that Palestinians would recognize to be in contrast with the decades of displacement that have followed." Granted, many Palestinians did not have a personal chauffeur or a country club membership, features that conflict indeed with the experience of dispossession and displacement. But most Palestinians, the Saids included, enjoyed "certain pleasures or habits of home that many Palestinians have shared across class and geography, like drinking tea surrounded by one's garden."[111] The intimacy of a family home and the simplicity of a life undisturbed by politics—such was the loss evoked in the book.

It remains hard to know whether the memoir appealed mainly to Said's fans or to Palestinian supporters or whether it reached audiences who had previously been less inclined to accept such political views. Yet one response from an old enemy was quite eloquent. Writing for *Forward*, American-born Israeli writer Hillel Halkin reviewed *Out of Place* in connection to Justus Weiner's allegations.[112] Halkin was convinced that Weiner was right and that Said had invented his West Jerusalem story. Nevertheless, he admitted, somewhat against himself, that the memoir had moved him deeply. He had read the book as a story of tribulation and triumph, and like Confino, had found parts of his own self, as a Jew, in Said. Said's lifelong dream of reconciliation between the Israelis and the Palestinians was thus achieved in a suspension of hostilities through narrative identification.[113]

CONCLUSION

Immersed for most of his life in the cosmopolitan world of New York and academia, Said neither aspired to Americanization nor was prevented from it. On the contrary, over the years he increasingly asserted his support for Palestinian liberation and a Palestinian identity that became a platform for his criticism of Israel and of its American supporters. His academic career as a scholar of Western high culture, along with a political commitment to the Palestinian indicate "the sign of an unevenness he actually lived, between a politics that was always about time and temporality and a culture than remained locked in fixed space if not in fantasy."[114] Yet this ambiguity only exists in a Western political tradition that separates reflection from action and the life of the mind from the life of the polis. While challenging this separation and advocating in passionate Benda fashion the responsibility intellectuals have to be politically engaged, Said admitted to struggling with the potential incompatibility between an academic and intellectual career and a political mission:

> My whole background in the Middle East, my frequent and sometimes protracted visits there, my political involvement: all this exists in a totally different box from the one out of which I pop as a literary critic, professor, etc. . . . I am as aware as anyone that the ivory-tower concerns of technical criticism . . . are very far removed from the world of political, power, domination, and struggle. But there are links between the two worlds which I for one am beginning to exploit in my own work.[115]

Said forged these links in his theory of representation, used to advance political claims on behalf of Palestinian self-determination, and his strategies of de-familiarization, which develop common tropes and themes in the Western canon but read them against their own logic. As he moved between the bright ivory tower of academia and the dark alleys of Arab-Israeli-American politics, he also shifted away from his interest in Orientalism as an ideology that represses difference toward an ever growing interest in humanism as philosophical reflection on the universality of the human condition. He viewed nations and cultures as mutually intelligible rather than incompatible, and in his late work, devoted himself to a scholarship grounded in the "secular notion that the historical world is made by men and women, and not by God, and that it can be understood rationally . . . [that] we can know things according to the way they were made."[116] Said died in 2003, the year that marked the launch of the second Iraq war and the official beginning of an era that saw significant changes in how America is perceived around the world as well as how many Americans relate to their own nation. In 2004, Samuel P. Huntington's book *Who We Are: The Challenges to America's National Identity* argued that America is not a nation of immigrants but descendent of European settlers and thus fundamentally a Western culture potentially threatened by every non-Western foreigner seeking to come here.

Asked whether he felt more at home in America or in the Middle East, Said responded: "I'm at home in both places. But I'm different, in a way. In the American context, I speak as an American and I can also speak as a Palestinian. But in neither case do I feel that I belong in a proprietary sense or, let's say, in an executive sense, to the central power establishment. I'm in the opposition in both places."[117] Those who saw him solely as a Palestinian activist often confused his arguments for the creation of a binational Israel with anti-Semitic banter. Those who only detected exilic melancholy in Said's work missed the significance of his Palestinian politics as well as the political implications of his literary ideas. It is significant and encouraging that it was in America where Said felt free to speak both as an American and as a Palestinian. Perhaps this explains why Said made his political home in the United States, no matter how much he may have felt, culturally and emotionally, at home in the Middle East.

CONCLUSION

I N VOLUME 2 of *Democracy in America*, published five years after the first
one had established the author's reputation as an admirer of American
society and its political system, Tocqueville noted that "in their relations
with strangers the Americans are impatient of the slightest criticism and
insatiable for praise."[1] He was a genuine admirer but complained nevertheless about the narcissism of many Americans:

> I tell an American that he lives in a beautiful country; he answers: "That
> is true. There is none like it in the world." I praise the freedom enjoyed by
> the inhabitants, and he answers: "Freedom is a precious gift, but very few
> peoples are worthy to enjoy it." I note the chastity of morals prevailing in
> the United States, and he replies: "I suppose that a stranger, struck by the
> immorality apparent in all other nations, must be astonished at this sight."
> Finally I leave him to his self-contemplation, but he returns to the charge
> and will not stop till he has made me repeat everything I have said. One
> cannot imagine a more obnoxious or boastful form of patriotism. Even ad-
> mirers are bored.[2]

Patriotism in this form is not only annoying but also dangerous as it continues to endorse familiar visions that might be socially and politically flawed

or even pernicious. The stranger persona is, most of all, a gateway to alternative representations that become visible once we renounce enamored perpetuations of what we already have. The stranger persona, as discussed in this book, is also the result of a tension between political subjectivities, the native and the foreigner. The persistent disagreement over visions of America between American intellectuals and the protagonists of this book is striking. Yet it is hardly surprising, as it reflects deep-seated differences in worldviews and commitments. These four intellectuals all arrived in America after experiencing traumatic events in their native country. Arendt was arrested by the Gestapo and was later interned as an enemy alien at Gurs, France. She could have shared the fate of historian Marc Bloch—among so many other Jewish intellectuals in Europe—who died in an extermination camp. Solzhenitsyn was in the Soviet Gulag and could have been interned again or executed if his growing international fame had not determined Soviet authorities to resort to deportation. Marcuse and Said did not experience directly such trauma, but they watched from up-close a politics of destruction affecting their people. All four came to the United States politically disenchanted. As the saying goes, they were not prophets in their own land. How then did they become prophets in America?

Disenchantment increases awareness of the wrongs of the world, both actual and possible. It breeds skepticism and pessimism and stimulates hypercritical evaluation. Such a mindset conflicted with the postwar optimism and enthusiasm of many Americans. For a lot of European intellectuals, the tragedy of World War II was to have called into question the very meaning of life and the fundamental goodness of human beings. If after Auschwitz poetry did not make sense any more, as Adorno put it, life itself, and with it politics, seemed to have come to an apocalyptic end.[3] By contrast, American intellectuals coming out of the war, and even more so those coming of age in the postwar era, had a keen sense of a new beginning. European pessimism clashed with American optimism as in each other's eyes one side looked grim and morose and the other naïve and gullible. In the case of the Frankfurt Institute leaders Adorno and Horkheimer, or writers like Mann and Brecht, this clash was never fully resolved and led to their decision to return to Europe. Arendt and Marcuse, on the other hand, were able to engage with American intellectuals in a way that allowed some cross-pollination rather than a constant locking of horns. Both displayed a certain amount of faith in American politics while also damping the national enthusiasm at times with their lucid analyses. For Solzhenitsyn and Said, adopting a critical stance toward American politics was part of maintaining a distinctively nationalized stranger persona, one as a Russian and the other as a Palestinian. Yet insofar as they continued to press their political goals, both were more optimistic than many Americans who feared that the Soviet Union was unstoppable or that the Israeli-Palestinian conflict is a case of irresolvable civilizational strife. The exchanges between these four foreigners and American intellectuals produced a political discourse that is itself a major gain, productive beyond immediate polling results and beyond an impact measurable in policy or regime change.

If these foreign intellectuals—white, Western educated, sophisticated, and highly articulate in English—encountered hostility when they expressed critical opinions of America, what does this say about Americans' willingness to grant the nonnative the right to participate in public discourse, and thus, the right to political membership? The objections against these foreign intellectuals' political ideas and their right to formulate them are indicative of a broader xenophobic politics and thus at least as troubling as the more blatant, institutionalized rejection of the foreigner in the person of an illegal alien, guest worker, or asylum seeker. To me, this illustrates the insidiousness of the national bond even in a country defined by civic patriotism rather than ethnic bonds, a country whose citizens commonly identify with a symbolic immigrant heritage. The challenge is to articulate a way in which this bond can maintain its strength while also allowing more receptiveness to the perspective of those who fall outside of it and thus creating a more complex and nuanced perspective on civic affairs. One possible way, which I sketch briefly by way of concluding, is through recognition of a mutual commitment to a shared world as part of a political friendship unconstrained by an ethics of nationality.

In her reflections on the legacy of *Brown v. Board of Education* for America's continuing struggle with racial inequality, Danielle Allen sees a possible solution in an increase in political friendship. She defines political friendship as a deliberate cultivation of, and engagement with, the ideas of people we do not know and do not resemble by way of measuring our own perspective against an unfamiliar one. As Allen stresses, "the final test of whether we have managed to cultivate political friendship in our own communities is . . . whether a stranger to our neighborhood, *including strangers from beyond the nation's borders*, could land here and flourish in conjunction with us." This would not simply require that "strangers from beyond the nation's border" receive more tolerance in American society but rather that they would feel they have a political membership in America and thus the right to reimagine their new country in a way that would reflect their own ideals, no matter how different from those held by their native-born fellow citizens. Allen urges us, as democratic citizens, "to develop [our] capacities for political imagination, particularly with reference to the strangers in [our] lives."[4]

This book has shown how difficult it is to engage in such an effort when the strangers are foreigners, people who were born and raised in different traditions. To imagine an alternative America, as envisioned in turn by Arendt, Marcuse, Solzhenitsyn, and Said, required a willingness to listen to them more carefully and to admit that their visions might be morally and politically justified, rather than assume them to be misguided or irrelevant to American life. Deeming the foreigner wrong by default is not only a mark of intolerance beyond social policies and rhetorical conceits; it is also a way of limiting political membership to those with whom we already share a bond. Seyla Benhabib has argued convincingly that allowing immigrants political membership in their new country is a fundamental right.[5] As she points out, "the human right to membership is an aspect of *the principle of right, i.e., of the recognition of the individual as a being who is entitled to moral respect, a being whose communicative freedom we must recognize.*"[6] I regard discursive acts of the kind put forth in these intellectuals' criticism of America as their attempted expressions of political membership. Political membership allows us to express particular views toward the polity we have entered and to expect such views to be heard and recognized as potentially valid and legitimate.

The criticism (occasionally quite harsh) that these intellectuals received in America suggests that they lacked such political membership even though they had the freedom of speech to articulate their views publicly and no matter how authoritative they might have been otherwise, intellectually or morally. The cause is not their rhetorical incompetence, far from it. It is not the case that foreign intellectuals simply needed to come up with a different set of rhetorical strategies. Such a demand would trivialize a rhetorical phenomenon that grew out of a complex political and ontological predicament. The stranger persona emerges from a historically and culturally situated form of political subjectivity. One could argue that these cases are exceptional and that there are counterexamples of foreign-born politicians and public intellectuals who have risen to the highest levels of power. Hans Morgenthau and Arendt were friends educated in similar intellectual traditions. National Security Advisor Zbigniew Brzezinski, a Polish native with direct knowledge of the communist bloc, successfully promoted as a member of the Jimmy Carter administration a political agenda similar to Solzhenitsyn's. At the same time, professional politicians like Morgenthau and Brzezinski spoke from within a discourse that was not uniquely theirs but created and shared by Americans. Morgenthau's conception of political realism found its practical grounding in George Kennan's Cold War containment doctrine. Brzezinski's conception of a non-antagonistic politics toward Eastern Europe matched President Jimmy Carter's vision (after having clashed earlier with the American official policy under President Dwight Eisenhower). Arendt, Marcuse, Solzhenitsyn, and Said were never professional politicians or government officials. If included in and subordinated to a native political vision, perhaps their political visions could have become part of an official agenda and even been incorporated in specific policies. Leo Strauss, while not a direct commentator of civic affairs himself, directly influenced the political thinking behind official decisions, which were nevertheless squared off on their own terms. The four intellectuals studied here were not members of the political establishment, and none an *eminence gris* mentoring powerful officials.

Through style and ideas, Arendt, Marcuse, Solzhenitsyn, and Said fell outside the bond of nationality shared by the audiences they addressed in America. At times, they may even have strengthened this exclusionary mechanism as Solzhenitsyn's Harvard speech did, just by mobilizing them against a common front, the foreigner's criticism of their country. The rhetorical fragility of the stranger persona is a consequence of its political and ontological framework. Irked by their style, Americans who rejected the views of Arendt, Marcuse, Solzhenitsyn, and Said rejected the voice of the stranger. I use the term "voice" in the same sense as Fred Evans, as both "conveyor of discourse" and material condition of existence, reflecting worldviews and subjectivities that interact in our forms of life. Evans describes society as a multivoiced body granting "equal audibility" to each voice in a creative interplay that values and maintains democratic diversity.[7] The value of unfamiliar voices lies in their capacity to stir up the imagination, but they risk being silenced forcefully by the oracular voice of the native. An oracle is a voice that tries to dominate and exclude others in the name of homogeneity and as an attempt at asserting hegemony. The native, here, is understood not in any biologically essentialist way but as a political construct made possible by the idea of the nation. Jürgen Habermas has stressed the role played historically by national identity in transcending regional particularistic ties and creating broader solidarities.[8] Yet nationality also limits solidarity, acting as an "ethical community," according to David Miller, that separates one national group from others and from humanity at large.[9] In Miller's view, such an ethical connection takes precedence over the more general bond we might feel with other human beings. It represents a commitment to people we do not know yet with whom we assume to have a certain familiarity. It is such a commitment that can justify in times of war the sacrifice of an individual's life for the good of not just family and close friends but also people one does not actually know. The "imagined community" that constitutes a nation, in Benedict Anderson's terms, creates an assumption of closeness where such a thing does not actually exist. An ethics of nationality involves a distribution of trust based on assumed familiarity. I trust fellow nationals because I assume that I know them, and even more important, that their judgment and actions and mine are likely to be at least based on a shared set of beliefs and values.

"Does the ethics of nationality not entail moral indifference to outsiders?" asks Miller, and the answer is surely positive, judging by what responses to international crises have repeatedly shown.[10] This book suggests that the ethics of nationality can shun outsiders at the level of discourse as much as at the level of policy even when those outsiders have become its newest members. American intellectuals repeatedly displayed a fundamental mistrust in the political ideas of Arendt, Marcuse, Solzhenitsyn, and Said, acting on behalf of an ethics of nationality troubled by, and alert to, the breach of familiarity. To be sure, there were ethnic, ideological, and philosophical bonds that these four intellectuals shared with American colleagues. These were strong connections but overall not as deep as those created by nationality.

Nationality can provide a bond that keeps out the foreigner on the assumption that foreignness will challenge the consensus or at least conventional wisdom of those sharing the national bond. The rejection of arguments proposed by Arendt, Marcuse, Solzhenitsyn, and Said reinforced the mechanism of statecraft by which the foreigner is the measuring rod against which states maintain control over the attribution of citizenship. As Nevgat Sozuk has argued, "the invention of the nation-state and the national citizen, outlining new forms of eligibility, could not have been achieved without defining those forms of ineligibility against which the forms of eligibility were presumed."[11] Insofar as *foreign* is a "political epithet," to use Rogers Brubaker's formulation, "condensing around itself pure outsiderhood,"[12] the politics of a nation would seem incompatible with foreign ideas.

Arendt, Marcuse, Solzhenitsyn, and Said faced an audience that, no matter how sophisticated intellectually, shared this strong national bond above other connections and commitments, which in turn presented these four foreign intellectuals with a daunting rhetorical task. Would they have faced it more effectively if they had avoided the stranger persona and tried instead to come across as naturalized Americans (or at least be less emphatic about their non-American identity, in Solzhenitsyn's case?) As I argued in chapter 1, the only rhetorical stance available to these foreigners was that of a stranger, which they employed with wisdom and dignity. Occasionally, one might wish they had displayed more diplomacy or sensitivity. Would it have been beneficial to American political discourse if the stranger persona I have examined had had an overall more favorable reception? My answer is yes, but not merely because I would rank the political beliefs of Arendt,

Marcuse, Solzhenitsyn, and Said superior to those of American-born intellectuals. The loss suffered by American political discourse in rejecting the arguments of these four is not reducible to a particular policy intervention or even broader reform—though it is interesting to speculate what would have happened, for example, if Arendt's plea for the abrogation of anti-miscegenation laws would have been heard and put into practice *then*, in 1959 rather than 1967, when the last anti-miscegenation legislation in America was abrogated. Beyond possibly missing the opportunity for enlightened sociopolitical reform, the American polis failed to look at itself through the eyes of another.

The stranger persona is central for an "intersubjective praxis of argumentation which enjoins those involved to an idealizing *enlargement* of their interpretive perspectives."[13] An enlarged perspective that included the criticism offered by these four intellectuals could have led to less reliance on American exceptionalism and an increased willingness and ability to situate and evaluate American politics in a broader international context without assuming America's superior status or its messianic mission. Each of these four intellectuals pleaded for such attitudes, directly or indirectly. An enlarged perspective would have also meant an increased skepticism toward the political trope of mythical America, a true nationalist strategy of disabling critical reflection on actual America and inhibiting reform. Finally, such an enlarged perspective would have made (as it did at times) disenchantment and estrangement part of political analysis, leading to fewer self-congratulatory assessments, and possibly to more daring visions. Creativity is the response to the interruption of habitual activity.[14] Such interruption requires "modes of argumentation that make use of innovative linguistic strategies and devices," as critical theorists recommend we use.[15] Estrangement led to original and sophisticated conceptions, rendering them at the same time unrecognizable to many American audiences.

Recognition implies a difficult task: to acknowledge another's identity in a way that shows an accurate understanding and without submitting it to a biased evaluation. Many New York intellectuals misunderstood Arendt's identity—in its complex relations to German culture, Jewish and Zionist politics, and abstract philosophical thought—and submitted her to a biased judgment. Similar misunderstandings and biased evaluations shaped the reception of Marcuse seen insistently as too German for a new American revolution, Solzhenitsyn as too Russian to appreciate true democracy, and Said, too Arab not to be anti-Semitic and anti-Western. As Charles Taylor has pointed out, the task of recognition involves a "politics of identity" but also actively seeks to avoid hierarchies of values and beliefs underlying different identities. In Taylor's view, every individual has a unique way of experiencing the world and should be allowed to hold those beliefs and convictions that reflect such a unique position. What we recognize, then, is another person's moral and epistemic scheme, the "background against which [her] tastes and desires and aspirations make sense."[16] On the same grounds, we can reject another person's views if we disapprove of the cultural, social, and political background against which these views make sense. To avoid such rejection, Nancy Fraser's conception of recognition focuses on the social divisions and the economic inequities that make recognition necessary in the first place by placing agents into privileged and oppressed positions—and thus assigning them a particular status. Recognition, when granted, is no longer measured by the extent to which a unique way of being in the world has been validated. Rather, recognition is possible when "institutionalized patterns of cultural value express equal respect for all participants and ensure equal opportunity for achieving social esteem."[17]

If we follow Taylor, the recognition of Arendt, Marcuse, Solzhenitsyn, and Said would have required an accurate understanding and acceptance of their worldviews. This can be exceedingly difficult under particular circumstances. How to convince some Americans caught in the panic of the Cold War that not all Russians are born either communists or religious nationalists? To make recognition predicated on accurate understanding also begs the question: what does it take to understand accurately the views of people who think so differently from us that we are bound to misunderstand them? Taylor can help us out of this dilemma, as I show shortly, but let us consider first Fraser's recommendation that recognition come from institutions and state practices. Where foreigners are concerned, institutions might be even less willing to recognize their perspective as valid, at least so long as they serve a nation-state founded on the a priori distinction between citizens and foreigners. Ironically, in the case of these four foreigners, the task of recognition did not benefit from the existence of an institutionalized setting that could guarantee equal opportunities for social esteem. Marcuse, for instance, ended up being seen by New Leftists as too much of a German, no matter how much their political ideals coincided and no matter how committed he was to American politics.

To avoid these pitfalls, we can think about recognition, along with Paul Ricoeur, as a relationship based on *reciprocity*: in the act of recognition, different actors recognize each other as mutually committed to one another and to their common world.[18] Rather than try to correct the understanding of Arendt, Marcuse, Solzhenitsyn, and Said or plead for institutional mechanisms more favorable to their acceptance, we can think about the relationship between these four foreign-born intellectuals and their American-born colleagues as part of a mutual commitment to America. Thus defined, recognition is not something granted by the native (or the state represented in institutions) to the foreigner—the New York intellectuals granting recognition to Arendt or the New Left to Marcuse—or indeed vice versa. It is mutually established. The foreign intellectuals would need to recognize the native' concern about their nation's welfare, just as the natives would recognize the right of the immigrants to be critical as an expression of their commitment to the country in which they have chosen to live. Arendt's dismissal of the NAACP's views was, by this logic, unacceptable, no matter whether wrong or right. Recognition based on mutuality offers one more important gain: it allows the expression of political membership through a common commitment to the American polis.

The main hang-up evidenced by some American readers in response to the stranger personae used in the texts I have analyzed here was that they could not imagine that those ideas could be worked into their own perspective as Americans. Although it was a source of insight for these four authors, estrangement sometimes also erected a barrier between them and the audience. It was this barrier that made recognition difficult, and with it, the enlargement of discursive perspectives. The obstacle was not insurmountable though. When these four thinkers achieved recognition by American peers, the result was not just intellectually superior but also politically expedient, as illustrated by the New Left mobilized alongside (if not behind) Marcuse or the emergence of postcolonialism, its own kind of revolution in cultural politics, inspired by the work of Said. Recognition of this kind, conceived as a reciprocal relation, can forge political friendship in the sense envisioned by Aristotle: a friendship among equals, born out of necessity and based on accepting difference. We are not friends only with those who resemble us but also with those different from us.

The stranger persona is the embodiment of mutuality as a product of recognition. An expanded political imagination can use a stranger persona as rhetorical artifice if not always the product of one's life circumstances. The stranger persona would facilitate a kind of intellectual activity promoting the "corporatism of the universal," actively encouraging a comparative analysis that acknowledges the uniqueness of historical situations and national polities while also regarding them from a "context-transcending" perspective.[19] Such an analysis can be described in Maeve Cooke's terms as "social criticism that challenges the validity of prevailing social institutions and arrangements through reference to some alternative idea of the good society."[20] Providing such an alternative idea is the political gain of a stranger persona.

To think of strangers as political friends and to accept their strange visions as our own requires us to rethink the "enemy-friend" distinction, which has a long tradition in political theory and is often viewed as a realistic take on political relations, one that involves, in the writings of Carl Schmitt, a permanent possibility of war, designed to defend and preserve a group's form of existence. The Cold War renewed this opposition and strengthened it in association with a rhetorical Manichaeism that is well suited for the age of a war on terror. Although many scholars have challenged this way of thinking and the discourse it creates, this book calls for a conscious and deliberate reversal of this distinction. How would our world be if we changed it on the basis of the criticism of enemies as readily as we do it in response to the advice of friends? To achieve such a world, we would need to suspend the assumption that foreigners are wrong by default and instead try out their ideas. This is a tall order not only because political mechanisms like the nation-state and ethical bonds like nationality sabotage such effort but also because our very capacity for understanding is, in Taylor's terms, an ethnocentric epistemic enterprise. Those responding to these foreign intellectuals' arguments by assessing them in their own familiar framework were bound to misunderstand those aspects that were most important and intriguing precisely because they were least familiar, such as Arendt's conception of segregation, Said's take on Zionism, Marcuse's notion of an aesthetic-political revolution, or Solzhenitsyn's criticism of American media and the legal system. The critics used their own language—in the broadest sense of the term, as a set of shared premises and argument techniques—and dismissed the language of the foreigners, and with it, their ideas. Taylor argues that "the adequate language in which we can understand another society is not our language of understanding, or theirs, but rather what one could call a language of perspicuous contrast."[21] An acceptance of the stranger persona does not require us to accept particular arguments as valid but to frame our response in such a language of perspicuous contrast. To this end, we could also use a strategy of estrangement, in order to develop a perspective that is radically different from our own. We can then compare the benefits of a world seen from that perspective and the ones of the world as we know it, before we make our final decision about the world we want.

The linguistic foreignness of these intellectuals—the fact that they came to English from another language—is, of course, a key dimension of their stranger persona. If poetic language is a foreign language, as Aristotle put it, then the language associated with the stranger persona is a poetic language, not because they relied so much on a tropological discourse, but because their was a language that "deepens the fundamental dichotomy of signs and objects," by bypassing or questioning shared meanings, and proposing new ones instead.[22] Our political order, to which Arendt, Marcuse, Solzhenitsyn, and Said contributed important ideas, is one in which tolerance needs to be supplemented with recognition, in order to not merely allow those who speak another language and have come from somewhere else the right to hospitability but also to give all of us a chance to embrace the changes foreigners can inspire.

NOTES

INTRODUCTION

1. Andrei Codrescu, "Arizona Education Loses the Accent of America," NPR, May 10, 2010.
2. The controversy surrounding President Barack Obama's birthplace in connection to his legitimacy as president is relevant in this regard, as is, of course, the fact that only a person born on American soil can become president.
3. Many foreign intellectuals were involved in diasporic politics, especially in the German exile community during the war years. Thomas Mann and Bertolt Brecht are cases in point, among others less famous. See Jean-Michel Palmer, *Weimar in Exile: The Antifascist Emigration in Europe and America*, trans. David Fernbach (London: Verso, 2006).
4. For a comprehensive treatment of Leo Strauss's influence on American political thought, including from the perspective of some of his former students who became government officials, see Kenneth L. Deutsch and John A. Murley, eds., *Leo Strauss, the Straussians, and the American Regime* (Lanham, Md.: Rowman and Littlefield, 1999).
5. For a discussion of Rand's influence on his views, see Alan Greenspan, *The Age of Turbulence: Adventures in a New World* (New York: Penguin, 2007).
6. See Jamie Stiehm, "Paul Ryan's Dangerous Obsession with Ayn Rand," *U.S. News and World Report*, April 14, 2012.
7. A notable exception, and possibly the definitive treatment of Rand, appears in Jennifer Burns, *Goddess of the Market: Ayn Rand and the American Right* (New York: Oxford University Press, 2009).
8. Seyla Benhabib, *The Rights of Others: Aliens, Residents, and Citizens* (Cambridge: Cambridge University Press, 2004).
9. Jürgen Habermas, *The Inclusion of the Other: Studies in Political Theory*, ed. Ciaran Cronin and Pablo De Greiff (Cambridge, Mass.: The MIT Press, 1998), 57.
10. Margarethe von Trotta, dir., *Hannah Arendt* (New York: Zeitgeist Films, 2012).

11. Aristotle's insights coincide with modern social scientific findings. A 1984 psychological study examined the way audience perception of a speaker (based on factors such as age, gender, and appearance) functioned as the main source of persuasion. The authors found that when audience members were unlikely to elaborate on the information presented, because they were not familiar with the content of the message or not especially interested in it (low likelihood of elaboration), they decided whether to accept the message based on how convincing they perceived the speaker to be. Once convinced by the speaker, an audience could conclude that the argument had intrinsic value. The audience members accepted the arguments as valid because they trusted the arguer. See R. E. Petty and J. T. Cacioppo, "The Effects of Involvement on Responses to Argument Quantity and Quality: Central and Peripheral Routes to Persuasion," *Journal of Personality and Social Psychology* 46 (1984): 69–81.

12. Eugene Garver, *Aristotle's Rhetoric: An Art of Character* (Chicago: University of Chicago Press, 1994), 192.

13. Pierre Bourdieu, *Language as Symbolic Power*, ed. John B. Thompson, trans. Gino Raymond and Matthew Adamson (Cambridge, Mass.: Harvard University Press, 1991), 48.

14. Jacques Le Goff, *Intellectuals in the Middle Ages* (Cambridge, Mass.: Blackwell, 1993).

15. Richard Pells, *The Liberal Mind in a Conservative Age: American Intellectuals in the 1940s and 1950s*, 2nd ed. (Middletown, Conn.: Wesleyan University Press, 1989).

16. Walter Lacquer, "The Arendt Cult: Hannah Arendt as Political Commentator," *Journal of Contemporary History* 33, no. 4 (1998): 289.

17. Benhabib, *Rights of Others*, 142–43.

18. Immanuel Kant, "Perpetual Peace" (1795), in *Kant: Political Writings*, ed. Hans Reiss, trans. H. B. Nisbett (Cambridge: Cambridge University Press, 1991), 105.

19. Alexis de Tocqueville, *Democracy in America* (1835–40), ed. J. P. Mayer, trans. George Lawrence (New York: Harper Perennial, 2006), back cover.

20. Sheldon Wolin, *Tocqueville Between Two Worlds: The Making of a Political and Theoretical Life* (Princeton, N.J.: Princeton University Press, 2009).

21. Ali Behdad, *A Forgetful Nation: On Immigration and Cultural Identity in the United States* (Durham, N.C.: Duke University Press, 2005), 60, 64, 51.

22. Tocqueville, *Democracy in America*, xiii.

23. Ibid., 50.

24. Ibid., 19.

25. Ibid., 9.

26. Ibid., 18. By some accounts, Tocqueville's image of America was, at heart, a representation of an idealized France. He presented the famous American practical sense as a form of Cartesianism perfected in ways never yet reached in Descartes's own country. Puzzling over the reference to something as distinctly French as Cartesianism, Susan Weiner argues that *Democracy in America* "presented French readers with their own idealized reflection" ("Terre à Terre: Tocqueville, Aron, Baudrillard, and the American Way of Life," *Yale French Studies* 100 [2001]: 16).

27. It goes without saying that pointing out this rhetorical effect in Tocqueville's writing does not amount to questioning the significance and originality of American political institu-

tions compared to other political institutions in the West. Traveling to America in 1899, Max Weber studied the working of American democracy in community councils and immigrants' schools, which inspired some of the key concepts in his *Protestant Ethic and the Spirit of Capitalism.*

28. Simon Schama, "The Unloved American: Two Centuries of Alienating Europe," *The New Yorker*, March 3, 2003.

29. Frances Trollope, *Domestic Manners of Americans* (1832), (New York: Knopf, 1949).

30. Charles Dickens, *American Notes for General Circulation* (New York: Harper and Brothers, 1842).

31. Matthew Arnold, *Civilization in the United States: First and Last Impressions of America* (Carlisle, Mass.: Applewood Books, 1888).

32. Albert Camus, *American Journals* (New York: Paragon House, 1987), 31.

33. Simone de Beauvoir, *America Day by Day*, trans. Carol Cosman (Berkeley, Calif.: University of California Press, 2000), 24.

34. William Barrett, *The Truants: Adventures Among Intellectuals* (Garden City, N.Y.: Anchor Press/Doubleday, 1982, 23.

35. Mary McCarthy, "America the Beautiful: The Humanist in the Bathtub," *Commentary* 4 (September 1947): 202, 207, 208.

36. Walter Lacquer, *Generation Exodus: The Fate of Young Jewish Refugees from Nazi Germany* (Boston: Brandeis University Press, 2001).

37. Lisa Fittko, *Escape Through the Pyrenees* (Evanston, Ill.: Northwestern University Press), 110.

38. See Daniel Tichenor, *Dividing Lines: The Politics of Immigration Control in America* (Princeton, N.J.: Princeton University Press), 151.

39. Charles Tilly, "Transplanted Networks," in *Immigration Reconsidered*, ed. Virginia Yans-McLaughlin (Oxford: Oxford University Press: 1990), 79–95.

40. Elisabeth Kessim Berman, "Moral Triage or Cultural Salvage? The Agendas of Varian Fry and the Emergency Rescue Committee," in *Exiles and Emigrés: The Flight of European Artists from Hitler*, ed. Stephanie Barron, Sabine Eckman, and Matthew Afferon (Los Angeles: Los Angeles Museum of Art; New York: H. N. Abrams, 1997), 109.

41. Stephanie Barron, "European Artists in Exile. A Reading Between the Lines," in *Exiles and Emigrés: The Flight of European Artists from Hitler*, ed. Stephanie Barron, Sabine Eckman and Matthew Afferon (Los Angeles: Los Angeles Museum of Art; New York: H. N. Abrams, 1997), 19.

42. Anthony Heilbut, *Exiled in Paradise: German Refugee Artists and Intellectuals in American from the 1930s to the Present* (Berkeley: University of California Press, 1997).

43. Francis Goffing, "The American and European Minds Compared: An Essay in Definition," *Commentary* vol. 28 No. 6 (1959): 506-14. Also quoted in Thomas Wheatland, *The Frankfurt School in Exile* (Minneapolis: University of Minnesota Press, 2009), 135.

44. Laurent Jeanpierre, "Pontigny-en-Amerique," in *Artists, Intellectuals, and World War II: The Pontigny Encounters at Mount Holyoke College, 1942–1944*, ed. Christopher Benfey and Karen Remmler (Amherst: University of Massachusetts Press, 2006), 34.

45. Theodor W. Adorno, "Scientific Experiences of a European Scholar in America," in *The Intellectual Migration: Europe and America 1930–1960*, ed. Donald Fleming and Bernard Bailyn, trans. Donald Fleming (Cambridge, Mass.: Belknap Press of Harvard University Press, 1969), 344, 348, 348–49.
46. Heilbut, *Exiled in Paradise*, 59.
47. Theodor W. Adorno, "On the Question: What Is German?," trans. Thomas Y. Levin, *New German Critique* 36 (1985): 127.
48. Ibid., 128.
49. Sander Gilman, *Smart Jews: The Construction of the Image of Jewish Superior Intelligence* (Lincoln: University of Nebraska Press, 1996), 7, 195.
50. Berman, "Moral Triage," 75.
51. Wulf Koepke, "Lifting the Cultural Blockade: The American Discovery of a New German Literature after World War I—Ten Years of Critical Commentary in the *Nation* and the *New Republic*," in *The Fortunes of German Writers in America: Studies in Literary Reception*, ed. Wofgang Elfe, James N. Hardin, and Gunther Holst (Columbia: University of South Carolina Press, 1992), 97.
52. See Barry Katz, *Foreign Intelligence Research and Analysis in the Office of Strategic Services, 1942–1945* (Cambridge, Mass.: Harvard University Press, 1989), 34.
53. Henry Hatfield, "Thomas Mann and America," *Salmagundi* 10–11 (1969–1970): 178.
54. See Daniel Kanstroom, *Deportation Nation: Outsiders in American History* (Cambridge, Mass.: Harvard University Press, 2007).
55. See Heilbut, *Exiled in Paradise*.
56. James K. Lyon, *Bertolt Brecht in America* (Princeton, N.J.: Princeton University Press, 1983), 4.
57. Bertolt Brecht, Foreign Bureau of Investigation File, File 100-190707 (emphasis mine).
58. Ibid.
59. Heilbut, *Exiled in Paradise*, 383.
60. Ironically, and in contrast to the German war refugees, Eastern and Central European found a cold reception precisely because they were not socialists. It is reported that Milosz was assured by his tenure committee at the University of California, Berkeley, that he would earn it "*despite*" the fact that he had fled communist Poland. See Jean Bethke Elshtain, *God, State, and Self* (New York: Basic Books, 2008), 234.
61. Bonnie Honig, *Democracy and the Foreigner* (Princeton, N.J.: Princeton University Press, 2001), 84.
62. Ibid., 75.
63. Hannah Arendt, "'What Remains? The Language Remains': A Conversation with Günter Gaus" (1964), in *The Portable Hannah Arendt*, ed. Peter Baehr (New York: Penguin, 2000), 13.
64. Paul Ricoeur, "Rhetoric and Poetics," in *Essays on Aristotle's Rhetoric*, ed. Amelie Rorty Oksenberg (Berkeley: University of California Press, 1996), 64.
65. Pierre Bourdieu, *Language as Symbolic Power*, ed. John B. Thompson, trans. Gino Raymond and Matthew Adamson (Cambridge, Mass.: Harvard University Press, 1991).

66. Benhabib, *Rights of Others*, 128.

67. Many earlier social and cultural histories focus on the academic and scholarly success of foreign intellectuals as indicators of enthusiastic reception in the United States. Fewer studies present the obstacles even the most famous of them had to overcome to become recognized in America. To offer an explanation for the foreign intellectuals' rise to distinction, many authors proceed by situating the foreigner in an institutional context, such as the Institute for Social Research (originally based in Frankfurt) or the New School for Research. Given the sheer size of the German group of scholars who found shelter in American institutions, a lot of effort has gone into comprehensive monographs, social and cultural histories aiming at an overall assessment of the role played by the émigrés in the United States. Some have also looked at the challenges facing the exiles. See Laura Fermi, *Illustrious Immigrants: The Intellectual Migration from Europe, 1930–1941* (Chicago: University of Chicago Press, 1968); Jeffrey Mehlman, *Émigré New York* (New Haven, Conn.: Yale University Press, 2000); Volkmar Zühlsdorff, *Hitler's Exiles: The German Cultural Resistance in America and Europe* (London: Continuum, 2004); Heilbut, *Exiled in Paradise*; Claus Dieter Krohn, *Intellectuals in Exile: Refugee Scholars and the New School for Social Research* (Amherst: University of Massachusetts Press, 1993). These books have made an invaluable contribution toward documenting the contribution of the exiles to postwar life in America. Later studies, especially Martin Jay, *Permanent Exiles: Essays on the Intellectual Migration from Germany to America* (New York: Columbia University Press, 1985), are more analytically oriented toward the sociological, cultural, and philosophical conflicts and confrontations that accompanied the entrance of the European intellectuals to American life. Although these authors do not deal explicitly with the political legitimation of the European intellectuals, they offer some valuable insights by showing how some decisions and choices (especially concerning institutional affiliation or personal ties to particular American academics) helped or hindered the process of acceptance into the American mainstream academia and intelligentsia. Two recent studies share my assumptions about the complex nature of the reception—both hostile and friendly—foreign intellectuals have had in American political discourse: Thomas Wheatland, *The Frankfurt Institute in Exile* (Minneapolis: University of Minnesota Press, 2009); David Jenemann, *Adorno in America* (Minneapolis: University of Minnesota Press, 2007). Both reveal that it is important not to assume a systematically oppositional or collaborative relation between the foreign and American intellectuals and to understand what led to opposition or collaboration, when either happened. Both Wheatland and Jenemann focus exclusively on German intellectuals: the members of the Institute for Social Research and Theodor W. Adorno, respectively.

1. THE STRANGER PERSONA

1. Robert E. Pierre and Paul Farhi, " 'Refugee': A Word of Trouble," *Washington Post*, September 7, 2005.

2. Ibid.

3. Liisa H. Malkki, "Speechless Emissaries: Refugees, Humanitarianism, and Dehistoriciza-tion," *Cultural Anthropology* 11, no. 3 (1996), 378 (emphasis mine).

4. Ibid.

5. "Refugees 'de Luxe,'" *Life Magazine*, July 22, 1940.

6. Quoted in Jeffrey Mehlman, *Émigré New York: French Intellectuals in Wartime Manhattan, 1940–1944* (Baltimore: The Johns Hopkins University Press, 2000), 2.

7. Daniel Kanstroom, *Deportation Nation: Outsiders in American History* (Cambridge, Mass.: Harvard University Press, 2007), 17.

8. Liisa Malkki, "National Geographic: The Rooting of Peoples and the Territorialization of National Identity among Scholars and Refugees," *Cultural Anthropology* 7, no. 1 (1992): 27.

9. Anthony Heilbut, *Exiled in Paradise: German Refugee Artists and Intellectuals in American from the 1930s to the Present* (Berkeley: University of California Press, 1997), 35.

10. National origin and race have generally influenced the reception of foreigners in a nation-state. In the United States, these categories have shaped immigration policy, limiting ac-cess and establishing preferential treatment. Class, economic standing, and gender have also been important factors but studies of immigration policy often focus primarily on the impact of national origin and race. This focus is justified, given some of the historic changes in immigration policy, such as the introduction of quotas for immigrants from non-European countries, which were driven by considerations of race and national origin.

11. Samuel P. Huntington, *Who Are We? The Challenges to America's National Identity* (New York: Simon and Schuster, 2004).

12. Desmond King, *The Liberty of Strangers* (Oxford: Oxford University Press, 2005), 25.

13. Nathan Glazer, "Hannah Arendt's America," *Commentary* 60 (1975): 61–67.

14. Laura Fermi, *Illustrious Immigrants: The Intellectual Migration from Europe, 1930–1941* (Chi-cago: University of Chicago Press, 1968).

15. Barry Katz, *Foreign Intelligence Research and Analysis in the Office of Strategic Services, 1942–1945* (Cambridge, Mass.: Harvard University Press, 1989).

16. Stephanie Barron, "European Artists in Exile: A Reading Between the Lines," in *Exiles and Emigrés: The Flight of European Artists from Hitler*, ed. Stephanie Barron, Sabine Eck-man, and Matthew Afferon (New York: H. N. Abrams, 1997), 19.

17. Aristotle, *Politics* 1.5.

18. Aristotle, *Rhetoric* 1.9, 3.16.9.1417a23–27.

19. Ingo Gildenhard, *Creative Eloquence: The Construction of Reality in Cicero's Speeches* (Ox-ford: Oxford University Press, 2011), 23.

20. Aristotle, *Nichomachean Ethics*, 2.1. See also Michael Halloran, "Aristotle's Concept of Ethos, or If Not His, Somebody Else's," *Rhetoric Review* 1, no. 1 (1982): 61.

21. Stephen Haliwell, "The Challenge of Rhetoric to Political and Ethical Theory in Aristo-tle," in *Essays on Aristotle's Rhetoric*, ed. Amelie Rorty Oksenberg (Berkeley: University of California Press, 1996), 178.

22. Arthur Walzer, "Blair's Ideal Orator: Civic Rhetoric and Christian Politeness in Lectures 25–34," *Rhetorica: A Journal of the History of Rhetoric* 25, no. 3 (2007): 274–75.

23. Cicero, *De Oratore* 1.40, 1.8.

24. Ibid., 1.8.

25. Cicero, *De Oratore* 2.

26. Anthony Giddens, *The Constitution of Society: Outline of the Theory of Structuration* (London: Polity, 1984).

27. Adam Seligman, *The Problem of Trust* (Princeton, N.J.: Princeton University Press, 1997), 107.

28. Walzer, "Blair's Ideal Orator," 295.

29. Luc Boltanski, *Distant Suffering: Morality, Media and Politics*, trans. Graham Burchell (Cambridge: Cambridge University Press, 1999), 37.

30. Jürgen Habermas, *The Inclusion of the Other: Studies in Political Theory*, ed. Ciaran Cronin and Pablo De Greiff (Cambridge, Mass.: MIT Press, 1998), 115.

31. Jean-Jacques Rousseau, *On the Social Contract*, Book II, 7, ed. and trans. Donald A. Cress (Indianapolis: Hackett, 1987).

32. Ibid

33. Bonnie Honig, *Democracy and the Foreigner* (Princeton, N.J.: Princeton University Press, 2001), 21, 32, 22.

34. Daniel Kanstroom, *Deportation Nation*, 7.

35. Saskia Sassen, *Guests and Aliens* (New York: The New Press, 1999), 77, 78.

36. Aristide Zolberg, *A Nation by Design: Immigration Policy in the Fashioning of America* (Cambridge, Mass.: Harvard University Press, 2006), 25.

37. Linda Bosniak, *The Citizen and the Alien: Dilemmas of Contemporary Membership* (Princeton, N.J.: Princeton University Press, 2006), 38.

38. Michael Walzer, *Spheres of Justice: A Defense of Pluralism and Equality* (New York: Basic, 1983), 54–55.

39. Bosniak, *The Citizen and the Alien*, 43, 84.

40. Desmond King, *A Nation of Strangers*, 166.

41. Sacvan Bercovitch, *The American Jeremiad* (Madison: University of Wisconsin Press, 1978), 50.

42. Seligman, *The Problem of Trust*, 118.

43. Zolberg, *Nation by Design*, 107–8.

44. Shawn J. Parry-Giles, *Hillary Clinton in the News: Gender and Authenticity in American Politics* (Urbana: University of Illinois Press, 2014).

45. Alan McPherson, "Americanism against American Empire," in *Americanism: New Perspectives on the History of an Ideal*, ed. Michael Kazin and Joseph A. McCartin (Chapel Hill: University of North Carolina Press, 2006), 117.

46. Honig, *Democracy and the Foreigner*, 74.

47. Georg Simmel, "The Stranger," in *The Sociology of Georg Simmel*, ed. Kurt H. Wolff (Glencoe, Ill.: Free Press, 1950), 404.

48. Montesquieu, *Persian Letters*, trans. C. J. Betts (London: Penguin, 2004), 83.

49. Simmel, "The Stranger," 402, 404, 405.

50. Pierre Birnbaum, *Geography of Hope: The Enlightenment and Disassimilation* (Stanford, Calif.: Stanford University Press, 2008), 141.

51. Simmel was accused of political utopianism. See Birnbaum, *Geography of Hope*.

52. Albert Salomon, "Georg Simmel Reconsidered," in *Georg Simmel and the American Prospect*, ed. Gary D. Jaworski (Albany: State University of New York Press, 1997).

53. Ibid.

54. Robert Park, "Human Migration and the Marginal Man," *American Journal of Sociology* 33, no. 6 (1928): 881–93.

55. Birnbaum, *Geography of Hope*, 150–51.

56. Simmel, "The Stranger," 403.

57. Ibid., 402.

58. Alfred Schutz, "The Stranger: An Essay in Social Psychology," *American Journal of Sociology* 49, no. 6 (1944): 506.

59. Aleksandra Alund, "Alterity in Modernity," *Acta Sociologica* 38 (1995): 314, 312.

60. *Philosophers in Exile: The Correspondence of Alfred Schutz and Aron Gurwitch, 1939–1959*, trans. Claude Evans (Bloomington: Indiana University Press, 1989).

61. Schutz, "The Stranger," 499–500, 501.

62. Ibid., 502.

63. Z. D. Gurevitch, "The Other Side of Dialogue: On Making the Other Strange and the Experience of Otherness," *American Journal of Sociology* 93, no. 5 (1988): 1180.

64. Ibid.

65. Carlo Ginzburg, "Making Things Strange: The Prehistory of a Literary Device," *Representations* 56 (1996): 15.

66. Viktor Shklovsky, *Theory of Prose*, trans. Benjamin Sher (Normal, Ill.: Dalkey Archive Press, 1990), 5.

67. Shklovsky, Theory of Prose, 10.

68. Svetlana Boym, *Another Freedom: The Alternative History of an Idea* (Chicago: University of Chicago Press, 2010), 208.

69. Viktor Shklovsky, *Zoo or Letters Not About Love*, trans. Richard Sheldon (Normal, Ill..: Dalkey Archive Press, 2001).

70. James Perrin Warren, *Culture of Eloquence: Oratory and Reform in Antebellum America* (University Park: Pennsylvania State University Press, 1999), 31.

71. Fredrick Antczak, *Thought and Character: The Rhetoric of Democratic Education* (Ames: Iowa State University Press, 1985), 9–10.

72. Svetlana Boym, "Estrangement as a Lifestyle: Shklovsky and Brodsky," *Poetics Today* 17, no. 4 (1996): 515.

73. Roman Jakobson, *Language in Literature*, ed. Krystyna Pomorska and Stephen Rushi (Cambridge, Mass.: The Belknap Press of Harvard University Press, 1987), 93.

74. Vladimir Nabokov, "The Art of Fiction no. 40," interview by Herbert Gold, *Paris Review* 41 (1967).

75. Simmel's essay was read as an argument against Zionism because he did not believe that Jews needed their own state in order to be recognized politically. Rather, he believed in a European political order that would incorporate the Jews organically. See Birnbaum, *Geography of Hope*.

2. HANNAH ARENDT: THE THINKER AND THE AMERICAN REPUBLIC

1. Hannah Arendt and Karl Jaspers, *Correspondence 1926–1969* (New York: Harcourt Brace, 1992).

2. Arendt is clearly referring to the distribution of power at the states level within the American Republic.

3. Hannah Arendt, "Reflections on Little Rock," *Dissent* 6, no. 1 (1959); Hannah Arendt, *Eichmann in Jerusalem: A Report on the Banality of Evil* (New York: Penguin, 1994).

4. Harvey Teres, *Renewing the Left: Politics, Imagination, and the New York Intellectuals* (Oxford: Oxford University Press, 1996).

5. In *On Revolution*, Arendt extols the political vision introduced by the American Revolution and the Founding Fathers, especially its ideal of equality, contrasting it to the vision of the French Revolution, which was quickly perverted, in her view, through corruption, power, and violence. Hannah Arendt, *On Revolution* (New York: Viking, 1991).

6. Hannah Arendt, " 'What Remains? The Language Remains': A Conversation with Günter Gaus," in *The Portable Hannah Arendt*, ed. Peter Baehr (New York: Penguin, 2000), 12.

7. Jenny Teichman, "Understanding Arendt," *The New Criterion* 12 (April 1994).

8. Jerome Kohn, "Evil: The Crime against Humanity," Hannah Arendt Papers, Library of Congress, http://memory.loc.gov/ammem/arendthtml/essayc1.html.

9. Kenneth Burke, "Terministic Screens," *Language as Symbolic Action: Essays on Life, Literature, and Method*. Berkeley: University of California Press, 1966.

10. Elisabeth Young-Bruehl, *Hannah Arendt: For Love of the World* (New Haven, Conn.: Yale University Press, 1982), 10, 14, 27.

11. Ibid., 11.

12. Ibid., 32.

13. See Young-Bruehl, *For Love of the World*, 61.

14. See Richard Wolin, *Heidegger's Children: Hannah Arendt, Karl Löwith, Hans Jonas, and Herbert Marcuse* (Princeton, N.J.: Princeton University Press, 2001).

15. Young-Bruehl, *For Love of the World*, 71.

16. Ibid., 108.

17. Ibid., 98.

18. The Soldiers' Council was mainly responsible for the revolution that led to the creation of the Weimar Republic.

19. Arendt's political theory has been amply discussed. For summarizing this vast body of thought in this chapter, I have relied especially on Margaret Canovan, *Hannah Arendt: A Reinterpretation of Her Political Thought* (Cambridge: Cambridge University Press, 1992) and Dagmar Barnouw, "Speaking about Modernity: Arendt's Construction of the Political," *New German Critique*, no. 50 (Spring–Summer 1990).

20. Lisa Fittko, *Escape Through the Pyrenees* (Evanston, Ill.: Northwestern University Press, 2000).

21. Hannah Arendt and Martin Heidegger, *Hannah Arendt and Martin Heidegger, Letters: 1925–1975*, ed. Ursula Ludz, trans. Andrew Shields (Boston: Harcourt, 2004), 12–13.

22. Julia Kristeva, *Hannah Arendt*, trans. Ross Guberman (New York: Columbia University Press, 2001).

23. Hannah Arendt, *Rahel Varnhagen: The Life of a Jewess* (London: East and West Library, 1957).

24. Arendt, *Rahel Varnhagen*, xv–xvi.

25. Seyla Benhabib, "The Pariah and Her Shadow: Hannah Arendt's Biography of Rahel Varnhagen," *Political Theory* 23, no. 1 (1995): 8.

26. Wolin, *Heidegger's Children*.

27. Ibid., 47.

28. Benhabib, "The Pariah and Her Shadow," 9.

29. Wolin, *Heidegger's Children*, 46.

30. Hannah Arendt, "The Jews and Society," in *The Jewish Writings*, ed. Jerome Kohn and Ron H. Feldman (New York: Schocken Books, 2007).

31. Lisa Jane Disch, *Hannah Arendt and the Limits of Philosophy* (Ithaca, N.Y.: Cornell University Press, 1996).

32. Wolin, *Heidegger's Children*, 56.

33. Benhabib, "The Pariah and Her Shadow," 11.

34. See Leerom Modovoi, *Rebels: Youth and the Cold War Origins of Identity* (Durham, N.C.: Duke University Press, 2005).

35. Hannah Arendt, *The Origins of Totalitarianism* (New York: Harcourt Brace, 1951).

36. Hannah Arendt, *Men in Dark Times* (New York: Harcourt Brace, 1955).

37. Disch, *Limits of Philosophy*, 191

38. Ibid., 176.

39. Hannah Arendt, *The Jew as Pariah: Jewish Identity and Politics in the Modern Age*, ed. Ron H. Feldman (New York: Grove Press, 1978), 77.

40. Disch, *Limits of Philosophy*, 187.

41. Arendt, *Men in Dark Times*, 29.

42. Hannah Arendt, " 'The Rights of Man': What They Are," *Modern Review* 31 (1949): 24–37.

43. Jeffrey Isaac, "Situating Hannah Arendt on Action and Politics," *Political Theory* 21, no. 3 (1993): 509–10.

44. Hannah Arendt, "We, Refugees," in *The Jew as Pariah: Jewish Identity and Politics in the Modern Age*, ed. Ron H. Feldman (New York: Grove Press, 1978), 55–66; Disch, *Limits of Philosophy*, 172.

45. Arendt, "We, Refugees," 58, 60.

46. Giorgio Agamben, "We, Refugees," *Symposium* 49, no. 2 (1995): 116.

47. Arnold Gennep, *The Rites of Passage*, trans. Monika B. Vizedom and Gavrielle L. Caffe (London: Routledge, 1960); Victor Turner, *The Forest of Symbols* (Ithaca, N.Y.: Cornell University Press, 1967).

48. Anthony Heilbut, *Exiled in Paradise: German Refugee Artists and Intellectuals in America from the 1930s to the Present* (Berkeley: University of California Press, 1983).

49. Many of the articles published in *Aufbau* have been included in an anthology that I used throughout this chapter: Arendt, *The Jewish Writings*.

50. Young-Bruehl, *For Love of the World*, 179.

51. *The Origins of Totalitarianism* was reviewed, among others, by Raymond Aron and David Riesman. The genesis of the book was complicated, as Arendt kept adding sections.

52. Young-Bruehl, *For Love of the World*, 211.

53. Ibid., 255.

54. David Riesman, Riesman-Arendt Correspondence, Hannah Arendt Papers, Library of Congress, Folder PO2, images 12, 26, 35, quoted in Peter Baehr, *Hannah Arendt, Totalitarianism, and the Social Sciences* (Stanford: Stanford University Press, 2010), 46.

55. See Bruce Lincoln, *Authority: Construction and Erosion* (Chicago: University of Chicago Press, 1994).

56. "Hannah Arendt on Hannah Arendt," in *Hannah Arendt: The Recovery of the Public World*, ed. M. A. Hill (New York: St. Martin Press, 1979), 333.

57. William Barrett, *The Truants: Adventures Among Intellectuals* (Garden City, N.Y.: Anchor/Doubleday, 1982), 101–2.

58. Ibid., 102.

59. This connection would become more and more common in later critiques of Arendt's work.

60. Martin Jay, "Force Fields: Intellectual Family Values: William Phillips, Hannah Arendt and the Partisan Review," *Salmagundi* 142 (2003): 43–55.

61. For a discussion of Arendt's essay from a legal perspective that considers the broader historical context, see Maribel Morey, "Reassessing Hannah Arendt's 'Reflections on Little Rock'" (1959), *Law, Culture, and the Humanities* (December 2011): http://lch.sagepub.com/content/early/2011/12/20/1743872111423795.full.pdf+html

62. Arendt, "Reflections on Little Rock," 46.

63. James Bohman, "The Moral Costs of Political Pluralism: The Dilemmas of Difference and Equality in Hannah Arendt's 'Reflections on Little Rock,'" in *Hannah Arendt: Twenty Years Later*, ed. Larry May and Jerome Kohn (Cambridge, Mass.: MIT Press, 1997), 54.

64. David Spitz, "Politics and the Realms of Being," *Dissent* 6, no. 1 (1959): 56–58; Melvin Tumin, "Pie in the Sky," *Dissent* 6, no. 1 (1959): 65–66.

65. Hannah Arendt, "A Reply to Critics," *Dissent* 6, no. 2 (1959): 179.

66. "Hannah Arendt and Little Rock: Reflections on the Fiftieth Anniversary of the Desegregation of Central High School," Princeton University Program in Law and Public Affairs, April 27, 2007.

67. See Bohman, "The Moral Costs of Political Pluralism"; Meili Steele, "Arendt Versus Ellison on Little Rock: The Role of Language in Political Judgment," *Constellations* 9, no. 2 (2002): 184–206.

68. I use the term in the sense of Chaim Perelman and L. Olbrechts-Tyteca, as a technique of argumentation that differentiates within aspects of reality or experience, which are otherwise assumed to be linked, in order to evaluate one of these aspects as positive and deem the other negative. In this case, Arendt was trying to present social discrimination as positive and political discrimination, tantamount to racism, as negative.

69. Jennifer Ring, "The Pariah as Hero: Hannah Arendt's Political Actor," *Political Theory* 19, no. 3 (1991): 436.

70. Hannah Arendt, *Crises of the Republic* (New York: Houghton Mifflin Harcourt, 1972).
71. Arendt, "Reflections on Little Rock," 46.
72. Ibid.
73. Arendt, *Crises of the Republic.*
74. Arendt, "Reflections on Little Rock," 46, 54.
75. Ibid., 49; Arendt, "A Reply to Critics," 181.
76. George Kateb, "The Questionable Influence of Arendt (and Strauss)," in *Hannah Arendt and Leo Strauss: German Emigres and American Political Thought After World War II*, ed. Peter Graf Kielmansegg, Horst Mewes, and Elisabeth Glaser-Schmidt (Cambridge: Cambridge University Press, 1995), 34.
77. See Carol Polsgrove, *Divided Minds: Intellectuals and the Civil Rights Movement* (New York: Norton, 2001).
78. Arendt, "A Reply to Critics," 181.
79. Sydney Hook, "Letter to the Editors," *Dissent* 6, no. 2 (1959): 203.
80. Spitz, "Politics and the Realms of Being," 58. Melvin Tumin, "Pie in the Sky," 65.
81. A further elucidated treatment of the topic is found in Hannah Arendt, *The Human Condition* (Chicago: University of Chicago Press, 1958).
82. Arendt, "Reflections on Little Rock," 57.
83. Ibid., 51.
84. Ibid.
85. For a comprehensive view, see Hanna Fenikel Pitkin, *The Attack of the Blob: Hannah Arendt's Concept of the Social* (Chicago: University of Chicago Press, 2000).
86. Norman Podhoretz, "My Negro Problem—and Ours," *Commentary* 35 (1963): 93–101.
87. Ibid., 93, 101.
88. Arendt, "Reflections on Little Rock," 46.
89. Young-Bruehl, *For Love of the World*, 311.
90. Philip Hansen, "Hannah Arendt and Bearing with Strangers," *Contemporary Political Theory* 3 (2004): 12.
91. Kenneth Warren, "Ralph Ellison and the Problem of Cultural Authority," *boundary 2* 30, no. 2 (2003): 15.
92. Quoted in Young-Bruehl, *For Love of the World*, 316.
93. Arendt, "Reflections on Little Rock," 50.
94. Arendt developed these views further in a lecture given in Bremen in 1958 and later published as "The Crisis in Education," *Partisan Review* 25, no. 4 (1958).
95. Arendt, "A Reply to Critics."
96. Tumin, "Pie in the Sky," 65.
97. Ralph Ellison, "The World and the Jug," in *The Collected Essays of Ralph Ellison* (New York: Modern Library, 1995), 156.
98. Martha Minow, *Making All the Difference: Inclusion, Exclusion, and American Law* (Ithaca, N.Y.: Cornell University Press, 1990): 19–23.
99. Henry Hampton, Steve Fayer, and Sarah Flynn, *Voices of Freedom: An Oral History of the Civil Rights Movement from the 1950s through the 1980s* (New York: Bantam, 1990).

100. Bohman, 58.

101. Polsgrove, *Divided Minds*, 59.

102. Bohman, 54.

103. Arendt, "Reflections on Little Rock," 232.

104. Daniel Tichenor, *Dividing Lines: The Politics of Immigration Control in America* (Princeton, N.J.: Princeton University Press), 151.

105. Ezra Pound, quoted in Alfred Kazin, *New York Jew* (Syracuse, N.Y.: Syracuse University Press, 1996), 32.

106. Kazin, *New York Jew*, 34.

107. Kazin, "Wisdom in Exile," *The New Republic* 7, no. 22 (1977): 28, 26.

108. A special issue of *Salmagundi* was dedicated to the impact of German émigrés on American thought and society. *Salmagundi: The Legacy of the German Refugee Intellectuals* 10–11 (1970).

109. Allan Bloom, *The Closing of the American Mind* (New York: Simon and Schuster, 1987).

110. Barrett, *The Truants*, 23.

111. Jacob Robinson, *And the Crooked Shall Be Made Straight: The Eichmann Trial, the Jewish Catastrophe, and Hannah Arendt's Narrative* (New York: Macmillan, 1965).

112. Lion Abel, "The Aesthetics of Evil: Hannah Arendt on Eichmann and the Jews," *Partisan Review* 30, no. 2 (1963): 211–30; "Eichmann in Jerusalem: An Exchange of Letters Between Gershom Scholem and Hannah Arendt," *Encounter* 1 (1964): 51–56; Irving Howe, "The New Yorker and Hannah Arendt," *Commentary* 36, no. 4: 318–19; Norman Podhoretz, "Hannah Arendt on Eichmann: A Study in the Perversity of Brilliance," *Commentary* 36, no. 3 (1963): 201–8; Anti-Defamation League, "A Report on the Evil of Banality: The Arendt Book," *Facts* 15, no. 1 (1963): 263–70.

113. Mary McCarthy, "The Hue and Cry," *Partisan Review* 31, no. 1 (1964): 82–94; Stephen Spender, "Death in Jerusalem," *The New York Review of Books* 1, no. 2 (1963); Daniel Bell, "The Alphabet of Justice: Reflections on Eichmann in Jerusalem," *Partisan Review* 30, no. 3 (1963): 417–29; Bruno Bettelheim, "Eichmann, the System, the Victims," *The New Republic* 148, no. 24 (1963): 22–33.

114. Irving Howe, " 'The New Yorker' and Hannah Arendt," *Commentary* 36, no. 4 (1963): 318–19.

115. Fred Kaplan, "The Woman Who Saw Banality in Evil," *New York Times*, May 24, 2013, http://www.nytimes.com/2013/05/26/movies/hannah-arendt-directed-by-margarethe-von-trotta.html.

116. See Deborah E. Lipstadt, *The Eichmann Trial* (New York: Schocken, 2011).

117. Gershom Scholem to Hannah Arendt, "An Exchange of Letters," in *The Jew as Pariah: Jewish Identity and Politics in the Modern* Age, ed. Ron H. Feldman (New York: Grove, 1978), 242.

118. Arendt to Scholem, "Exchange of Letters," 248.

119. Walter Lacquer, "Footnotes to the Holocaust," *The New York Review of Books* 5, no. 7 (1965).

120. See Richard Piro, *Hannah Arendt and the Tragedy of Politics* (DeKalb: Northern Illinois University Press, 2000); David Douglas Klusmeyer, "Beyond Tragedy: Hannah Arendt

and Hans Morgenthau on Responsibility, Evil, and Political Ethics," *International Studies Review* 11 (2009): 332–51.

121. Klusmeyer, "Beyond Tragedy," 336.

122. Arendt, *Eichmann in Jerusalem*, 251.

123. Dagmar Barnouw, "Hannah Arendt Revisited: Eichmann in Jerusalem," *Shofar: An Interdisciplinary Journal of Jewish Studies* 21 (2003): 22.

124. Arendt, *Eichmann in Jerusalem*, 4.

125. Ibid., 7, 8.

126. According to Lipstadt, Arendt was absent from the courtroom for most of the trial.

127. Arendt, *Eichmann in Jerusalem*, 8 (emphasis mine).

128. Ibid., 48.

129. Mieke Bal, *Narratology: Introduction to the Theory of Narrative* (Toronto: Toronto University Press, 1997), 23.

130. Arendt, *Eichmann in Jerusalem*, 84–85.

131. Ibid., 51.

132. Ibid.

133. David Velleman, "Narrative Explanation," *Philosophical Review* 112 (2003): 23.

134. For Arendt's conception of evil, I have relied on Steven Aschheim, "Nazism, Culture, and the Origins of Totalitarianism: Hannah Arendt and the Discourse of Evil," *New German Critique* 70 (1997): 117–39.

135. Berel Lang, "The Limits of Irony," *New Literary History* 27, no. 3 (1996): 571–88.

136. Richard Rorty, *Contingency, Irony, and Solidarity* (Cambridge: Cambridge University Press, 1989).

137. Lang, "The Limits of Irony," 574.

138. Arendt, *Eichmann in Jerusalem*, 58.

139. Karl Jaspers, *The Question of German Guilt*, trans. E. B. Ashton (New York: Fordham University Press, 2000).

140. Arendt, *Eichmann in Jerusalem*, 152.

141. James Baldwin, "A Letter from the South: Nobody Knows My Name," *Partisan Review* 26, no. 1 (1959).

142. Aron Rabinbach, "Eichmann in New York: The New York Intellectuals and the Hannah Arendt Controversy," *October* 108 (2004): 110.

143. Norman Podhoretz, *Ex-Friends: Falling Out with Allen Ginsberg, Lionel and Diana Trilling, Lilian Hellman, Hannah Arendt, and Norman Mailer* (New York: The Free Press, 1999).

144. Sophisticated as it is in its take on what constitutes true commitment to one's "own people," this statement did not convince Scholem, or many other members of the Jewish American community. It did not help that Arendt addressed him in her letter as Gerhardt rather than by the Jewish name he had been using after moving to Israel, Gershom. Yet she probably used the German name not intending offense as much as scorn for the ostentatious change her friend had made to signal that he was Jewish. That does not mean she did not feel Jewish. In a letter sent to Jaspers, who questioned the right of the Israeli

police to arrest Eichmann by abducting him in Argentina, Arendt defended the decision passionately in the name of the Jewish people, using repeatedly the first person plural "we."

145. Dana Villa, "The Philosopher Versus the Citizen: Arendt, Strauss, and Socrates," *Political Theory* 26, no. 2 (1998): 147–72.

146. Arendt, "What Remains," 3.

147. Kateb, "The Questionable Influence," 30.

148. Hannah Arendt, "Philosophy and Politics," *Social Research* 57, no. 1 (1990): 73, 74.

149. Villa, "The Philosopher," 148.

150. Anthony Grafton, "Arendt and Eichmann at the Dinner Table," *The American Scholar* 68, no. 1 (1999): 105–119.

151. Arendt, "Philosophy and Politics," 80.

152. Ibid., 81.

153. Villa, "The Philosopher Versus the Citizen," 168.

154. Shirley Samuels, ed., *The Culture of Sentiment: Race, Gender, and Sentimentality in Nineteenth-Century America* (Oxford: Oxford University Press, 1992).

155. Arendt to Scholem, "Exchange of Letters," 246.

156. Hannah Arendt to Georg Lichtenstein, 23 November 1957, Hannah Arendt Papers, Library of Congress, quoted in Polsgrove, *Divided Minds*, 56.

3. HERBERT MARCUSE'S GERMAN REVOLUTION IN AMERICA

1. Carlo Romani "Occupy This: Is It Comeback for Herbert Marcuse?" *The Chronicle of Higher Education*, December 11, 2011, http://chronicle.com/article/Occupy-This-Is-It-Comeback/130028.

2. Ibid.

3. Leo Löwenthal, *Mitmachen wollte Ich nie: Ein autobiographisches Gespräch mit Helmut Dubiel* (Frankfurt: Suhrkampf, 1980).

4. Paul Breines, "From Guru to Specter: Marcuse and the Implosion of the Movement," in *Critical Interruptions: New Left Perspectives on Herbert Marcuse*, ed. Paul Breines (New York: Herder and Herder, 1970), 1–21; Richard Wolin, *The Frankfurt School Revisited and Other Essays in Politics and Society* (London: Routledge, 2006).

5. Anthony Heilbut, *Exiled in Paradise: German Refugee Artists and Intellectuals in America from the 1930s to the Present* (Berkeley: University of California Press, 1983).

6. Michael G. Horowitz, "Portrait of the Marxist as an Old Trouper," *Playboy*, September 1970, http://www.marcuse.org/herbert/newsevents/1970/709PlayboyInt.htm.

7. The information is presented in Paul Alexander Juutilainen's documentary *Herbert's Hippopotamus: Marcuse and Revolution in Paradise*, University of California at San Diego (1996).

8. Thomas Wheatland, *The Frankfurt School in America* (Minneapolis: University of Minnesota Press, 2009).

9. See Kevin Mattson, *Intellectuals in Action: The Origins of the New Left and Radical Liberalism, 1945–1970* (State Park: Pennsylvania State University Press, 2002); Mattson, "Between

Despair and Hope: Revisiting Studies on the Left," in *The New Left Revisited*, ed. John M. Millian and Paul Buhle (Philadelphia: Temple University Press, 2000).

10. David Jones, *The Lost Debate: German Socialist Intellectuals and Totalitarianism* (Chicago: University of Illinois Press, 1999), 67.

11. Barry Katz, "Praxis and Poiesis: Toward an Intellectual Biography of Herbert Marcuse (1898–1979)," *New German Critique* 18 (1979): 13.

12. Ibid., 16.

13. For comprehensive accounts of the Frankfurt School, see Martin Jay, *The Dialectical Imagination. A History of the Frankfurt School and the Institute of Social Research, 1923–1950* (Boston: Little, Brown, 1973); Wheatland, *The Frankfurt School in America*; and Rolf Wiggershaus, *The Frankfurt School* (Cambridge: Polity Press, 1995).

14. Martin Jay, *The Dialectical Imagination: A History of the Frankfurt School and the Institute of Social Research, 1923–1950* (Boston: Little, Brown, 1973), 35.

15. Ibid., 9 (emphasis mine).

16. Fritz Ringer, *The Decline of the German Mandarins: The German Academic Community, 1890–1933* (Hanover, N.H.: University Press of New England, 1990), 122.

17. Wiggershaus, *The Frankfurt School*, 105.

18. Jay, *Dialectical Imagination*, 4.

19. Katz, "Praxis and Poiesis," 16.

20. Wheatland, *The Frankfurt School in America*, 73.

21. Stephen Gennaro and Douglas Kellner, "Under Surveillance: Herbert Marcuse and the FBI," *Nature, Knowledge and Negation: Current Perspectives in Social Theory* 26 (2009): 285.

22. Herbert Marcuse, *Gespräche mit Herbert Marcuse* (Frankfurt: Suhrkamp, 1978).

23. See Barry Katz, *Foreign Intelligence: Research and Analysis in the Office of Strategic Services, 1942–1945* (Cambridge, Mass.: Harvard University Press, 1989).

24. Wheatland, *Frankfurt School in America*, 99.

25. Both Jay and Wiggershaus follow this line.

26. Jay, *Dialectical Imagination*, 30.

27. Wheatland, *The Frankfurt School in America*, 72.

28. See Wheatland, *The Frankfurt School in America*.

29. Peter Marcuse, "Herbert Marcuse's Identity," in *Herbert Marcuse: A Critical Reader*, ed. John Abromeit and W. Mark Cobb (London: Routledge, 2004), 249.

30. Jay, *Dialectical Imagination*, 32.

31. Max Horkheimer and Theodor W. Adorno, *The Dialectic of Enlightenment*, trans. Edmund Jephcott (Stanford, Calif.: Stanford University Press, 2007).

32. Jonathan Judaken, "Blindness and Insight: The Conceptual Jew in Adorno and Arendt's Post Holocaust Reflections on the Anti-Semitic Questions," in *Arendt and Adorno: Political and Philosophical Investigations*, ed. Lars Rensmann and Samir Gandesha (Stanford, Calif.: Stanford University Press, 2012), 173–96.

33. See Elliot Cohen, "Jewish Culture in America," *Commentary* 3 (1947): 412–20.

34. Marcuse, "Herbert Marcuse's Identity," 251.

35. See Wheatland, *The Frankfurt School in America*.

36. Marcuse, "Herbert Marcuse's Identity," 250.

37. Katz, "Poiesis and Praxis," 18.

38. Bryan Magee, "Marcuse and the Frankfurt School: Dialogue with Herbert Marcuse," in *Men of Ideas* (New York: Viking, 1978), 55.

39. See Jay, *Dialectical Imagination*.

40. Wiggershaus, *The Frankfurt School*, 221.

41. See Marianne DeKovic, *Utopia Limited: The Sixties and the Emergence of the Postmodern* (Durham, N.C.: Duke University Press, 2004).

42. See my discussion of Adorno's philosophical style in chapter 1.

43. Enzo Traverso, "Theodor W. Adorno: Portrait of a Marxist Mandarin," *Queen's Quarterly* 111, no. 4 (2004): 525.

44. Jay, *Dialectical Imagination*, 71, 70.

45. Fredric Jamieson, *Marxism and Form* (Princeton, N.J.: Princeton University Press, 1971), xiii.

46. See Magee, "Marcuse and the Frankfurt School."

47. Wiggershaus, *The Frankfurt School*, 498.

48. Andrew Jamison and Ron Eyerman, *Seeds of the Sixties* (Berkeley: University of California Press, 1994), 123.

49. Traverso, "Theodor W. Adorno," 526.

50. Angela Y. Davis, "Preface," in *The Collected Papers of Herbert Marcuse: The New Left and the 1960s*, vol. 3, ed. Douglas Kellner (London: Routledge, 2004).

51. Herbert Marcuse, "Dear Angela," in *The New Left and the 1960s*, 49–50.

52. Brian Thill, "Black Power and the New Left: The Dialectics of Liberation, 1967," in *Mediations: Journal of the Marxist Literary Group* 23, no. 2 (2008), http://www.mediationsjournal.org/articles/black-power-and-the-new-left.

53. Wolin, *The Frankfurt School Revisited*, 83.

54. See "Reading Between the Lines," letters between Herbert Marcuse and Theodor W. Adorno, trans. Esther Leslie, http://hutnyk.files.wordpress.com/2013/06/adornomarcuse_germannewleft.pdf.

55. Wheatland, *The Frankfurt School in America*, 326.

56. Jamison and Eyerman, *Seeds of the Sixties*, 103.

57. Paul Breines, "Germans, Journals, and Jews/Madison, Men, Marxism, and Mosse: A Tale of Jewish-Leftist Identity Confusion in America," *New German Critique* 20, no. 2 (1980): 82.

58. Ibid., 84.

59. Paul Buhle, "Radical America and Me," in *History and the New Left: Madison, Wisconsin, 1950–1970*, ed. Paul Buhle (Philadelphia: Temple University Press, 1991).

60. Sydney Hook, "Review of Herbert Marcuse's *Reason and Revolution*," *The New Republic* 105 (1941): 91.

61. Ibid.

62. John Patrick Diggins, "The Man Who Knew Too Much," *The New Republic* 203, no. 23 (1990): 27.

63. Herbert Marcuse, *Eros and Civilization* (Boston: Beacon Press, 1955), 12.

64. Norman Brown, *Love's Body* (New York: Vintage, 1966).

65. The book marked an important stage in the development of Marcuse's career for another reason: it brought utopia and art into the discussion, presenting them as sources of "liberation" from "repression."

66. Herbert Marcuse, *Reason and Revolution: Hegel and the Rise of Social Theory* (London: Humanities Press, 1941).

67. Douglas Kellner, *Herbert Marcuse and the Crisis of Marxism* (Berkeley: University of California Press, 1984), 235.

68. Detlev Claussen, "The American Experience of the Critical Theorists," in *Herbert Marcuse: A Critical Reader*, 58.

69. Kellner, *Herbert Marcuse*, 262.

70. Wolin, *The Frankfurt School Revisited*.

71. See Jones, *The Lost Debate*, 34.

72. Herbert Marcuse, "Repressive Tolerance," in *A Critique of Pure Tolerance*, ed. Robert Paul Wolff and Barrington Moore Jr. (Boston: Beacon, 1965); Marcuse, *Essay on Liberation* (London: Allen Lane, 1969).

73. Russell Jacoby, *The Last Intellectuals: American Culture in the Age of Academe* (New York: Basic Books, 2000).

74. Marcuse, "Repressive Tolerance," 111, quoted in Wolin, *The Frankfurt School Revisited*, 92.

75. Ibid.

76. Carl Schorske, "Encountering Marcuse," in *Herbert Marcuse: A Critical Reader*, 253–59.

77. Angela Davis, *An Autobiography* (New York: Random House, 1974).

78. Herbert Marcuse, "Liberation from the Affluent Society," in *The Dialectic of Liberation*, ed. David Cooper (New York: Penguin, 1968), 176.

79. Ibid.

80. Ibid.

81. Marcuse, *Essay on Liberation*, 30.

82. Ibid, 36.

83. While Marcuse was putting together his political-philosophical program in America, in Turkey, his compatriot Erich Auerbach was writing his study on mimesis. See Erich Auerbach, *Mimesis: The Representation of Reality in Western Literature*, trans. Willard A. Trask (Princeton, N.J.: Princeton University Press, 1963, 2003). Auerbach's analysis of aesthetic realism traced the mimetic function of literature and art through the history of Western culture, examining ways in which artistic representation reflects the social world as well as challenges and transcends it. Auerbach's book contained no explicit political comments, although its political subtext has been recognized. See Terry Eagleton, "Pork Chops and Pineapples," *The London Review of Books* 25, no. 20 (2003): 17–19.

84. The fullest elaboration of the political dimension of aesthetics, both as an emancipator and as a conservative force, appears in Marcuse's essay, "The Affirmative Character of Culture," in Herbert Marcuse, *Negations: Essays in Critical Theory* (Boston, Mass.: Beacon, 1968).

85. Marcuse, *Essay on Liberation*, 38–39.

86. Karl Mannheim, *Sociology as Political Education*, ed. David Kettler and Colin Loader (New Brunswick, N.J.: Transaction, 2001), 23, 25.

87. W. Mark Cobb, "Diatribes and Distortions: Marcuse's Academic Reception," in *Herbert Marcuse: A Critical Reader*, 165.

88. Alasdair MacIntyre, *Herbert Marcuse: An Exposition and a Polemic* (New York: Viking, 1970), 13, 97, 2, 105.

89. George Kateb, "The Political Thought of Herbert Marcuse," *Commentary* 49 (1970): 48–63.

90. Ibid., 48, 49, 54.

91. Ibid., 53, 54.

92. Ibid., 55, 63.

93 Ibid., 63.

94. Pierre Nora, "America and the French Intellectuals," trans. Michael Taylor, *Daedalus* 107, no. 1 (1978): 325–37.

95. Jeffrey Herf, "One-Dimensional Man," *The New Republic* (February 1, 1999): 4.

96. Ibid.

97. Hans Joas, *Creativity of Action*, trans. Jeremy Gaines and Paul Keist (Chicago: University of Chicago Press, 1996), 71, 113.

98. Herbert Marcuse, *One-Dimensional Man: Studies in the Ideology of Advanced Industrial Society* (Boston: Beacon, 1964).

99. Erich Fromm, *The Revolution of Hope* (New York: Holt, Rinehart, and Winston, 1941), 8–9.

100. Walter Benjamin, "Leftwing Melancholia," in *The Weimar Republic Sourcebook*, ed. Kaes Anton and Martin Jay (Berkeley: University of California Press, 1994).

101. Hugh Bredin, "Metonymy," *Poetics Today* 5, no. 1 (1984): 57, 48.

102. C. Wright Mills, *The Power Elite* (London: Oxford University Press, 1956).

103. Marcuse, *One-Dimensional Man*, 88, 97.

104. Ibid., 87.

105. Ibid., 86.

106. Ibid., 95.

107. Herbert Marcuse, "The Individual in the 'Great Society,'" http://www.sfu.ca/~andrewf/individual.pdf. The text has also been published in Herbert Marcuse, *Towards a Critical Theory of Society*, ed. Douglas Kellner (London: Psychology, 2001).

108. Marcuse, "The Individual in the 'Great Society,'" 14.

109. Ibid., 14, 15, 16.

110. Marcuse, "The Individual and the Great Society."

111. Ibid.

112. Harold Keen, "Interview with Dr. Herbert Marcuse," in Kellner, *Herbert Marcuse: The New Left*, 133.

113. Keen, "Interview," 131.

114. Ringer, *The Decline of the German Mandarins*, 123.

115. David Spitz, "Pure Tolerance: A Critique of Criticisms," *Dissent* 13, no. 5 (1966): 521.

116. Letter from Mike Davis to Herbert Marcuse, *Herbert Marcuse Achiv,* file 1458, Universitätstbibliothek, Frankfurt, quoted in Wheatland, *The Frankfurt School in America*, 312.

117. Herbert Marcuse, "The Failure of the New Left," in *Herbert Marcuse: A Critical Reader*, 185.

118. Bill Moyers, "A Conversation with Herbert Marcuse," in *Herbert Marcuse: A Critical Reader*, 161–62.

4. COLD WAR PROPHESIES: ALEXANDER SOLZHENITSYN AND MYTHOLOGICAL AMERICA

1. Sara Rimer, "Cavendish Journal; Shielding Solzhenitsyn, Respectfully," *New York Times*, March 3, 1994.

2. Alexander Solzhenitsyn, "Alexander Solzhenitsyn Biographical," in *Nobel Lectures, Literature 1968–1980*, ed. Tore Fränsmir (Singapore: World Scientific Publishing Co., 1993). http://www.nobelprize.org/nobel_prizes/literature/laureates/1970/solzhenitsyn-lecture.html

3. Tony Judt, *Postwar: A History of Europe Since 1945* (New York: Penguin, 2005), 561.

4. Philip Wander, "The Rhetoric of American Foreign Policy," in *Cold War Rhetoric: Strategy, Metaphor, and Ideology*, ed. Martin Medhurst et al. (East Lansing: Michigan State University Press, 1997).

5. Mark Stoda and George Dionisopoulos, "Jeremiad at Harvard: Solzhenitsyn and 'The World Split Apart,'" *Western Journal of Communication* 64, no. 1 (2000): 31.

6. Sacvan Bercovitch, *The American Jeremiad* (Madison: University of Wisconsin Press, 1978), 7, 23.

7. David Foglesong, *The American Crusade and the "Evil Empire"* (New York: Cambridge University Press, 2007), 168.

8. Jeremi Suri, *Power and Protest: Global Revolution and the Rise of Detente* (Cambridge, Mass.: Harvard University Press, 2005), 215, 258.

9. Alexander Solzhenitsyn, AFLO-CIO Speech, New York, 9 July 1975, quoted in Michael Scammell, *Solzhenitsyn: A Biography* (London: Paladin, 1986), 915.

10. Foglesong, *The American Crusade*, 120.

11. These early attempts at finding a common ground found expression in international forums such as the American Committee for Cultural Freedom. Created in 1949 to promote international intellectual cooperation, its members included both Western and Soviet intellectuals. By 1956, however, the Soviet delegation to the annual congress included darker figures such as Konstantin Fedin, who was responsible for the decision to ban the publication in the USSR of Solzhenitsyn's *Cancer Ward*. See Peter Coleman, *The Liberal Conspiracy: The Congress for Cultural Freedom and the Struggle for the Mind of Postwar Europe* (New York: The Free Press [Macmillan], 1989).

12. William Philips, *A Partisan View: Five Decades in the Politics of Literature* (New Brunswick, N.J.: Transaction, 2004), 151.

13. Volker Berghan, *America and the Intellectual Cold Wars in Europe* (Princeton, N.J.: Princeton University Press, 2001), 127.

14. Marc Selverstein, *Constructing the Monolith: The United States, Great Britain, and International Communism, 1945–1950* (Cambridge, Mass.: Harvard University Press, 2009), 2.

15. Robert Latham, *The Liberal Movement* (New York: Columbia University Press, 1997), 57.

16. Judt, *Postwar*, 221.

17. Akira Iriye, *Cultural Internationalism and World Order* (Baltimore, Md.: John Hopkins University Press, 2000), 157.

18. "Our Country, Our Culture," in *A Partisan Century: Political Writings from* Partisan Review, Edith Kurzweil, ed. (New York: Columbia University Press, 1996), 117.

19. Ibid.

20. Irye, *Cultural Internationalism*, 157.

21. Kurzweil, *A Partisan Century*, 118.

22. Ibid., 136.

23. Suri, *Power and Protest*, 215.

24. Theodore Draper, "Appeasement and Détente," *Commentary* 61 (1976), http://www.commentarymagazine.com/article/appeasement-detente/.

25. Quoted in David Mayers, *George Kennan and the Dilemmas of U.S. Foreign Policy* (New York: Oxford University Press, 1988), 296.

26. Andrei Sakharov, *My Country and the World* (New York: Knopf, 1975), 34.

27. Mayers, *George Kennan*, 297.

28. John Dunlop, "Solzhenitsyn's Reception in the U.S.," in *Solzhenitsyn in Exile: Critical Essays and Documentary Materials*, ed. John Dunlop, Richard Haugh, and Michael Nicholson (Stanford, Calif.: Hoover Institution Press, 1985), 25.

29. Ibid., 28.

30. Ibid., 29.

31. Alexander Solzhenitsyn, *One Day in the Life of Ivan Denisovich* (New York: Knopf, 1963).

32. Scammel, *Solzhenitsyn: A Biography*, 936; Bernard Henri Lévy, *Barbarism with a Human Face* (New York: HarperCollins, 1980), 153.

33. Robert Horvath, "The Solzhenitsyn Effect: East European Dissidents and the Demise of the Revolutionary Privilege," *Human Rights Quarterly* 29, no. 4 (2007): 898.

34. Pierre Nora and Michael Taylor, "America and the French Intellectuals," *Daedalus* 107, no. 1 (1978): 333.

35. André Glucksmann, *La cuisiniere et le mangeur d'hommes: Reflexions sur l'etat, le marxisme, et les camps de concentration* (Paris: Editions du Seuil, 1976).

36. Lévy, *Barbarism*, 154.

37. Nora and Taylor, "America and the French Intellectuals," 332.

38. Irving Howe, "Lukacs and Solzhenitsyn," *Dissent* 18, no. 6 (1971): 643, 644.

39. Ibid.

40. Walter Kaufmann, "Solzhenitsyn and Autonomy," in *Solzhenitsyn: A Collection of Critical Essays*, ed. Kathryn Feuer (Englewood Cliffs, N.J.: Prentice-Hall 1976).

41. Foglesong, *The American Crusade*, 168.

42. Sidney Monas, "Fourteen Years of Aleksandr Isaevich," *Slavic Review* 35, no. 3 (1976): 521.

43. Scammel, *Solzhenitsyn: A Biography*, 822.

44. Ana Siljak, "Between East and West: Hegel and the Origins of the Russian Dilemma," *Journal of the History of Ideas* 62, no. 2 (2001): 352, 357.

45. Alexander Solzhenitsyn, "Cavendish Farewell," in *The Solzhenitsyn Reader: New and Essential Writings, 1947–2005* (Wilmington, Del.: ISI Books, 2006).

46. Scammel, *Solzhenitsyn: A Biography*, 993.

47. Bernard Pivot, "Centerpiece: Solzhenitsyn at Work Amidst Peace of Vermont Hills, Russian Exile Writes of Revolution," *Boston Globe*, February 24, 1984.

48. Horvath, "The Solzhenitsyn Effect," 880.

49. Susan L. Carruthers, "Between Camps: Eastern Bloc 'Escapees' and Cold War Borderlands," *American Quarterly* 57, no. 3 (2005): 911.

50. See Scammel, *Solzhenitsyn: A Biography*.

51. Carruthers, "Between Camps," 914.

52. Alexander Solzhenitsyn, *The Gulag Archipelago: 1918–1956* (New York: Harper and Row, 1978).

53. Kelly Oliver, *Witnessing: Beyond Recognition* (Minneapolis: University of Minnesota Press, 2001), 89.

54. Ibid., 99.

55. Horvath, "The Solzhenitsyn Effect," 883–84.

56. Roger Baldwin, *Liberty Under the Soviets* (New York: Vanguard, 1928), 4.

57. Alexander Solzhenitsyn, *Letters to Soviet Leaders* (London: Harvill, 1974).

58. Alexander Solzhenitsyn, *Publitsistika*, vol. 1 (Yaroslavl: Verkhne-Volzhskoe Knizhnoe Izdadel'svo, 1995), 179, quoted in Horvath, "The Solzhenitsyn Effect," 898.

59. Michel Foucault, *Dits et écrits*, vol. 2, ed. Daniel Defert et François Ewald (Paris: Gallimard, 1994), 289–99, quoted in Jan Palmer, "Foucault's Gulag," *Kritika: Explorations in Russian and Eurasian History* 3, no. 2 (2002): 255–80.

60. Foglesong, *The American Crusade*, 164.

61. Scammel, *Solzhenitsyn: A Biography*, 968.

62. Here is a telling example, which criticizes the Western concept of freedom as a fundamental component of a democratic society: "Freedom! To fill people's mailboxes, eyes, cars, and brains with commercial rubbish against their will. . . . Freedom! To force information on people. . . . Freedom! To spit in the eyes and souls of passersby with advertisements" (*Solzhenitsyn Speaks at the Hoover Institution* [Stanford, Calif.: Hoover Institution, 1976], quoted in Scammel, *Solzhenitsyn: A Biography*, 954).

63. Kenneth Burke, *A Grammar of Motives* (Los Angeles: University of California Press, 1945), 508.

64. Karlyn Kohrs Campbell, "An Exercise in the Rhetoric of Mythical America," in *Readings in Rhetorical Criticism*, ed. Carl R. Burgchardt (State College, Pa.: Strata Publishing), 202.

65. Alexander Solzhenitsyn, "A World Split Apart," in *Solzhenitsyn at Harvard: The Address, Twelve Early Responses, and Six Later Reflections*, ed. Ronald Berman (Lanham, Md.: University Press of America, 1980), 17–18.

66. Ibid., 18.

67. Ibid., 14, 13, 8.

68. Ibid., 11.

69. Ibid., 20.

70. Ibid., 21.

71. Bercovitch, *The American Jeremiad*, 28.

72. Maurice Isserman and Michael Kazin, *America Divided: The Civil War of the 1960s*, 2nd ed. (New York: Oxford University Press, 2004), 4.

73. James Darsey, *The Prophetic Tradition and Radical Rhetoric in America* (New York: New York University Press, 1997), 436.

74. George Meany, "No Voice More Eloquent," *Time*, June 26, 1978.

75. Archibald MacLeish, "Our Will Endures," in *Solzhenitsyn at Harvard*, ed. Ronald Berman (Lanham, Md.: University Press of America, 1980), 59; Meany, "No Voice More Eloquent," 22.

76. Michael Novak, "On God and Man," in Berman, *Solzhenitsyn at Harvard*, 131.

77. Alexander Solzhenitsyn, "Misconceptions about Russia area Threat to America," *Foreign Affairs*, Spring 1980, 830.

78. *Washington Post*, "Solzhenitsyn as Witness," in Berman, *Solzhenitsyn at Harvard*, 26, emphasis mine.

79. *The National Review*, "Thoughts on Solzhenitsyn," in Berman, *Solzhenitsyn at Harvard*, 32.

80. James Reston, "A Russian at Harvard," in Berman, *Solzhenitsyn at Harvard*, 36.

81. George Will, "Solzhenitsyn's Critics," in Berman, *Solzhenitsyn at Harvard*, 35.

82. *Washington Star*, "Solzhenitsyn at Harvard," in Berman, *Solzhenitsyn at Harvard*, 28.

83. Olga Andreyev Carlisle, "Solzhenitsyn's Invisible Audience," in Berman, *Solzhenitsyn at Harvard*, 40.

84. Mary McGrory, "Solzhenitsyn Doesn't Love Us," in Berman, *Solzhenitsyn at Harvard*, 62.

85. MacLeish, "Our Will Endures," 59.

86. John Dunlop points out that Solzhenitsyn participated in town meetings in Cavendish, Vermont and insists that he thus had met and talked to "real" Americans. Yet in his biography, Scammel recounts this differently, claiming that Solzhenitsyn only attended the meeting for the purpose of justifying building a tall fence around his property and that he left immediately after he spoke. See Scammel, *Solzhenitsyn: A Biography*, 956–57.

87. Sydney Hook, "On Western Freedom," in Berman, *Solzhenitsyn at Harvard*, 85.

88. *New York Times*, "The Obsession of Solzhenitsyn," in Berman, *Solzhenitsyn at Harvard*, 24.

89. *Washington Star*, "Solzhenitsyn at Harvard," 29.

90. Reston, "A Russian at Harvard," 38.

91. MacLeish, "Our Will Endures," 59–60.

92. Arthur Schlesinger Jr., "The Solzhenitsyn We Refuse to See," in Berman, *Solzhenitsyn at Harvard*, 72.

93. Hook, "On Western Freedom," 90–91.

94. Michael Mandelbaum, *The Case for Goliath: How America Acts as the World's Government in the Twentieth Century* (New York: PublicAffairs, 2005).

95. Max Boot, "American Imperialism? No Need to Run Away from Label," *USA Today*, May 5, 2003, http://usatoday30.usatoday.com/news/opinion/editorials/2003-05-05-boot_x.htm.

5. EDWARD SAID AND THE CLASH OF IDENTITIES

1. Mary McCarthy, *The Company She Keeps* (San Diego: Harcourt Brace, 1942).

2. John Carlos Rowe, "Edward Said and American Studies," *American Quarterly* 56, no. 1 (2004): 42 (emphasis mine).

3. Edward Said, "The Clash of Ignorance," *The Nation* 273, no. 12 (2001): 11.

4. Tony Judt, *Reappraisals: Reflections on the Forgotten Twentieth Century* (New York: Penguin, 2008), 163.

5. Jeffrey Williams, "Romance of the Amateur Intellectual," *Review of Education, Pedagogy, and Cultural Studies* 17, no. 4 (1995): 405.

6. Bruce Bawer, "Edward W. Said, Intellectual," *The Hudson Review* 54, no. 4 (2002): 625.

7. Edward Said, *Representations of the Intellectual* (New York: Pantheon, 1994), 50, 53.

8. Edward Said, *The Politics of Dispossession: The Struggle for Palestinian Self-Determination, 1969–1994* (New York: Pantheon, 1994), 54.

9. See Amritjit Singh and Bruce G. Johnson, eds., *Interviews with Edward W. Said* (Jackson: University Press of Mississippi, 2004); Tariq Ali, *Conversations with Edward Said* (Calcutta: Seagull, 2005).

10. Luc Boltanski, *Distant Suffering: Morality, Media and Politics*, trans. Graham Burchell (Cambridge: Cambridge University Press, 1999), 58.

11. Edward Said, *Out of Place: A Memoir* (New York: Vintage, 1999).

12. Gyan Prakash, "Edward Said in Bombay," in *Edward Said: Continuing the Conversation*, ed. Homi Bhaba and W. J. T. Mitchell (Chicago: University of Chicago Press, 2005), 135–42.

13. Boltanski, *Distant Suffering*, 58, 60.

14. Boltanski, *Distant Suffering*, 64–65.

15. Homi Bhabha, "Untimely Ends," *Artforum* (February 2004): 19, quoted in Joseph Massad, "The Intellectual Life of Edward Said," *Journal of Palestine Studies* 33, no. 3 (2004): 15.

16. Leon Wieseltier, "Review of *Orientalism*," *The New Republic* 180, no. 14 (1979): 27–33.

17. Boltanski, *Distant Suffering*, 64, 65.

18. Said, *Representations*, 7, 6, 8.

19. Williams, "Romance of the Amateur Intellectual," 404.

20. Said, *Representations*, 4.

21. Ibid., 30.

22. Rowe, "Edward Said and American Studies," 39.

23. Judt, *Reappraisals*, 166.

24. Ibid., 165.

25. Edward Said, *After the Last Sky: Photographs by Jean Mohr* (New York: Pantheon, 1986), 107.

26. Edward Said, *On Late Style: Music and Literature Against the Grain* (New York: Vintage, 2004), 55, 57.

27. Ari Shavit, "My Right of Return: Interview with Edward Said," *Haaretz*, August 18, 2000, http://www.middleeast.org/archives/8-00-31.htm.

28. Edward Said, "On Jean Genet's Late Works," *Grand Street Magazine* 36, no. 9 (1990): 3, 6, 5, http://www.grandstreet.com/gsissues/gs36/gs36c.html.

29. Harry Harootunian, "Conjunctural Traces: Said's 'Inventory,'" in *Edward Said: Continuing the Conversation*, 71.

30. Edward Said, *The Question of Palestine* (New York: Times Books, 1979), xliii.

31. Said, "A Visit to Sartre," *The London Review of Books* 22, no. 11 (2000): 5.

32. Ibid.

33. Jacqueline Rose, *The Question of Zion* (Princeton, N.J.: Princeton University Press, 2005), 118.

34. Timothy Brennan, "The Critic and the Public: Edward Said and World Literature," in *Edward Said: A Legacy of Emancipation and Representation*, ed. Adel Iskandar and Hakem Rustom (Berkeley: University of California Press, 2010), 102, 103.

35. Edward Said, *Humanism and Democratic Criticism* (New York: Columbia University Press, 2004), 38.

36. Karlis Racevskis, "Edward Said and Michel Foucault: Affinities and Dissonances," *Research in African Literature* 36, no. 3 (2005): 86.

37. Said, *Humanism*, 9–10.

38. Edward Said, *Orientalism* (New York: Random House, 1978) 2–3.

39. Ibid., 239 (emphasis mine).

40. Nicholas B. Dirks, "Edward Said and Anthropology," *Journal of Palestine Studies* 33, no. 3 (2004): 39.

41. Harootunian, "Conjunctural Traces," 73.

42. William Spanos, *The Legacy of Edward Said* (Urbana: University of Illinois Press, 2009), 77.

43. Massad, "The Intellectual Life of Edward Said," 10.

44. Dirks, "Edward Said and Anthropology," 46–47.

45. Michael Richardson, "Enough Said: Reflections on Orientalism," *Anthropology Today* 6, no. 4 (1990): 16–19.

46. Clifford Geertz, "Conjuring with Islam," *The New York Review of Books*, May 27, 1982, 28.

47. Robert Griffin, "Ideology and Misrepresentations: A Response to Edward Said," *Critical Inquiry* 15, no. 3 (1989): 624.

48. Valerie Kennedy, *Edward Said: A Critical Introduction* (Cambridge: Polity, 2000), 29.

49. Bawer, "Edward W. Said, Intellectual," 662.

50. Foucault's seemingly implacable conception of power as a force inescapable precisely because so diffuse (rather than concentrated in a monarch or state institution) has brought him frequent charges of political conservatism. See Nancy Fraser, "Michel Foucault: A Young Conservative?" *Ethics* 96, no. 1 (1985): 165–84.

51. Bernard Lewis, "Review of *Orientalism*," *New York Review of Books*, June 24, 1982, 3, 4, 5.

52. Ibid., 10.

53. Ibid., 1.

54. Ibid., 1–2.

55. Lila Abu-Lughod, "About Politics, Palestine, and Friendship: A Letter to Edward from Egypt," in *Edward Said: Continuing the Conversation*, 21.

56. Said, *Politics of Dispossession*, 34.

57. Said, *Question of Palestine*, 8.

58. Avi Shlaim, "Edward Said and the Palestine Question," in Iskandar and Rustom, *Edward Said: A Legacy of Emancipation and Representation*, 283.

59. Melvin I. Urofsky, "A Cause in Search of Itself: American Zionism After the State," in *Solidarity and Kinship*, ed. Nathan M. Kaganoff (Boston: American Jewish Historical Society, 1980), 102.

60. Evyatar Friesel, "Brandeis' Role in American Zionism Historically Reconsidered," in Kaganoff, *Solidarity and Kinship*, 61.

61. Said, *Politics of Dispossession*, 32.

62. Said, *Question of Palestine*, 60.

63. Ibid., 25.

64. Ibid., 30.

65. Ibid., 35.

66. Edmund Wilson, quoted in Said, *Question of Palestine*, 35 (emphasis mine).

67. Said, *Question of Palestine*, 36.

68. Ibid., 89, 37, 97.

69. William Spanos, "Edward W. Said and Zionism: Rethinking the Exodus Story," *boundary 2* 37, no. 1 (2010): 127.

70. Said, *Question of Palestine*, 21, 25.

71. Cameron S. Brown, "Answering Edward Said's *The Question of Palestine*," *Israel Affairs* 13, no. 1 (2007): 55–79.

72. Said, *Question of Palestine*, 87, 9, 87.

73. Ibid., 71–72 (emphasis mine).

74. Brown, "Answering," 71; Said, *Question of Palestine*, 107.

75. Said, *Question of Palestine*, 37, 66.

76. See Griffin, "Ideology and Representation."

77. Michael Walzer, *Exodus and Revolution* (New York: Basic Books, 1985).

78. Edward Said, "Michael Walzer's *Exodus and Revolution*: A Canaanite Reading," in *Blaming the Victim: Spurious Scholarship and the Palestinian Question*, ed. Edward W. Said and Christopher Hitchins (London: Verso, 1988), 161. Originally published in *Grand Street* 5, no. 2 (1986): 86–106.

79. Edward Said, *Freud and the Non-European* (London: Freud Museum, 2003), 43–44.

80. See R. H. Armstrong, "Contrapuntal Affiliations: Edward Said and Freud's Moses," *American Imago* 62, no. 2 (2005): 235–57.

81. Leon Wieseltier, "The Ego and the Yid," *The New Republic* 228, no. 13 (2003), 38.

82. Ibid.

83. See my discussion in the introduction.

84. Eugene Alexander, "Professor of Terror," *Commentary* 88, no. 2 (1989): 49.

85. Said, *Question of Palestine*, 103.

86. Ibid., 51.

87. I rely on the understanding of presence as an argumentation technique advanced in Chaim Perelman and Lucie Olbrechts-Tyteca, *The New Rhetoric: A Treatise on Argumentation* (Notre Dame, Ind.: Notre Dame University Press, 1969).

88. Edward Said, *Reflections on Exile and Other Essays* (Cambridge, Mass.: Harvard University Press, 2000), 194.

89. Edward Said, "Permission to Narrate," *The London Review of Books* 6, no. 3 (1984).

90. Said, *After the Last Sky*, 30.

91. Said, "Permission to Narrate."

92. Said, *After the Last Sky*, 69–70.

93. Richard Locke, *Critical Children: The Use of Childhood in Ten Great Novels* (New York: Columbia University Press, 2011).

94. Justus Reid Weiner, " 'My Beautiful Old House' and Other Fabrications by Edward Said," *Commentary* 108, no. 2 (1999): 29.

95. Alexander Cockburn, "Said as a Jew," *CounterPunch* 6 (1999), 1.

96. Hannah Arendt, *The Human Condition* (Chicago: University of Chicago Press, 1958).

97. Said, *Out of Place*, 21.

98. Said, *After the Last Sky*, 88.

99. Martin Buber, *On Zion: The History of an Idea* (Syracuse, N.Y.: Syracuse University Press, 1973).

100. Amahl Bishara, "House and Homeland: Examining Sentiments about and Claims to Jerusalem and Its Houses," *Social Text* 75, no. 2 (2003): 143.

101. Robert Werman, letter to the editor, *Commentary*, January 1999, 6.

102. Said, *Out of Place*, 87, 68, 65.

103. Ibid., 127, 80, 82, 83, 100.

104. Edward Said, "Setting the Record Straight: Edward Said Confronts His Future, His Past, and His Critics' Accusations," *The Atlantic Online*, September 22, 1999, http://www.theatlantic.com/past/docs/unbound/interviews/ba990922.htm.

105. Ian Buruma, "Misplaced Person," *New York Times*, October 3, 1999.

106. Ibid.

107. Alon Confino, "Remembering Talbiyah: On Edward Said's *Out of Place*," *Israel Studies* 5, no. 2 (2000): 187, 188.

108. Edward Grossman, "Speaking For Himself," *The American Spectator* 23, no. 12 (1999): 43.

109. Meron Benvenisti, "Blank Spaces: Talbiyah and Rehavia," *The SAIS Review of International Affairs* 20, no. 1 (2000): 220, 219.

110. Confino, "Remembering Talbiyah," 196.

111. Bishara, "House and Homeland," 152.

112. Hillel Halkin, "Self-Made Man: Looking for the Real Edward Said," *Forward*, October 22, 1999.

113. Although both found the story appealing, Halkin's response differed from Confino's. While Confino emphasized the *human* experience conveyed in the memoir that resonated with him, Halkin read it specifically as the story of a Palestinian and was moved.

114. Harootunian, "Conjectural Traces," 78.

115. Edward Said, "Beginnings, " *Power, Politics, and Culture: Interviews with Edward W. Said*, ed. Gauri Viswanathan (New York: Vintage Books, 2001), 14.

116. Said, *Humanism and Democratic Criticism*, 11.

117. Said, *Power, Politics, and Culture*, 227.

CONCLUSION

1. Alexis de Tocqueville, *Democracy in America*, ed. J. P. Mayer, trans. George Lawrence. (New York: HarperCollins/Perennial Classics, 2000), 612.

2. Ibid.

3. Theodor W. Adorno, *Negative Dialectics*, trans. E. B. Ashton (London: Routledge, 1990).

4. Danielle S. Allen, *Talking to Strangers: Anxieties of Citizenship Since Brown v. Board of Education* (Chicago: University of Chicago Press, 2004), 186 (emphasis mine).

5. Seyla Benhabib, *The Rights of Others: Aliens, Residents, and Citizens.* (Cambridge: Cambridge University Press, 2004).

6. Ibid., 142–43.

7. Fred Evans, *The Multivoiced Body* (New York: Columbia University Press, 2008), 267.

8. Jürgen Habermas, *The Inclusion of the Other: Studies in Political Theory*, ed. Ciaran Cronin and Pablo De Greiff (Cambridge, Mass.: MIT Press, 1998), 131.

9. David Miller, *On Nationality* (Oxford: Claredon, 1995), 49.

10. Ibid., 73.

11. Nevgat Sozuk, *States and Strangers: Refugees and Displacements of Statecraft* (Minneapolis: University of Minnesota Press, 1999), 74.

12. Rogers Brubaker, *Citizenship and Nationhood in France and Germany* (Cambridge, Mass.: Harvard University Press, 1992), 47.

13. Habermas, *The Inclusion of the Other*, 57 (emphasis mine).

14. Barbara Misztal, *Intellectuals and the Public Good: Creativity and Civil Courage* (Cambridge: Cambridge University Press, 2007), 55.

15. Maeve Cooke, *Re-presenting the Good* Society (Boston, Mass.: MIT Press, 2006), 155.

16. Charles Taylor, "Politics of Recognition," in *Philosophical Arguments* (Cambridge, Mass.: Harvard University Press, 1995), 226, 231.

17. Nancy Fraser, "Rethinking Recognition," *New Left Review* 3 (2000): 103.

18. I have explored this possibility in Andreea Deciu Ritivoi, "Ricoeur and Rhetorical Theory: Paul Ricoeur on Recognition in the Public Sphere," in *Ricoeur Across the Disciplines*, ed. Scott Davidson (London: Continuum, 2010), 122–41.

19. Misztal, *Intellectuals and Public Good*, 26.

20. Cooke, *Re-presenting the Good Society*, 155.

21. Charles Taylor, "Understanding and Ethnocentricity," in *Relativism: A Contemporary Anthology*, ed. Michael Krausz (New York: Columbia University Press, 2010), 479.

22. Roman Jakobson, *Language in Literature*, ed. Krystyna Pomorska and Stephen Rushi (Cambridge, Mass.: The Belknap Press of Harvard University Press, 1987), 70.

INDEX

academic institutions: German intellectuals and American, 22, 265n67. *See also* universities; *specific academic institutions*

academics, and Marcuse, 108–20

accents: of Arendt, 88; education and, 1, 30; inferiority associated with, 29; stranger persona and, 30. *See also* language

activism: Marcuse and, 109–12, 118, 125–27, 129, 130, 137, 139, 146; philosophy and, 124. *See also* New Left

Adams, John Quincy, 46

Adorno, Theodor W., 22–24, 116–18; Marcuse and, 108, 109, 111, 113–15, 120–24, 130; Said and, 206–7, 208

aesthetics: Marcuse on, 135, 136, 138–40; politics and, 139, 140, 278n83

affluent society, 135, 137–38, 148, 151

African Americans, 103; American Jews and, 85, 104; Arendt on, 77–79, 82–84; Marcuse and, 125, 149. *See also* racism; segregation

After the Last Sky (Said), 206, 233–35, 241

aliens: foreigners as, 45. *See also* foreigners

Allen, Danielle, 251

America: academic institutions and German intellectuals, 22, 265n67; Arendt and, 5, 8–9, 17, 47–48, 56, 58, 69–107, 269n2, 269n5;

capitalism, 9, 31, 112, 128, 131, 132, 143–44, 146, 151; communism and, 184, 190, 193; Europe and, 163; foreign intellectuals leaving, 28; German intellectuals and, 109; German thought and spirit of, 88; investigations, 116; Israel and, 222; jeremiad, 159, 182, 185, 186, 187; Marcuse and, 8–9, 47–48, 108–55; mythological, 156, 158, 181, 184, 192, 195; patriotism, 249; postwar hegemony of, 163–64; press, 180, 183–84, 187–89, 192; revolution and, 144; Said and, 8–9, 47–48, 196–248; Solzhenitsyn and, 8–9, 31, 47–48, 156–68, 170–95; as Soviet Union, 182–84, 190; stranger persona and, 39; totalitarianism and, 133, 164, 184, 190; Western world as, 180–82, 184, 187, 189, 191–92, 194; Zionism and, 222, 224–26. *See also* Cold War; *specific U.S. topics*

America Day by Day (de Beauvoir), 15–16

American citizens, 47. *See also* citizens

American culture, 145; American intellectuals and, 163–64; "Our Country and Our Culture" symposium, 163–64

American democracy, 163, 192; Solzhenitsyn on, 181, 182; Tocqueville on, 10–13, 164–65, 249, 262nn26–27